Gender and French Identity after the Second World War, 1944–1954

Gender and French Identity after the Second World War, 1944–1954

Engendering Frenchness

Kelly Ricciardi Colvin

BLOOMSBURY ACADEMIC
LONDON • NEW YORK • OXFORD • NEW DELHI • SYDNEY

BLOOMSBURY ACADEMIC
Bloomsbury Publishing Plc
50 Bedford Square, London, WC1B 3DP, UK
1385 Broadway, New York, NY 10018, USA

BLOOMSBURY, BLOOMSBURY ACADEMIC and the Diana logo
are trademarks of Bloomsbury Publishing Plc

First published 2017
Paperback edition first published 2019

A catalogue record for this book is available from the British Library.

Library of Congress Cataloging-in-Publication Data
Names: Colvin, Kelly Ricciardi, author.
Title: Gender and French identity after the Second World War, 1944-1954 :
engendering Frenchness / Kelly Ricciardi Colvin.
Description: London ; New York, NY : Bloomsbury Academic, 2017. |
Includes bibliographical references.
Identifiers: LCCN 2017010665| ISBN 9781350031104 (hb) |
ISBN 9781350031135 (epub)
Subjects: LCSH: Women–France–Social conditions–20th century. |
Sex role–France–History–20th century. | Femininity–France–History–20th century. |
Women–Identity–History–20th century. |
Nationalism–France–History–20th century. | World War,
1939-1945–Women–France. | France–Civilization–20th century.
Classification: LCC HQ1613 .C7337 2017 | DDC 305.40944/0904–dc23
LC record available at https://lccn.loc.gov/2017010665

ISBN: HB: 978-1-3500-3110-4
PB: 978-1-3501-0555-3
ePDF: 978-1-3500-3112-8
ePub: 978-1-3500-3113-5

Typeset by Deanta Global Publishing Services, Chennai, India

To find out more about our authors and books visit
www.bloomsbury.com and sign up for our newsletters.

Contents

List of Illustrations

Acknowledgments

The ability to acknowledge some of the many people who toiled generously on my behalf is a gift; my debts are great in number and depth. Carolyn Dean fundamentally changed the way I think about history, gender, and the possibilities of the scholarly voice. There is no possible way this book would exist if not for her inspiration and guidance. Maud Mandel has been an unending source of support as a mentor and colleague. The amount of time and effort she has expended on this project and my career stretches well beyond what she signed up for all those years ago. Sarah Fishman and Michèle Plott have had a significant impact both on the development of this project and on me as a scholar. I am fortunate to know them both.

Colleagues at Brown University and beyond have contributed immensely to the ideas and substance within these pages. In particular, the modern European history colloquium at Brown has been a safe space in which to express academic creativity, often awkwardly in my case. Ethan Pollock and Mary Gluck took extra time to work with me on honing my argument and voice in the book. At a critical moment, Joel Revill read through parts of the manuscript and improved it immensely. I am grateful to them all.

Rhodri Mogford and the team at Bloomsbury have made the process of publishing my first book feel smooth; I greatly appreciate their enthusiasm and deep reserves of patience. The anonymous readers at Bloomsbury went far beyond normal efforts in this project; I hope they see their influence in the book as a sign of my gratitude.

Writing about my family makes me reflect on the great luck I have enjoyed. Pat and Joanne Ricciardi built the foundation of love and help from which my four siblings and I have benefited immensely. Ryan, Thomas, Tracy, and Katie Ricciardi offer a web of hilarity, support, and feedback without which I would be lost.

I think my greatest fortune in life was meeting Will Colvin over twenty years ago. His warmth, humor, and steadiness have been immeasurably important to me. His example of partnership gives me hope that all things, including equality, are possible. Our children, Alex and William, have defined for me what happiness looks like, and I love them more than I can begin to express.
Thank you all.

Introduction: France is Beginning Again

given a right to vote

"*Freedom—France is beginning again.*"
— Jean Guéhenno, August 25, 1944[1]

At the end of the Second World War, women were enfranchised in France. And yet it was a writer contemporary to this book, Simone de Beauvoir, who in 1949, just five years after women's enfranchisement, wrote that political rights are insufficient to addressing gender inequalities in society. "Abstract rights," she argued, "have never been sufficient to guarantee woman a concrete hold on the world: there is not yet real equality today between the two sexes."[2] That she would consider women voting such an unremarkable achievement after generations of activists had worked to achieve it begs explanation; the disparity between the promise of the moment and the reality of its lived experience seems particularly wide.

The circumstances of the Second World War in France—and its conclusion—created a moment of possibility, when the nature of liberal democracy there could have shifted to a more gender-neutral status. Historians have convincingly demonstrated that French republicanism is fundamentally conceived of as male.[3] Women's enfranchisement presented a serious contradiction in that it carried the potential to alter the basic makeup of the underpinnings of the French state. Other fights, like secularization, had managed to define suffrage as out of the mainstream under the Third Republic, or even as a danger to the Republic in cases where women were assumed to be swayed by priests.[4] But after the military and political embarrassment of the Second World War, France needed to reassert its place at the head of Western democratic values, which included human rights. Male suffrage was a stain on that reputation that was relatively easily removed in the unsettled moment of the postwar when the Catholic right had been discredited for its wartime conduct and the constitution was being rewritten. Joan Scott has argued that by 1944, "the definition of democracy had expanded to include sexual democracy (in the form of the vote for women)."[5] In enfranchising women, France made a correction, bringing the nation in line with other major democratic powers.

vs a being with a person's general capacity to possess rights

FRENCHINESS!

However, changing voting rights did not alter French cultural assumptions about women's roles in politics and society that had been structured by (at least) seventy-five years of masculinist republicanism. This book will explain that continuity through an exploration of how the process of confining women's possibilities worked. If women's accession to political rights was a surface-level shift, then the place to look for continuity is not in the realm of politics per se, but in culture. What this book has found in the cultural realm is a pervasive drive toward disunity and confinement.

Other major democracies had collaborated with the Germans and faced the task of reorganizing their governments and their reputations at the end of the war, but France was unique in folding women's suffrage into the rebuilding effort.[6] France, arguably the birthplace of human rights, had fouled its reputation on that front during the war, but the opportunity to enfranchise half the population of the Republic presented a chance to rewrite the war years. The realities of fascist overthrow now combined with the possibility of patriarchal overthrow, and a real occasion for expanded human rights seemed to loom.

French women's enfranchisement in 1944 came a full generation later than the bulk of their Western compatriots. The struggle for rights had been the work of many feminist activists' lifetimes, dating from the Enlightenment and the French Revolution through the nineteenth century and the interwar period. Women like Olympe de Gouges, Jeanne Deroin, and Louise Weiss fought for enfranchisement over three centuries, for an official voice in the body politic of France. What was new in 1944 was the sense of possibility surrounding women's roles in France. Charles de Gaulle referred to women's enfranchisement as "tremendous," and feminist Louise Weiss called it "the most important collective phenomenon of the first half of this century."[7] The fractious debates of the Third Republic about the natural, inherent unfitness of women to vote could, it seemed, be put to bed by a simple political edict in 1944.[8]

Or could they? Despite this rhetoric about the importance of women's suffrage, very little resistance arose to challenge the larger structures of male hegemony at the time of women's enfranchisement. There was no blossoming of consciousness or solidarity among women, no major feminist movement or even moment. Women did not vote together, nor did they occupy positions of power in any serious numbers.[9] In fact the opposite was true. As Joan Scott notes, when women became legal subjects in 1944, "the limits of formal rights for redressing inequities of economic and social power became more evident."[10] To be clear, this is not at all to suggest that women inevitably would have come together and voted as a bloc without the efforts to confine them. However, there is a difference between the concerted creation of political disunity and the construction of a monolithic coalition. This book takes as its subject the former. What occurred in the postwar stew was the active confinement of women to a narrow definition of what it meant to be proper at the same time that they became political actors and presumably became more politically consequential.[11]

Employing gender as an analytical lens, this book places cultural sources in dialogue with political developments to understand the limitations on femininity, the disempowerment of women, and the reinforcement of the French political actor as masculine at the end of the war, despite women's enfranchisement. In effect, it demonstrates how France culturally tempered the potential energy in voting rights. In doing so, it asks difficult questions about the celebration of voting rights that is common in the West, and it also advances the gendered history of liberal democracy as a system of government.

Historians have convincingly demonstrated that the origins of modern republican democracy in France are masculine, as are the assumed political actors.[12] Addressing the time preceding the tumult of the Second World War, Judith Surkis's work on the Third Republic persuasively argues that a heterosexual masculinity was foundational to that government.[13] When it came to forming the Fourth Republic, though, the question of women's enfranchisement was settled, at least officially, when women's accession to full citizenship was secured in 1944. As historian Anne-Sarah Bouglé-Moalic has posited, women gaining the right to vote came at a moment when the state was remaking itself. This state reconstruction, she notes, took its cues from contemporary global trends. By the time of reconstruction, full suffrage for women had long been the norm among Western democracies outside of France. As Bouglé-Moalic goes on to argue, "That which seemed abnormal in 1848 had become normal, logical in 1944."[14] If Bouglé-Moalic refers to a state-level correction, it is crucial to also examine the vote and women's elevation to full citizenship from another perspective. The story manifests quite differently with a focus on culture. The addition of women to the official body politic necessitated the cultural negation of their potential impact on that body. If men were "sexed" in the Third Republic, as Surkis shows, after the war women were yoked to a definition of womanhood that delineated their lives quite clearly, if extralegally.

In addressing the inequities of a gendered republic in France, feminists and historians have faced a particularly French hurdle. France defines its sense of justice and citizenship based on an absence of difference: the citizen is a neutral actor who carries no gender, race, or religion in the eyes of the law. Joan Scott has shown how feminists' attempts to engage with the government since the time of the French Revolution faced a stubborn paradox. In France's universalist system, feminists advocating for their own equality have inevitably called attention to their difference from the normal political actor, who is male.[15] Despite their long-standing call for rights and opportunities, French women thus have had extremely limited space in which to operate as political, public subjects.[16]

The sources examined in this book worked to reaffirm France's masculine status at a time when the state had enfranchised women. Joan Scott has argued that "citizenship had made women men's equals as subjects before the law in a formal, procedural sense, but it had failed to win for them autonomy—social, economic, or subjective."[17] In order to understand how femininity became a limiting agent politically, this book identifies narratives of gender that prevailed in post–Second World War France, placing the cultural in dialogue with the political to determine how women failed to achieve parity, despite achieving ostensible equality.[18]

This book breaks down the process of diminishing the possibilities of womanhood in the wake of receiving the vote. It exposes the contemporary cultural trends that emphasized femininity and docility, not publicity and empowerment. If, as cultural historian Raylene L. Ramsay suggests, "it is the premium placed on being feminine that most dissuades French women from entering the masculine world of politics," then it is crucial to explore how the state and other cultural entities prioritized that femininity at the very moment of women's enfranchisement.[19] In exposing the methods by which these entities articulated womanhood, the book also reveals how femininity functioned as a limiting political force in postwar France.

The experience of womanhood in any context is not monolithic; differences of class, region, race, and religion all played a role in how women experienced the end of the Second World War. However, in attempting to diminish women's power and privilege masculinity, forces from state institutions to the media "taught" women what a normal vision of French womanhood looked like.[20] There was a very narrow definition of proper feminine performance, one that hinged implicitly on narratives of female confinement. This book takes as its subject the articulation of that confinement.

The book begins in 1944, the year when the war ended and women were enfranchised, and it traces cultural developments until 1954, when the French underwent a paradigmatic shift with respect to their memory of the war, their society, and their global role. Historian Karen Adler has termed this time the "long Liberation."[21] Her characterization is useful, as it re-periodizes the history of postwar French history in a way that does not reenact the myths propagated by the French during the time itself.[22] The war was not simply over in 1944/5, instead there was a large amount of political, social, economic, and cultural work done by people in all fields to recover. Some of this work was public and transparent, while other work took a less obvious form, and it resulted in complicated webs of reality and myth that have long defined the French memory of the Second World War.

The creation of political disunity and the negation of the power of the vote among women in the long Liberation were not natural phenomena. Just as the French worked actively to create a myth about their wartime experience, so the French put effort into delineating the terms of public womanhood appropriate to a postwar era. Each chapter in the book addresses a specific theme regarding female comportment in the postwar years. The first chapter looks at the way artists, writers, and the government painted France itself as a victimized woman at the end of the war. It demonstrates how the use of gender worked to reinforce national myths about France's simultaneous female victimization and masculine prowess. Chapter 2 expands that analysis to include the image of victimhood as a political identity for women, as articulated in memoirs and court cases. Victimhood was a way for women to rehabilitate France as a whole and conform to the myth of *résistancialisme*,[23] but it was also pointedly temporary; there was no lasting autonomous political gain for a female victim of war. The third chapter turns to how love became a charged topic in the postwar years, when the responsibility for constructing a heteronormative family fell on women alone. Women's magazines, a postwar juggernaut, encouraged, cajoled, and frightened women into privileging the man in their lives above all else. A reinvigorated beauty culture is the subject of Chapter 4. Women's priorities in the postwar period included their own personal appearances, as well as those of their families and their homes, trumping any outside work commitments they may also shoulder. Magazines articulated the very specific requirements of feminine appearance, and they warned of the major consequence of nonconformity: social isolation. The fifth chapter focuses on women who disobeyed or challenged the imperatives set forth in the first four chapters, either consciously or not. These women included torturers and spies; their danger to the French state and the French people comes across clearly in the public exposure, punishments, and excoriations meted out to them by the state and the media. This chapter also addresses how male threats to the state did not face the same kinds of hostility experienced by the women. The final chapter turns to the vote and identifies reasons for the lack of female solidarity. It looks to women's magazines again, which offered multiple messages of anti-solidarity in the postwar era. Magazines warned women not to trust one another, arguing for general female duplicity and covetousness. Confidence, even in one's female friends and relatives, magazines cautioned, would lead to the breakdown of a woman's family and, consequently, her happiness. Taken together, these themes articulate an "ideal type" of femininity, as well as the perils faced by women who challenged it.

This book, as suggested above, mines a wide variety of sources, including women's magazines, memoirs, popular artwork, novels, political speeches, and newspaper articles. I have tried to gather widely read materials in order to examine the most prevalent, most common visions of gender and French identity in the postwar era. I do this in order to understand French identity not as monolithic, but certainly as a powerful organizational force for conformity in people's lives.

The boundary between cultural and political history can be both porous and perilous, but traversing it is a valuable effort, as this boundary is also highly instructive for scholars, particularly those who work with marginalized communities, whose opinions and influences rarely grace official narratives. The "mechanics of power," as Michel Foucault described it, is a form of discipline aimed at producing "'docile' bodies," and this is what is at stake in postwar France.[24] In order to produce a standard set of behaviors, the possible repercussions of potential transformative change were reformed and articulated to reflect a new definition of normal; the desire for normalcy in postwar France was palpable.[25] To uncover how these processes functioned, it is not always possible to interrogate the inner workings of French minds. As some scholars have posited, in examining practices for the formation of femininity, it is perhaps not even preferable. "The disciplinary power that inscribes femininity on the female body is everywhere and it is nowhere," writes theorist Sandra Bartky, "the disciplinarian is everyone and yet no one in particular."[26] In order to truly examine the processes by which women's lives are controlled by external discipline, she states, it is crucial to realize "the extent to which discipline can be institutionally *unbound* as well as institutionally bound."[27] [original emphasis]

French women and men reacted to the many messages that propagated at this time in different ways, and, with rare exceptions, historians cannot know how people understood what they were reading or whether they were absorbing it. It is not the intention of this book to query the mind of the postwar French layperson as to what he or she internalized. Instead, the sources, which, as individual chapters will note, were mainstream and widely read, speak to how an ideal vision of national identity formed and crystallized around a series of narratives about France's experience of war and postwar, as well as how these myths functioned to benefit the nation at this time. In this way, the feminine identity that emerged from wartime France represented an idealized vision of what it meant to belong to the nation and is instructive about women's relationship to a democracy. There is fluidity in this gendered ideal precisely because it is a marker of power relations, responding to particular contexts, not despite that fact.[28] Analyzing how power disseminated at the end of the war illustrates the processes by which women became "docile" participants in a new, twentieth-century government, despite winning the right to vote. "Instead of eliminating the general problem of sexual difference," Joan Scott has argued, "the vote drew attention to it with greater force."[29] This book will attempt to explain that gap.

[handwritten annotation: offered up to God can remit the just punishment for one's sins.]

The Re-Victimization of France *[handwritten annotation: personified]*

In Charles de Gaulle's famous speech at the Hôtel de Ville in Paris on August 25, 1944, he proclaimed: "Paris! Outraged Paris! Broken Paris! Martyred Paris, but liberated Paris!" The crowd was enormous and animated, with thousands of people clapping, cheering, and crying at the words of their leader, who had been in exile in England since 1940. De Gaulle went on to intone: "France returns to Paris, to her home. She returns bloody, but quite resolute. She returns there enlightened by the immense lesson, but more certain than ever of her duties and of her rights." In this charged moment, de Gaulle was not simply stating a historical truth. Instead, he was actually creating an identity of victimization—which in the case of postwar France signified redemptive suffering—for the city of Paris and for the Parisians: Paris had been brutalized by the German Occupation, but now the city was free. He was recounting and teaching the audience a version of history that distorted and simplified the more complex reality. To that history, de Gaulle added femininity, arguing in the same speech that France itself was a victimized woman: "bloody, but quite resolute." De Gaulle's historicizing effort did not take into account the complex daily acts of collaboration and resistance that marked life in the occupied city and elsewhere in the nation. Rather, using gendered narrative, it imposed a singular history of victimization upon the city and the people.

This chapter demonstrates how the portrayal of the nation as a pointedly female victim operated at this particular moment to benefit France. It first examines some of the many representations of France as a woman victim, which at first glance feels inharmonious with the need for a masculine nation. In depicting France as a brutalized woman, artists and writers presented the nation as simultaneously intent on repelling the Germans and ready to rebuild; she quietly regained her forces and then emerged as a strong, masculine, even virile power.[1] In contemporary imagery, France's victimhood—portrayed as feminine—reinforced the myth that all of the French had been oppressed by a German aggressor. It also revealed how the French had purportedly drawn on a masculine strength to put the Germans back in their place. The chapter then turns to an analysis of how Charles de Gaulle presented himself as Joan of Arc at the time of the Liberation, which again seems dissonant with the need for a strong, virile nation and the negation of femininity's relationship with power. However, a closer look reveals how de Gaulle—and other contemporary writers and commentators—used the Jehannic image to craft a narrative about France's experience of war and the best way for individual men and women to comport themselves going forward. These narratives of victimhood and gender combined to "teach" a universal experience of war.

A brief analysis of the Resistance myth provides a compelling explanation for why gendered imagery of victimhood might have been appealing to the French at this time. Historian Henry Rousso has argued that the Resistance myth, which stated that all of the French had heroically resisted the German enemy—aside from a few errant French traitors—allowed the French nation to rebuild around a "collective memory of still fresh events [which] quickly crystallized around a small set of central ideas and images." In fact, according to Rousso, when de Gaulle announced the Liberation of Paris, he "established the founding myth of the post-Vichy period."[2] In this retelling, the French were the heroes of the war, their nation was strong and stable, and France deserved a place among the Great Powers of the time. This stood in marked contrast to the reality of the wartime situation in France, when most French people simply survived.[3]

Rousso does not deal with the gendered aspects of the Resistance myth, which called for virility in French men, while historians of women in the Resistance have emphasized female participants' absence in the historical record. An analysis that incorporates gender reveals the extent to which such national myths addressed far more than the Resistance. The Resistance myth was part of a larger structure of national stories, many of which dealt with gender, which allowed the French to travel past the ambiguities of war, albeit temporarily. Gendered discourses about victimization served the French nation by portraying France as a universal female victim facing a masculine German aggressor. They figured into a larger effort to shape the French experience of war in a way that benefited the nation. The confinement of women happened on a large scale as well as an individual one: this chapter articulates how gendered imagery of France itself functioned to limit the possibilities of women's lives in the postwar era.

France as a victimized woman

During the postwar period, even the nation of France took the form of a victimized woman in contemporary productions. Writers and artists during the Liberation commonly equated the wartime experience of France with that of female suffering, providing a language that allowed them to avoid the many complexities and contradictions that embodied life during the Occupation. When writer and deportee Simone Saint-Clair returned to France in the spring of 1945 from her time in German camps, she was so overcome by emotion that she found it difficult to express how she was feeling. All of the lost time, all of the lost people—Saint-Clair's own son had died in battle—what were they for? Saint-Clair wondered. Some of the answers, she recalled, came when the train she was riding crossed the border between France and Switzerland. As she wrote in her memoir, upon first glance, "We saw France under a veil of mourning, but her face, hollowed out from deprivation and sadness, shone with purity. Her clear eyes, lifted toward high peaks, bespoke her faith in a better future. This was France battered, but courageous, proud, hard-working and ardent, the France of former, nobler days."[4] Saint-Clair's account characterizes France purely as a victim, and more specifically a victimized woman. France is neither triumphant nor wracked with guilt over its ambiguous wartime activities. Instead France is a woman who has been beaten down by others, and who is just now beginning to revive herself.[5] Her revival is particularly important because it betrays the notion that France's strength was not completely lost during the Occupation, showing that France could be a forceful world power. Just as de Gaulle portrayed himself as the best of both French men and women, so the discourse of victimization depicted France as simultaneously a feminine victim and a survivor regaining his manhood. Consequently, writers, memoirists, and others used a gendered discourse of victimization to universalize and shape French experiences of war and Liberation.

There is a seeming incongruity here: the symbolic face of France was feminine at a time when the French were reasserting their masculinity after the quick defeat in the German invasion and the experience of the Occupation. Why not simply use one masculine image to unite the image and project virility? There are a variety of responses to this question. First, Marianne was strongly tied to imagery of the French Republic, which distanced the new government from that of the Vichy regime. In fact Maurice Agulhon argues that Marianne, a representative of the republican state, had no "logically tolerable" place and "had to be attacked" by the Vichy government because of the threat she posed to her symbolic replacements, images of Maréchal Pétain and, curiously, Joan of Arc.[6] Additionally, the female imagery reinforced the notion that France was a victimized nation rather than an active participant in the Nazi program. France's passive depiction supports the Resistance myth, and the feminization of the country renders that portrayal all the more powerful.[7]

This feminine allegory is still less surprising when taking into account France's—and indeed the West's—long history of feminine symbols that do not translate into improved conditions for actual female citizens.[8] The use of a female symbol as a public representation of the nation could have been— seemingly paradoxically—intended to discourage women's public participation. At the very least, it reflected the reality that later parts of the book will address: female political progress was highly unlikely in the context of the Liberation.[9] Finally, the symbolic feminization of France within victimization metaphors ultimately gave way to the imagery of France as a powerful, masculine nation, prepared to reassert itself in the wake of Nazi aggression, rather than dealing with the reality of defeat and collaboration. France was thus both feminine and masculine through victimhood imagery. This image of Marianne physically defeating the German eagle from the May 8, 1945 edition of the newspaper *Les nouvelles du matin*, clearly highlights the masculine aspects of Marianne, who lords her dominance over the fallen German eagle.

(Dessin de A. GALLAND), (C.P. 3.520).

Cette fois tu ne te relèveras pas !

Figure 1 This time you won't get back up![10]

The lines of action trace the trajectory of Marianne's fist, which was powerful enough to knock out Germany. In the depiction, France's flag stands first in line with those of the Soviet Union, the United States, and Great Britain. Here, despite clearly being a woman, France is a masculine force, strong enough to fell Germany with its physicality and stand among the Great Powers.

Cultural productions echoed depictions of France as a female victim, but they also took care to reinforce the notion that France was a strong power. In January 1945, for example, *Marie-France* printed a poem by Simone Fresneau entitled, "France is a Soul." In this poem, Fresneau articulated the notion that France's wartime experience was one of suffering at the hands of her enemies, and ultimately one of self-actualized strength and redemption:

As long as France stops herself at the brink of death
And says that she will not fall,
As long as the Other still laughs and makes the blows rain down
And the blood stream
And life slip away
As long as he only sees his demented actions,
And his dismembered body
And his dismantled being
As long as he can no longer retain his life,
Just when he thinks that all is lost,
She discovers in her bereft and dreary breast
The fragile shock of a heart that still beats.
And rain the blows down
And stream the blood
And slip away life
She knows that she is saved
For this divine power comes to her all at once
To bring together from all of the parts of her stricken heart
The smallest jolts, the tiniest waves
In a gigantic flood of resurrection.
And the Other, terrified, watches this beaten woman
Who returns and rises up,
And yells right in front of him, that She wants to live.
He can only shrink back
Before this woman in chains who walks toward liberty,
This disfigured woman walks toward light
This annihilated woman who walks toward.
He had thought her flesh and blood
And discovers in that instant that France is a soul.[11]

France appears here as a beaten-down, tired, even "annihilated" woman, a classic victim. However, she is a victim who will not submit to the enemy, even when at the brink of death—just as France's citizens would not submit to the Germans.[12] Indeed the poem portrays France as having rescued itself—a concept of whose importance Charles de Gaulle was quite conscious—and betrays a masculine strength within the nation, thereby echoing the developing notions of the Resistance myth. The ambiguity of the French experience of war does not emerge in the text of the poem. Instead, national identity is singular and solid: France was battered and beaten, and now she has freed herself. Here France was once again ready to retake her place at the fore of national and international power.

Fresneau's poem confirms as well that France was more than a physical state, it was an idea, or a "soul" to which the people could turn their hope. For people like Saint-Clair and Fresneau, a victimized France was a symbol whose fluidity allowed it to assume the characteristics the French population was attempting to express about itself in the context of the Liberation. This poem and this testimony are creating the "soul," the identity, of France in the postwar moment: France is a victimized woman who withstood the evil enemy and now is returning to life— in a display of masculine strength—to the dismay of those who doubted her and the satisfaction of those who always trusted in her. The singularity of purpose in Fresneau's poem is illustrative of the state of affairs in France at this time. These works begin to show a positive definition of France and what it meant to experience the Occupation as a true French citizen, for both men and women.

Another cultural format, the poster (*affiche*), played a crucial role in transmitting such messages about the sexed symbolism of France—both subversive and official—during and immediately after the war. Indeed Margaret Collins Weitz has argued that "Posters conveyed messages at a time when television did not exist and newsreels were censored (as was the press)."[13] During the war, the Resistance battled Vichy and the Germans both militarily and in terms of propaganda. During the Liberation, though, one *affiche* stood out as particularly powerful.

The person behind the poster, Paul Colin, was a fairly well-known artist of the middle of the twentieth century who founded a popular art school in Paris before the war. Known as the "magician of *les années folles*," Colin was most famous for his drawings of dancers like Josephine Baker and Loïe Fuller in the 1920s.[14] His work in the interwar period became so well known that Colin is credited with reviving the poster as an art form, one which had waned since the

days of Toulouse Lautrec.[15] Even more impactful was his influence on Parisians'
interest in black American culture in the 1920s through his art, which historian
Henry Louis Gates Jr refers to as a combination of "delight and disorientation."[16]
Colin ceased creating posters for the duration of the war, citing his "inexpressible
confusion" about current events.[17] The atmosphere was quite different in France
at the end of the Second World War, but Colin still attempted to read and reflect
on the mood of the people.

Colin's 1944 *affiche*, entitled *Libération*, depicts a victimized woman
embodying the nation in a way even more abstract and potentially evocative
than the Fresneau poem. This poster was affixed to buildings all over Paris when
the first Allied troops entered to liberate the city. In fact, on August 17, 1944,
Colin heard that the American troops were approaching the city and drew the
image explicitly so that it could be posted throughout the town by the time they
arrived. According to one biographer, Colin completed this process so quickly
that even departing Germans saw it.[18] Unlike the normal process for *affiche* work,
nobody commissioned the piece; Colin "simply wanted to express his joy"[19]
spontaneously at the end of Occupation. The potent aspect of that statement,
however, is exactly how Colin chose to depict that "joy": through the image of a
downtrodden woman facing the light.

Contemporary commentators on this piece agreed that no words were
necessary to describe it; its meaning, they argue, comes through clearly,
simply, and evocatively.[20] In their analysis, there is evident gender-blindness.
In his illustration Colin selected as his subject Marianne, the famous symbol
of republican France since the time of the French Revolution. This selection
is particularly striking considering that Marianne's image was banished from
Vichy propaganda.[21] In *Libération*, Colin draws Marianne using the red, white,
and blue of the French national flag to represent the return of republicanism on
a symbolic level. Such imagery posed a contrast to Vichy's aggressive celebration
of paternalism and masculinity. After the war, though, republican France called
upon Marianne's image not simply to represent the republic, but also, according
to Maurice Agulhon, to manifestly express the notion—famously espoused by
de Gaulle—that the French Republic had never ceased to exist.[22]

Perhaps most evocative of Colin's visual language of martyrdom is that despite
Marianne's determinedly secular past, her hands bear the marks of stigmata,
linking her with a potent Christian story of betrayal, suffering, and, ultimately,
redemption. Marianne here reflects the secular, discursive victimhood which is
so evident in France at this time. Marianne as victim is an evocative stand-in for

Figure 2 Libération.

the nation. She is a Christ-like figure who has emerged from the tomb, bearing the scars of her suffering, the blood of war, and the physical damage sustained by France, but she is hopeful for the future. In Colin's rendition, the symbol of France has been crucified in a powerful articulation of France's experience during the war. France's new metaphorical body is that of a destroyed female who will rise again.[23] Colin presents an immediate analysis of France's experience during the war as one of suffering and yet the promise of redemption. Colin's piece offers a powerful coalescence of the gendered messages of national victimhood of the time: France was a victim of Nazi aggression rather than an active collaborator, but she is still strong and powerful.

In the Colin image, Marianne holds one bloody hand up to her forehead, as if in a gesture of weariness, yet the position of her body is turned squarely toward the light, as if to show that despite all of the painful baggage she carries, both physical (bombed-out buildings) and emotional (her grief-filled fatigue is evident), she will not yield to the pain of what she has endured. Instead, she faces the future buoyed by republicanism, in this case represented by the flag of France and the Revolutionary cockade. Marianne is both victim and inspiration, both death and hope, all embodied in the symbol of a woman who is to represent France. The poster captures a moment in French life and an artist's reaction to this moment, but it was also meant to be displayed widely in public; that is the express purpose of an *affiche*. Colin drew upon traditional republican and religious symbolism to illustrate a story about the war that depicted France as a woman whose strength was not bested by the pain of Occupation.[24]

Colin himself stated that the point of a poster like this was to "seduce" the audience.[25] As Colin was primarily an *affichiste* by commission, he openly stated that he needed to figure out how to "appeal" to the public, to attract people's attention to the artistic message he was representing.[26] The art historian Robert Rey, writing in the introduction to an exposition of Colin's work in 1949, expressed wonderment at this fundamental problem of any *affichiste*: "To evoke in a passerby the desire to go see a play about which he knows nothing except the title and to evoke intrigue and interest." His evocation of emotion, Rey said, was Colin's genius: "Every time, Paul Colin finds the solution."[27] The solution for Colin at the time of the Liberation was the utilization of emotional, familiar images.

Colin's *affiche* did seem to provoke the kinds of reactions that he himself had felt in drawing it. When the famous Resistance member and writer Vercors was commissioned to write an article articulating the French experience of war and the Liberation to American readers in *Life* magazine immediately following the Liberation of Paris, he immediately turned to the *affiche* to explain his feelings about his country.[28] The poster, he wrote, gave him great joy every time he saw this "young woman" representing France:

> as the day is dawning. She is not happy—oh no! she is proud. But she is also timid and uncertain. She is like those people who have been confined by sickness to their beds for long months, who are not yet cured, but who are getting up for the first time, and who are filled with anguish at the idea of trusting their legs which have been immobile for so long: are they still going to work? . . . This country that suffers so much that joy dares not show itself, this country is so unhappy that it doesn't know if it can really believe in its deliverance. It is this France that the artist represents and that I love more than ever.[29]

Vercors adopted the visual language of Colin's *affiche* to explain to Americans the experience of his country during the war: it had suffered, and the experience was painful, but there was hope for the future.[30] Attesting to the potency of Colin's *affiche* is the fact that it was more widely reproduced than any other image in France for decades.[31] Certainly it was true that the French did not have an easy time under the Occupation, and were not enjoying an immediate prosperity by any means now that the war was over, but this easy visual narrative provided by the *affiche* overlooks the undeniable facts of the Vichy regime and the purge, both of which were important parts of the French reality at this time.

Newspapers and magazines also employed the image of France as a victim in their issues. In 1944, the influential journalist Georges Hourdin published a story in *Marie-France* in honor of the upcoming Easter holiday, which for him signified the Catholic ideas of martyrdom and ultimately redemption, all embodied in the image of France as a beaten woman. He wrote:

> A new France emerges from the tomb on this day of Easter 1945 and breathes the air of liberty with full lungs. She sees the great devastation of modern war recede away from her. She is intoxicated by the first warm days and the coming of victory. But when she takes stock of her strength, when she trips during her first steps, France must remember that she has been, for four years, nailed to the Cross. She is battered. The blood has not yet dried on her body, the wounds still seep on her feet and on her hands.[32]

Hourdin uses this same martyr-driven imagery, of France as a female victim—in fact of France literally as Jesus during the Ascension—to make a point both about the struggles of France and about the future of France. Here again, France's experience is depicted as one of unanimity: it can be embodied in the story of a victimized female figure transcending her physical realities. And on the very first day of its publication, *Marie-France* told its readers that France herself was counting on her female citizens to be her very soul, "as she has never done before," and to help her restore her strength and her good name.[33] Ultimately, though, such images betray the masculine strength that France purportedly still carried within her soul.

Joan of Arc, Charles de Gaulle

In 1946, Charles de Gaulle told his transportation minister, Jules Moch, about his decision to resign from the government. In a thinly veiled reference to his distaste for having to share power, he purportedly explained, "I don't imagine Joan of *dictator?*

Arc married, a mother, and, who knows, maybe betrayed by her husband."[34] So began one of several direct identifications de Gaulle made between himself and the storied, and often-referenced, French heroine. Robert Aron cites de Gaulle, in discussing his future plans with the provisional commissioner of Toulouse in 1944, as stating, "As for me, I shall withdraw.... I have a mission; and it is coming to an end. I must disappear. France may again one day have need of a pure image. That image must be left with her. Had Joan of Arc been married, she would no longer have been Joan of Arc. I must disappear." According to Raoul Aglion, an aide to de Gaulle, the general also referred to himself as Joan of Arc in an exchange with Franklin Roosevelt when he stated, "Joan of Arc was not elected," during a conversation about his place in France's political future. (On hearing of this, Winston Churchill retorted, "Yes, Mr. President, he thinks he is Joan of Arc, but unfortunately my bishops won't let me burn him."[35]) Thus the president of France repeatedly self-identified with a teenage girl from centuries past, a tactic which initially seems at odds with French efforts at establishing virility.

Charles de Gaulle did not merely use Joan's story to make a point about history and historical legacies and responsibilities, as he did with many other historical figures during the war, including Danton, Poincaré, and Clémenceau.[36] Instead, de Gaulle metaphorically became Joan, raising certain gender problems evident in this curious blending, which one historian has referred to as "the perfect osmosis ... of political mission[s]."[37] The literary critic Françoise Meltzer argues that the figure of Joan of Arc has ceased to have much meaning in and of itself, and representations of her instead can be read as a critical allegory of the "assumptions and gender prejudices of each succeeding era."[38] Thus her image has become a vessel for people to articulate and attempt to legitimate their anxieties and dogmas about gender.

To provide a brief context, Joan of Arc lived in the fifteenth century, a time when France and England were engaged in what would become known as the Hundred Years' War. In 1429, Joan was probably seventeen and living in Domrémy, a small village in Lorraine, when she heard what she described at her later trial as a voice from God, which told her to help the French dauphin rid France of the English invaders. Prince Charles was apparently convinced, and under Joan, the French repelled the English at Orléans. The prince became Charles VII of France, having undergone the traditional crowning in the Reims Cathedral in July 1429. In 1431, during an attempt to take back territory in Burgundy, Joan was captured, bared (to determine that she was in fact female), her virginity tested, and placed on trial. Found guilty of heresy, she was ultimately burned at the stake in 1431.

It is crucial to consider the extent to which de Gaulle himself reflects these gender-based "assumptions and prejudices" through his own personage. This is especially provocative considering de Gaulle's metaphorical embodiment of the nation. In his *Vichy Syndrome*, Rousso states that it is possible to reduce the wartime de Gaulle mystique to a simple equation: de Gaulle resisted, and de Gaulle was France, so France's wartime experience was one of resistance.[39] This places his self-equation with Joan of Arc on an even grander scale.

By looking beyond de Gaulle and examining other kinds of the many evocations of Joan from the same period it is possible to explain his motivations. The cultural theorist Marina Warner has written extensively on Joan of Arc, and she argues that the Jehannic figure has been deployed in different eras to reify norms, particularly gendered ones.[40] Thus in using Joan of Arc, Charles de Gaulle made an explicit statement about what behaviors would be acceptable for both men and women during the long Liberation. This section will analyze the figure of Joan of Arc through writings and speeches from a selection of Jehannic sources that appeared during the immediate postwar era to show how Joan of Arc's nebulous gender assignation allowed for her symbolic usage by Charles de Gaulle in the immediate postwar years, and then examine the potential meanings of this usage.

French historical actors of all stripes have invoked Joan of Arc, intending to assign some meaning or validity to their specific causes and circumstances.[41] During the time surrounding the Second World War alone, the Jehannic image was employed concurrently by both the Right and the Left, by people as seemingly disparate as the infamous fascist intellectual Robert Brasillach[42] and the Resistance writer Vercors.[43] Robert Gildea argues that there was a serious battle over who was allowed to claim her during the Second World War; Marshall Pétain invoked her, as did French Communists. But, he states, at the end of the war, she was "firmly located in the camp of the Communists and Charles de Gaulle, who marched together in procession to her statue on 12 May 1945."[44]

As the Vichy regime had so actively attempted to claim the figure of Joan of Arc as its own, Charles de Gaulle vigorously reclaimed her at the Liberation. Marianne had been banned under Vichy, but Joan of Arc was Vichy's preferred symbol. Charles de Gaulle needed to bring her back under the umbrella of republican France in order to diminish the Vichy regime. André Rauch has argued that Marianne, despite her enduring status as a symbol for the French Republic and the value of liberty, is occasionally supplanted by other female symbols, if the historical moment demands it.[45] In order to eliminate the historical stain of Vichy, it was necessary to win the ultimate battle for Joan of

Arc. In embodying her fully, Charles de Gaulle accomplished both a Jehannic rehabilitation and an erasure of her Vichy roots.

Charles de Gaulle often used the figure of Joan of Arc historically (as opposed to his more purely symbolic usage) to appeal to the French people both during and after the war. As early as July 1940, a mere two weeks after his first broadcast from London, he cited her name, among others, in an address to the French people. He implored his listeners not to surrender their weapons, asking if French heroes like Joan "would have agreed to surrender all of France's arms to her enemies so that they might use them against her Allies?"[46] Again in May 1941, in an effort to combat the Vichy-sponsored celebrations of Joan of Arc Day, de Gaulle called upon the French to oppose Vichy in Joan's name, saying:

> A country three-quarters conquered. Most of her men who lived there collaborating with the enemy. Paris, Bordeaux, Orléans, Reims, had become foreign garrisons. A representative of the invader dictating law in the capital. Treason displayed everywhere. A chronic state of famine. An ignoble regime of terror and informing organized in the fields as well as in the cities. Soldiers hiding their arms, leaders their chagrin, the French their fury. Such was, on the surface, France, five hundred and twelve years ago, when Joan of Arc appeared to fulfill her mission. Such is, on the surface, the France of today.[47]

With these evocations, the personage of Joan of Arc was split into two rival images, belonging to Vichy and the Resistance, which were both competing for legitimacy as the rightful heir to the French past. As Robert Gildea argues, Joan's character was divided between [Vichy] Joan, the symbol of national suffering and redemption, on the one hand, and [Resistance] Joan, the rebel and freedom fighter, on the other.[48] This battle between Vichy and the Resistance for the historical Jehannic legacy was likely part of de Gaulle's motivation to invoke Joan's name.[49] The question of why Charles de Gaulle would identify so directly with a teenage girl at a time of crisis for French masculinity remains.

On May 8, 1945, the archbishop of Luçon, Monsignor Antoine-Marie Cazaux, delivered a tribute to Joan of Arc in the Saint-Croix Cathedral in Orléans before an audience which held many government and military representatives.[50] Cazaux was a well-known soldier, priest, and thinker, and in his sermon, he told of how during his preparations for the day he had struggled to understand the meaning of Joan of Arc—so much had been said about her already, and thus he felt it best to use her own words to explain her importance on such a profound day— V-E Day—and in such a symbolic setting. In his talk, Cazaux did not simply quote from official trial transcripts or other well-known writings attributed to Joan. Instead, he constructed a fairly complex argument about what Joan of Arc represented at that particular moment in French history.

Like many authors who chose to focus on Joan of Arc as a subject in the immediate postwar years (including Charles de Gaulle), Cazaux seized upon the historical parallels between the German Occupation of the Second World War and the English Occupation in the fifteenth century. France was a demoralized country for those long war years, he wrote, "her liberties shackled, her life paralyzed, the very best of her sons imprisoned, deported, shot, she is hard to recognize . . ."[51]

Cazaux then broke with his purely historical comparison and went on to argue that Joan of Arc embodied the very essence of what *both* French women and French men should strive to be. In the postwar era, when the confinement of women was the order of the day, this gender flexibility seems initially puzzling. And yet it allows Cazaux to make an argument that narrowed the possibilities of womanhood quite distinctly. Cazaux first points out that Joan was a girl from Lorraine who proved herself to be

> ours [French] by her very heart. A veritable flower of France, we find in her that which every little girl from our house [France] has in its purest, most kindly, most delicate form. . . . Nowadays, some people have wanted to portray her as a veritable "girl of the camps," as having borrowed from the soldiers of her army the most incredibly masculine traits. Grave error! The "Libératrice" of Orleans did not change since her childhood. In the midst of her triumphs, sitting firmly on her steed, she keeps, under her heavy armor, still intact, the heart of that humble peasant woman from Domrémy.[52]

In Cazaux's retelling, Joan reflects the best of every French female. Like female victims, who also stood in for all French women, Joan steps into the public sphere only when necessary, when her country or her own very Frenchness are under attack, but she never forgets that she is but a humble Frenchwoman, and, if she survives the crisis, she returns to those simple roots, seeking no glory. In fact, Cazaux directly states this maxim in his sermon, saying that before Joan heard the heavenly voices, she had never had any ambition other than to stay home with her family, and he adds that the voices had to be particularly loud and persistent to convince her to leave.[53] Cazaux then returns to France's present situation and links it with Joan of Arc, saying: "Today, at the end of a war that has caused so many tears amongst mothers and wives, who is the woman of France who does not recognize the cry of her own soul in the words of Joan?"[54] Through a rhetorical linking of past and present, Cazaux has delivered a lesson to French women in how to embody their Frenchness most fully: they must fight only when absolutely crucial and then they must go home.

Cazaux goes on to highlight Joan of Arc's "candor" and "finesse" which make her character so charming. These, he argues, are the traits that she inherited from every young French girl: "She has taste, good sense, and a spiritual gaiety, along with a delicate sensibility."[55] In this quote, Cazaux is creating a descending and ascending inheritance in terms of femininity and Frenchness in the sense that Joan of Arc both gave and received the traits of a good young French girl. This construction suggests that these traits are innate and do not have to be learned. In this way, Cazaux communicates a mode of behavior that is universal and has no beginning or end. This is simply how French women are and always have been. Here, he is no longer referring to anything that has to do with Joan of Arc, or even anything close, such as a discourse on symbolic female martyrization or wartime sacrifice. He is instead describing a purportedly timeless combination of coquetry and refinement natural to French women.

However, as Cazaux goes on to state, Joan of Arc represents much more than the quintessentially simple, humble, yet beautiful French girl; she also embodies the very best traits of the French man, as seen in the figure of the knight. "Certainly," he argues, "the French soldier has neither the phlegmatic calm of his English counterpart nor the German's mechanic discipline. But the whole world envies and fears the French soldier's quick decision-making, his vivacity in maneuvers, the resources which allow him to gather himself after a moment of weakness." Here Cazaux is presumably making a historical and prescriptive reference both to the French army's quick defeat at the hands of the Germans at the beginning of the war and to Joan of Arc's injury in the battle of Orléans, when she was hit with an arrow and began to cry, but then, as Cazaux himself notes earlier in his sermon, rallied herself and took the position. These types of events, according to Cazaux, constitute momentary setbacks for France in a long and triumphant history. It is better to focus on another inherent aspect of French masculinity, he argues, "this impetuosity in attack that surprises and disconcerts the enemy." For Cazaux, this, combined with the other exalted "qualities of the race . . . Joan eminently possesses them."[56]

Cazaux alters Joan's essential character to be gender neutral and yet simultaneously gendered and prescriptive. According to Cazaux, "She fears neither another woman from Rouen's sewing or spinning skills nor crossing a French military captain to lead and train troops in battle."[57] Because Joan of Arc can stand as both humble peasant woman and valiant knight, she can serve as an instructive figure for all of the French as they leave the war years behind them.

Joan's image was also desexualized while it was simultaneously imbued with traits traditionally linked to both genders, lending it an extra layer of flexibility for the postwar commentator. Under the Vichy regime, Joan of Arc was mystically feminine, yet in the Liberation era the emphasis on her sexuality dealt with its inherent absence. In famed writer and member of the Resistance Édith Thomas's 1947 history *Jeanne d'Arc*, she discusses how Joan traveled to see the dauphin with a group of seven male knights. She highlights the fact that none of these knights felt attracted to Joan in the slightest, a fact that they found "stunning," as they described her as "pretty and well formed, and [the knights] were quite young. The only feeling they had for Joan was a completely religious respect."[58] A rector speaking in the Rouen cathedral in 1947 echoed themes of Joan's desexualization, intoning that "she devoted herself wholly to the mission: she belongs to it body and soul."[59] Her marriage was to France, not a corporeal man. Additionally, in René Bronner's 1948 children's play, he writes, "At 14 years old, her heart began to beat, but only for France, for she would only ever know one love: the holy love of the Patrie."[60] Her sexuality was gone, replaced by a neutral, patriotic religiosity which ironically rendered her more of a woman, and hence less of a temptress and, consequently, more able to lead France.

So at the same time that postwar commentators like Thomas and Bronner both sexed and sexually stripped Joan of Arc's image (and hence rendered her able to embody the very best essentialized qualities of Frenchness for both men and women), Charles de Gaulle chose to call upon that image as a symbolic justification for his own arrival and relationship to power. In doing so, he created a connection between this historical French heroine, the experience of France during the war, and this new French hero who had set himself up to lead the country out of its languor.

Charles de Gaulle acted as a model for the country, actualizing within his very being what it meant to be French at all both during and after the tumult of the Second World War. Indeed de Gaulle himself famously said later in his career, "I am a man who belongs to no one person and yet who belongs to everyone."[61] But if de Gaulle was France, and he had to be an icon of normative French identity during this period when France was in a state of national and international confusion, then he also had to serve as an example for both French men and French women. In this vein, it is perhaps more understandable that he drew upon a personage whose own gender flexibility would allow him to call upon the most honorable aspects of both French masculinity and femininity.

Charles de Gaulle stepped into the symbolic gap in guidance that appeared after the war. The literary critic Julia Kristeva has stated that in this moment of

Liberation de Gaulle understood that the issue at hand was not simply that the French had lost a leader or leadership between the Third Republic and the Vichy regime. Instead, de Gaulle recognized that a "regicide" had taken place and the people had been orphaned.[62] By employing Joan of Arc, de Gaulle positioned himself to be both mother and father to this apparently abandoned people.[63] De Gaulle was again able to embody a bi-gendered vision of France, and through this, he could set an example for the entire populace to emulate.

In the postwar years, when de Gaulle was an outsized persona for the French nation, his particular message was both desexualized and doubly gendered. This charged messaging is significant because Charles de Gaulle was positioning himself directly as Joan of Arc in a moment when gender stability—and national stability in general, which gender stability was meant to reinforce—was widely present in a variety of cultural productions.[64]

In this context, the fact that Charles de Gaulle was both mother and father to the French people through the symbolic usage of Joan of Arc becomes more comprehensible because Joan was not simply a teenage girl. Instead she was victimized in the name of France, and as such she could be a symbol of all that was right with French men and French women in a time of uncertainty that followed the end of the Second World War. For his part, Charles de Gaulle was there to channel the gendered images of Joan and funnel them into his particular Jehannic vessel: a gendered discourse about a timeless, honorable, and well-ordered France.[65] Joan of Arc represents, according to the literary critic Marina Warner, "the yearning . . . for stasis and constancy and comprehensibleness."[66] In choosing to employ Joan of Arc as a figurehead, Charles de Gaulle tapped into the deep need for gender normalcy during the long Liberation.

Conclusion

For writers and artists such as Vercors, Paul Colin, and Simone Fresneau, as well as members of government and the press, the feeling of the Liberation period was most evocatively articulated with images of redemptive suffering. These images reflected a unified singularity of experience during the war, and thus they served to construct, in this moment of Liberation, a national identity of Resistance and republicanism in the face of a non-French oppressor. The theme of a phoenix-like ascent in the images allowed the artists and writers to communicate a resurgent masculine strength within the nation, which would allow France to regain its status as a world power. France's categorization as a female victim helped to allow the French to forget the disturbing ambiguities of the recent past, find consensus, and look to the future and rebuild. The gendered victimization of France thus constitutes a significant element of France's reconstruction.[67]

The idea of France as a female victim carried power because it was a familiar image in both secular and religious contexts, through symbols like Marianne as well as the Catholic Virgin Mary. As scholars have shown, female symbols often function well when representing male power precisely because of the distance between symbol and the reality of women's lives. During the Liberation, however, the discourse of martyrdom was used to respond to a new context and new perceived threats to the French nation. Cultural representations of female victimhood served to universalize the national experience of war as one of historical victimization and renewed strength. Female victimization was particularly useful in postwar France because it did not threaten fragile social boundaries or challenge male authority.

If France itself was a victim, particularly a female one, then it could confirm the Resistance myth. In the French mind, France would not be the country that fell quickly to the Germans and went through four years of occupation and collaboration. Instead, it would be the nation that bore the weight of repression, but also the nation of people who had endured, and had never lost sight of the meaning of France, or the nation's identity. This is why Charles de Gaulle references Joan of Arc as though he is *la pucelle*; he is tapping into an idea of Frenchness that is presumably fixed. This constancy also emerges in the Paul Colin *affiche*, when he depicts France as a brutalized Marianne. These symbols or concepts comprised part of a larger idea of Frenchness which purported to transcend the events of recent history. In actuality, rather than being references for an eternal notion of French identity, as Charles de Gaulle tried to demonstrate in his adoption of the Joan of Arc persona, these symbols and concepts combined to construct that identity concurrently.

2

Women as Victims

In 1953, Mlle Marie Medard, a resistor who was tortured by the *milice* and who later testified against her torturers, was described by the conservative newspaper *Le Figaro* as "heroic" for her continued resistance to their entreaties, despite enduring intense physical duress:

> As Mlle Marie Medard advanced to the stand, M. Chadefeux [the presiding judge] recalled for the courtroom how her heroic acceptance of suffering had so impressed her torturers that these people called her Joan of Arc! . . . They tied her hands behind her back and burned her fingers with a cigarette, then they hit her with a rod on her shins and on the soles of her feet.[1]

On the other side of the political spectrum, the leftist newspaper *Combat* echoed these sentiments in describing Medard, saying, "It was her that [the torturers] set upon most fiercely. She experienced it all, the bathtub, the blows, the whip, the burns. She did not speak."[2] The language here is not particularly subtle: Mlle Medard is heroic by the very virtue of her suffering and her silence.

This chapter will examine the postwar portrayals of actual women victims from France in the Second World War. Their often-pointed depictions, written *after* the war was over in a sort of *à la minute* analysis of their war and postwar experiences, reflect a focus on the confinement of femininity that was so important to the reconstruction of France. This chapter will focus on several prominent themes that arose in postwar coverage and memoirs of French female victims: the image of the caregiver; feminine strength and duty; religious principles; patriotism and duty; guilt and modesty; and the link between femininity and national pride. These themes reinforced the idea that the women were largely passive supporters of the French nation, not active fighters, like French men. Postwar coverage of women's wartime participation reinforced specific values of French womanhood that women ought to emulate: passivity, compliance, cheerfulness, and nurturing.

This chapter analyzes these values in female victims' memoirs to elucidate postwar ideals of French womanhood and reveal how they ultimately confined definitions of proper behavior. It also delves into how male and female experiences of victimhood were quite different, owing to the exigencies of the postwar period. While the male role in postwar France was one of strength and power in order to project such an image on to the world stage as well as the nation, it was unclear whether or how French femininity would be altered by the war, as well as what women's relationship to the nation would be. This was especially the case in lieu of female participation in the Resistance as well as women's enfranchisement at the end of the war. In this context, through specific images of women sufferers, victimhood became an acceptable public, political identity for women at a time when cultural forces strongly encouraged them to return to the private sphere. However, while victimization represented a voice for women in public, this voice was not akin to self-actualization. The vision that public female victimhood transmitted to the French, and to French women in particular, portrayed French women's public experiences during the war as exceptional, for their true place was in the domestic arena. There, they would pose no threat to the masculine hierarchy so important to France at this time. While memoirs describe experiences that occurred during the war, they were all published or released in the postwar period. The tropes that they describe or even embody, then, are functioning for postwar readers.

Defining victimhood as feminine and honoring female victims served to limit and control women's roles and lives in postwar France. Through the label of victim, women acquired a very specific public identity that could complement the notion of the honorable, masculine hero who had fallen for France. It masked both men and women's actual wartime activities, complex as they were. This book has touched upon the notion that most French people neither resisted nor collaborated to any great degree during the war. Rather, they survived in a climate that was shifting and could be hostile. However, women did make up a significant percentage of Resistance participators, as historians like Christine Bard, Margaret Collins Weitz, Claire Duchen, and Margaret Rossiter have shown in their work.[3] These scholars have proven that women were largely written out of the history—and historiography—of the Resistance. For example, Duchen points to the fact that the "prestigious" *Croix de la Libération* was awarded to "1,030 men, five towns, eighteen combat units and six women (four of these being posthumous awards)."[4] And Bard cites the account of a young woman who states that only her father assumed the title of resistor, but her mother's work—preparing food for him to eat while out, for example, or facing down the police when they called—at the very least enabled the Resistance.[5] These historians' works have contributed to the restoration of women's presence within the historical legacy of the Resistance. Having proved that women did indeed participate, the question then becomes why this erasure of female resistors occurred at all. After the war, when stability and legitimacy became important for France's internal and external image, gender roles were defined anew in order to support a specific image of the strength and prowess of the nation.

The women described in this chapter faced detention, torture, and in some instances even death. French female deportees typically went to Ravensbrück, the women's camp in Germany. Around ten thousand French women were deported there, of whom two thousand survived.[6] It is undoubtedly the case that these French women faced their extraordinarily difficult circumstances in many ways, including with grace, deep kindness, pluckiness, and courage. This book seeks not to judge those experiences and reactions negatively or positively, but rather to place them in a context of postwar cultural pedagogy. It looks at why and how people described these women (or how they described themselves) in a particular time and place, the Liberation, and how their language and stories functioned in terms of the reconstruction of gender and French identity *after* the war.

Characteristics of the female victim

Perhaps the most salient characteristic of the French female victim, both in the detention camps and outside of them, was the poise she showed under extreme duress: she would not talk and betray her fellow resistors. After the war, however, when her testimony served the interests of the nation, she would speak, but only temporarily. Her testimony was not akin to a sanctioned public role.

Silence typified the female victim's experience during the war, demonstrating her great strength for France in the face of pain and potential suffering. One female resistor, Daisy Georges-Martin, showed the same poise as Mlle Medard when she submitted to prolonged torture. Her cellmate, Mlle Micinska, remembered her fortitude during this time:

> After three days of tortures, beaten, with one arm dislocated, they threw her in the cave like a wreck. German torturers spit on her and insulted her. One *milicien* proposed inflicting a level of torture on her that had never been applied before. Eventually all of them left. Finally alone, she stayed in the cave half dead, but proud and happy because despite all her suffering, she did not speak.[7]

Even then, according to the memoir, she "always had a smile." Georges-Martin is content because of her suffering, and the author of this memoir, Germaine Mornand, emphasizes the combination of pain and joy in the face of extreme tactics. What is important here, for Mornand, who is writing in the immediate postwar era, is that Georges-Martin continued to smile through the pain. French women's pride lay in retaining silence in the name of France and not allowing exceptional public moments to affect their true, essential selves.

One striking dichotomy that arises in the accounts of women who faced extreme pressure to speak is that of silence vs. testimony. First, the women are lauded for their ability to stay silent: they are better, more French even, because they do not talk and betray their fellow countrymen with their speech. They stay silent for France. In many ways, this quality speaks to women's natural abilities to stay in the private sphere, to retain silence in public and try to remain invisible. Yet several years after the war, the need for justice arose in postwar trials of war criminals, as in the case of Medard, and the Resistance myth was in full bloom. Women like Medard were now celebrated by politicians and the mass media for their courage in making their stories public through testifying. For example, when Suzanne Busson "finally" decided to publish her memoirs in 1946, apparently after much consideration, the president of the National Association of the Fighting Press, Camille Delétang, himself a deportee, wrote of how he appreciated her contribution to the national memory of heroic resistance.[8] However, these women were allowed to be public, and even congratulated as such, only while acting in the role of victims for their country. They are not heroes because they were resistors, they are not heroes for their actions; these women are heroes because of what was done to them and to their femininity. It is under this pretext, and the caveat that they have retained their femininity, that they are allowed to publicly represent France. In both cases their positions do not harm the nation's postwar goals.

This notion of the female victim as confirmation of the postwar gender order is highlighted through the accounts that stressed modesty, a desire to remain private, as a dominating characteristic of female victims. Christine Bard has noted that many oral interviews with *résistantes* include them saying, "Oh, I really didn't do anything much."[9] Most often the sense of modesty manifested itself in a desire to want to downplay any heroism or tribulation that these women experienced during the war. When Simone Téry went to interview fellow female resistors for her book on famous communist resistor Danielle Casanova, many of them insisted upon anonymity: "They were not afraid of the Gestapo or of torture, but they were frightened at the idea that I would pronounce their names here."[10] These women had been courageous and bold in the name of France, but they shunned any public recognition of their experiences and achievements, preferring to stay anonymously in the private sphere. In fact one woman from Brittany, Suzanne Wilborts, even wrote her memoir in the third person, as though the events she lived during the war were an anomaly or had happened to someone else. They were an anomalous rupture from her real life as wife and mother, rather than part of a whole. Putting one's voice in the public sphere in the guise of a martyr did not fundamentally challenge women's traditional "Frenchness," and could therefore be lauded. Deportee Simone Saint-Clair expressed a similar sentiment upon her return to France from Ravensbrück. According to her memoir, Charles de Gaulle happened to be in Annemasse when her train arrived there, and he greeted the women, saying, "You have done your duty. Well done." Saint-Clair remembered thinking to herself, "Doing one's duty? Isn't that the natural thing?" Her experience of deportation and deprivation, all of the difficulties she endured, she interpreted as "natural," as it was for France.[11] De Gaulle and Saint-Clair assumed that the experience of Resistance, deportation, deprivation, and even torture were inimical to women's wartime experience and to French female identity. In this way, normalized, "natural," French female identity is constructed as having undergone a difficult wartime experience. Perhaps these assumptions contributed to the lack of official recognition that women received after the war.[12] Either way, they reinforce the notion that women were acting extraordinarily in these specific circumstances, and afterwards they neither sought nor desired public roles or gratitude. They wanted to resume their "real" lives in the private sphere.

These sentiments of modesty and duty are echoed in the words of Manon Cormier, who died soon after her return to France from the camps in Germany. Cormier was the first woman in the Bordeaux region to receive a doctorate, she was an agitator for women's rights, and she actively participated in the Resistance. When her Resistance activities were discovered by the authorities during the Occupation, she was deported to Germany, where she suffered in the camps because of her already poor health. While in the camps, Manon was physically unable to work. Rather than wallow, her memoir asserts, she tried to lift the spirits of all those around her by giving lectures and lessons on topics as varied as the loves of the French kings and the rights of women. In her abbreviated time in France at the very end of her life, Manon never complained about her lot. Her sister, who transcribed Cormier's own account of her life, wrote: "Despite the endured sufferings, [Manon] regretted nothing. She simply stated these words: 'I did my duty. If I had to do it again, I would start all over. . . .'"[13] Both Cormier and Saint-Clair downplayed their experience during the war as exceptional, and they asked for nothing for their sacrifices for France. In doing so, the women reinforced the conceptualization of French women's wartime activities as selfless and temporal.

The addition of motherhood to accounts of torture and deprivation represented a heightened symbolism to characterizations of victimization. When the famed writer Charlotte Delbo wrote about Auschwitz, one of the images of bleakness she drew on was this: "Here mothers are no longer mothers to their children."[14] In her memoir, Sabine Hoisne recalled a woman from Nancy who was sentenced to death for issuing 357 false demobilization papers. Despite her dire fate, she never "cried for herself," Hoisne reported, but rather for her six-year-old son. Hoisne found herself admiring the woman's great "courage."[15] In December 1944, the Resistance newspaper *Ceux du Maquis* ran a series of vignettes called the "Gallery of Martyrs." It featured the story of Madame Menut, a pharmacist from Riom, a small town in the Auvergne region, who participated in the local branch of the *maquis*. After her husband joined the Resistance, she left her pharmacy and child behind to join him.[16] Mme Menut acted as a nurse in several battles, and then she was injured and taken prisoner. She was several months pregnant, but, as the article points out, she

> submitted to the most horrendous tortures at the hands of the Nazis. Despite her [pregnant] state, she resisted and never delivered one name of her comrades or *maquisards*. She must have been massacred by these cowards, and her horrendously mutilated body was recovered, along with so many others, in a mass grave in Aulnat.[17]

The article mentions the many other bodies in the mass grave, but it places specific weight on the body and life of Mme Menut. Because of her pregnancy and her symbolic potency, her story is highlighted. Here, the emphasis on Mme Menut and her pregnancy signifies the most powerful symbolic public role a woman can have—women can serve France best by providing more children. Anyone who interferes with this is an animal and a "coward."[18]

Similarly, in the famous tragedy at Oradour-sur-Glane, there was one survivor when the Germans set fire to the church with the townspeople inside: a mother who, according to Sarah Farmer's work, made the greatest impact in court. Here is how this woman, Madame Rouffanche, was described in an account of the trial by *Le Figaro*:

What great writers achieve by the power of art: a stripping away, concision, the power of sober lines and density like marble, Mme. Rouffanche, a peasant of the Limousin, achieves effortlessly. . . . A perfectly sober account, and, in that, overwhelming, reduced to the essential facts. . . . She holds herself dignified and austere, dressed in clothes of deepest mourning. . . . Her face under her black hat is white as chalk. . . . Her voice, without the least trace of easy sentiment, reaches us clear and implacable. She is Nemesis, calm and inexorable.[19]

Mme Rouffanche describes her loss in terms that are full of maternal imagery: "In her final words to the court, she spoke with 'the intense illumination of a visionary'[20]: 'I ask that justice be done with God's help. I came out alive from the crematory oven, I am the sacred witness from the church. I am a mother who has lost everything.'"[21] Here Mme Rouffanche constructs her own harrowing experience in a way that echoes the rhetoric of Resistance women victims and also taps into the powerful symbolism of motherhood. It is Rouffanche's motherhood that sanctions her speech and adds a level of potency and validity to her account.

The examples of Rouffanche and Menut depict women who are not idealized participants in the Resistance, hiding out in the hills and making daring raids on enemy positions, or even gathering information on behalf of the Resistance. Instead, they entered into public view somewhat reluctantly, in the case of the famous Mme Rouffanche, as an innocent victim, or, in the case of Mme Menut, as a caregiver to her husband. In each circumstance, directly or indirectly, their feminine qualities are a constant throughout their story, rather than an additional characteristic. Menut is not mourned or respected for her personal heroic exploits, but for the fact of her maternity. Through the account of Mme Menut and the testimony of Mme Rouffanche, it is clear that the enemy has so little respect for life that it will torture and kill mothers, or kill children in front of mothers. Mme Rouffanche represents hope and integrity: it is as though a part of France has died and it is left to the mothers to pursue justice.[22] The maternity of French victims is a powerful blow to the psyche of the nation, as it suggests that the torture extends to the future of France.[23]

Many women resistors were portrayed after the war as caregivers, an identity which dovetailed nicely with characteristics that France required in women at this time. Daisy Georges-Martin, who died in Ravensbrück, nursed fellow deportees back to health when they were ill, and encouraged them when they were down. As Mlle Yvonne Margerit, a fellow detainee, recollected, "Her good humor, her perpetual smile were a precious comfort for us."[24] Even in the worst of times, when all of the women were starving in the camps, Daisy made sure to share her food with the sickest or hungriest. Another detainee, Mme Roche, remembered Daisy as incredibly kind, despite the fact that she was half-naked (because it was so hot) and her skin was yellowed from poor health. Still, Daisy gave each new deportee "a bit of her heart."[25] In a display of national sacrifice for the future, Suzanne Wilborts recalled seeing older French women who were "dying of hunger" giving their food to younger ones in the camps in a sign of pure generosity.[26] Charlotte Delbo remembered urging the sick to eat, to remain strong in the face of despair.[27] Older French inmates thus acted as surrogate mothers, taking care of their younger national counterparts. This was not limited to random acts by individuals, either. The famous academic Germaine Tillion, who is now interred in the Pantheon, asserted that the French block in Ravensbrück was "the only one with a regular system of helping the sick with small portions of extra food—hungry women would give up a potato or the spoon of ersatz jam they received once a week to help a tubercular live a little longer."[28] Whether in groups or as individuals, French women drew upon their purported natural ability to care to survive the camps. Their actual experience may have known great generosity and caring, but how they address it in postwar memoirs, as a fundamental characteristic of French female identity, is what is most pertinent here.

Even the newly founded women's magazine *Marie-France* emphasized the nurturing trait innate in French women in its vignette about Mme Annie de Montfort, who passed away in the camps.[29] Montfort was arrested in 1943 in Grenoble because of her illicit nursing of Polish prisoners of war, and she was eventually transferred to the "sinister" Ravensbrück camp. There, the article noted, "The deprivations and bad treatment got the best of her health, and Mme de Montfort died, victim of her indefatigable generosity which the Gestapo could neither understand nor excuse. A great Frenchwoman has just died."[30] De Montfort was punished by the enemy precisely for her caregiving, and here *Marie-France* highlights how nurturing is both natural for French women and incomprehensible for Germans and for French betrayers.

Likewise, in February 1946, another new women's magazine, *Elle*, published an article, "It is not by coquetry that these women wear the red ribbon," which featured four French women out of the twenty-six who had recently received the Legion of Honor. Three of the four had faced torture, and one of the four had died in Auschwitz. One of these women, Marie-Claude Vaillant-Couturier, was transferred to Auschwitz and then later to Ravensbrück, lived through the experience, and testified against her torturers after the war. Vaillant-Couturier was from a prominent French family, had been a journalist in the interwar period, and was an early exposer of Hitler's camps in that role: "So valuable was Marie-Claude's testimony considered," historian Sarah Helm wrote, "that after the war she was called to give evidence at Nuremberg."[31] Yet Vaillant-Couturier's profile did not emphasize her Resistance activities or her courage in testifying against those who imprisoned her. Instead, the magazine focused on how she provided care and sustenance to her companions in the Resistance and in the camps. The magazine noted that her "devotion" to her fellow detainees was so great that she even stayed in the camps long after she was due to leave so that she could minister to the sick until they could be evacuated.[32] French women like Annie de Montfort and Marie-Claude Vaillant-Couturier cared for one another and for strangers, displaying maternal tendencies that were intrinsic to femininity and the real France (as opposed to the Gestapo). Similarly, Rosane (the pseudonym for professor and Resistance member Renée Lascraux) remembered an incident at the very end of her internment when, at Bergen-Belsen, a male and a female guard came around looking for four French women for a brothel. The man put his hand on Rosane's shoulder, and the French woman next to her "horrified, leaps forward, thanks to her gray hair, and without losing her composure, says in German that I am her daughter, she protests and wrests me from the soldier's hands." The maternal instinct displayed by that woman in that moment saved Rosane from a "shameful ordeal."[33] French women's nurturing was thus highlighted in various cultural productions, showing its importance for the reconstruction.

French women were proud of their patriotism in the camps, which they often measured by their comportment compared to women of other nationalities. For example, Marie Jeanne Bouteille-Garagnon proudly reported that no French woman would agree to work as policewomen, a privileged position, in the foreign camps, unlike some of their counterparts from places like Poland. Any French woman who might even have thought of it, she wrote, would have been "lynched" by their fellow French prisoners.[34] Police women, Germaine Tillion recalled, were chosen for their innate "instincts of domination and cruelty."[35] Similarly, Tillion argued, "out of patriotism and a sense of revulsion for German discipline," no French woman would consider working in the camp's factories, thus aiding the war effort against the Allies, a fact she argues led to a far higher death rate for French women, as they hence received no extra rations.[36] And Rosane recalled how nary a French prisoner established warm relations with any camp guards: "We didn't want to speak German, and I refused to give French lessons to those bitches (*chiennes*)."[37] Accounts suggested that French women's innate moral nationalism prevented them from supporting the Nazi cause.

Aesthetics, so crucial to the postwar gender order, were also present in the camps, and the proper performance of them often took on nationalist tinges. French women's perceived beauty superiority became a source of national pride, for, according to their own accounts, it separated them from the "ugly" German women and gave them a sense of supremacy. That aesthetic distance between French and German women could also provide political distance, in the sense that the French were wholly different from Germans and had an entirely different experience of war, thus supporting the myth of universal Resistance. In her memoir, Marie Jeanne Bouteille-Garagnon wrote of riding the train from France in February 1944 along with a group of French women prisoners. When the train crossed the border into Germany, it stopped, and a group of "dumpy and classless" women from the German Red Cross boarded and drearily served the prisoners barley soup. As Bouteille-Garagnon relates it, the contrast between the two nationalities—and femininities—was striking: the French women were all beautifully dressed and well-coiffed. They did not lose their manners, either: "The detained women thanked [the servers] with a most French politesse," which, Bouteille-Garagnon alleges, took the Germans aback. For the French, the beauty and manners of the French woman in the face of danger stood in strong contrast to the brutish German women and a great expression of French national pride.[38] Even Danielle Casanova, the famous communist resistor, took notice of her changed appearance. She quipped that her weight loss due to nutritional deprivation was all for naught: "I have lost a lot of weight. . . . I can't remember ever having a figure like this one, and just when there's nobody around to admire my elegance."[39] Here, Casanova jokingly sought public recognition for her newly appealing figure. The French allegedly cared so much about how they looked that prisoners in Ravensbrück of other nationalities attributed this vanity to French women's high death rates.[40] Prisoner Sabine Hoisne, accused of sheltering two English soldiers, recalled in her memoir how, for a holiday, female detainees would "make ourselves beautiful; the makeup is impeccable, the dresses carefully chosen."[41] French women's national pride was located in retaining one's outward appearances of femininity and traditional beauty in the face of oppression and ugliness, symbolized by German women.

French women described the shaving of their heads upon their arrival in the camps as detainees as one of the most difficult experiences they had.[42]

Journalist and writer Simone Téry describes the arrival in Auschwitz of a group of French female prisoners, all of whom had attractive French hair: "The silky hair, the blond or brunette curls, their most beautiful female finery and their pride, was stolen from them even after everything else. For it is very precious, women's hair, and the Nazis let nothing go to waste. They had a peculiar look to them, our little French girls, with their skulls as naked as marbles."[43] Téry describes how the women made sure they laughed off this blow to their vanity and their very selves so that the Germans would not see them cry. Marie Jeanne Bouteille-Garagnon describes her absolute horror at the realization that women were being shaved; she bristles that the Germans said that French women had "lice-ridden heads."[44] In fact, Germaine Tillion asserted that the French block in the camp was the only one "free of lice."[45] Simone Saint-Clair, a prisoner in Ravensbrück, also registered disgust at the notion that French women would have dirty heads in her own memoir. Still, she notes, French women bore the loss of this symbol of their femininity bravely, "smiling despite feeling like crying." Thankfully they had no mirrors to see what they really looked like, Saint-Clair writes, for that would have been truly devastating.[46] Charlotte Delbo remembered primping with her fellow prisoners in preparation for Christmas, ironing dresses and "combing our hair. A few experts devoted their efforts to setting hair. 'Cécile, it's my turn, after Gilberte.—No, mine!' We enjoyed the new growth of our hair [since having been shaved upon arrival] which, however, did not enable the volunteer hairdressers to set large curls."[47] Appearances, especially those linked to hair, carried such heft among French prisoners that Tillion recalled how the first indication that a fellow prisoner had given up on life was her surrender in the constant battle with lice.[48] French women's pride in themselves and in their nation was tied up in their hair and overall appearance, but they were determined to carry on and act like French women despite the loss of such a potent symbol of their femininity.

French women's bodily health also took on extra nationalistic and symbolic import in postwar accounts. In her memoir, Sabine Hoisne remembered feeling "outraged" at a "fat" German girl's inspection of her for syphilis. Hoisne was disgusted that this guard was implying that "all the French women are sick and that most of them were arrested for contamination."[49] This affront to Hoisne's morals—and the morals of her countrywomen—left her incensed. The insinuation that she might be dirty or damaged, especially coming from a well-fed German, was a blow.

Even at or near death, the French woman prisoner did not lose a sense of her public face of beauty. Suzanne Bouvard wrote an eyewitness account of the death of Rose-Marie Lafitte, a young woman who had suffered greatly on the trip to the camp. She was extremely sick, and even had a large abscess on her hip, which was quite painful. Despite being near death in the camps, Lafitte made sure to put on makeup and do her hair when she had the chance. Bouvard remembered seeing Lafitte happy for the last time when she thought herself pretty:

> The final vision I keep of her smiling dates from [March 26] where, in a barrack of bloc 26 (I believe), again young and impish for a few hours, she had "made herself a beauty again" with accessories discovered by chance. As she examined herself in a shard of broken mirror, Rose-Marie asked one of her companions: "I haven't changed so much since Toulouse, right, Madeleine?"[50]

Bouvard writes that her beautified appearance seemed to breathe life into Lafitte, albeit briefly, as she died five days later. The opportunity to feel feminine again afforded both Lafitte and Bouvard some temporary comfort and even hope. Here, Bouvard is emphasizing how beauty allowed Lafitte to retain a semblance of her own identity in a time when, as later chapters will show, cultural productions were showing French women how beauty was part of their duty.

Suzanne Wilborts, an older woman who was arrested on suspicion of Resistance activities, also emphasized the power of appearance and the nation when she wrote in her 1946 memoir, *For France*, about a moment in the Angers prison, when she thought her execution was imminent. Immediately upon hearing this news, she "freshened up, one must die in beauty. But there is no water in that cell, nothing. She tries to fix her hair, all the while thinking that it is a beautiful thing to die for her country."[51] Wilborts was not killed, and was instead sent on, eventually landing in Germany. There, she noticed how all of the German women were quite jealous of how well dressed and well kempt the French women were. Rosane meditated on how ironic this was: "If we had marched in the streets of France, with our camp clothes, our shaved heads, our purulent legs covered in paper, horrified passersby would have cried or screamed."[52] And yet maintaining that sense of beauty—and reporting on its importance after the war—was paramount for these women.

In postwar French memoirs, women defined their experiences in ways that privileged proper appearance and comportment, which they retained in the name of national pride even in difficult circumstances.[53] In delineating these aesthetic and behavioral boundaries, postwar memoirists created an ideal image of Frenchness, well after the end of their time in detention.

Male victims

While the focus of this book is postwar feminine representations, and feminine victimhood in this chapter specifically, many French men endured torture and death during the war. However, memoirs reveal marked differences in processing male and female victimhood. Male suffering had more to do with a specific, singular sacrifice for France, rather than a national tragedy and indignity. Their deaths were heroic and contributed to the future. Political theorist Carole Pateman has conceptualized the relationship of men and the state, arguing that male citizenship is best achieved through fighting and dying for the nation.[54] The postwar notion of male physical obligation to the state reinforces that "ideal type" of masculinity. An additional justification for this is, perhaps, as Sarah Farmer argues, "martyrdom . . . suggests physical weakness."[55] In this time of reconstruction and national and international repositioning, France needed forceful and strong men, as seen in the masculine aspects of metaphorical depictions of France as a victim, when the nation's desire to rebuild was manifested in depictions of physical stamina. The state of victimhood was thus constructed as feminine, both to present France as a universal victim and, seemingly paradoxically, as a masculine, active power.

Fictional accounts published during the postwar period bore out notions of difference in the symbolic weight carried by male and female victims. In 1945, Marie Brillant wrote a short story in *Marie-France* around the time of the Easter holiday which detailed the experiences of France's treasured church bells. None of the bells were in the churches on Easter morning, and the parishioners were shocked. The bells had, in fact, flown off to Rome for the traditional papal blessing, and some of them regaled the other bells with war stories on the way back to France. For example, one rang just in time to alert Americans not to shell the town because the Germans were gone—"I rang for liberty!" Instead of heading directly to France, they decided to make a detour to Germany to play for the French who were still in camps. The bells played above several camps, but at Ravensbrück, the women's detention center, their sound was different: "As opposed to other camps, loud joy did not dominate, rather the women below cried softly."[56] The bells lost track of time while playing for the women, hence their late arrival back in France.[57] This story exemplifies how the experience of France's female victims was perceived as different from that of male ones: the women suffered, and the people (whose greatest wish, to visit their fellow French in the camps, here is symbolically fulfilled) must observe this solemnly and soberly.

Nonfiction accounts of male victimhood told of a sense of duty and pride, rather than the suffering and pain common in accounts of female victimization. For example, in Bernard Busson's 1947 anthology of French athlete-warriors, he described Léo Lagrange, a "tall, robust" and talented athlete in many sports who was also the former minister of sport under the Popular Front. Lagrange had joined the military in 1939, only to be killed in 1940. For Lagrange, Busson writes, "Being strong, or becoming strong, was an obligation, putting this strength to service in the name of France, an obligation." Where women could express their gendered allegiance to France through silence and propriety, for men, Frenchness signified a noble physicality. Busson implores the young athletes of France, who he says owe Lagrange a great debt, to honor him by showing that they, too, would know how to die when France is threatened.[58] Similarly, in the Resistance newspaper *Ceux du Maquis* in 1944, the column "Échos des grands bois" reprinted the final letter of a Robert B., a Resistance hero who had killed a German officer in Clermont-Ferrand, who had written to his parents just two hours before his execution in 1943. In this note, he told them to be brave: "Do not cry; that would serve nothing. Try to live in the future that I will be there in death. . . . I hope that once the war is finished, you will again find the happiness for which I give my life." The paper reported that Robert B.'s last words before the firing squad were: "Vive la France!"[59] These accounts reflect a sense that death, for both of these men, was a matter of solemn obligation in the name of France.[60]

If male citizenship is indeed defined as the ability to die for the nation, the French men who died were simply performing their citizenship to the utmost. In doing so, they were presenting the nation and the world with a vision of postwar French masculinity. Charles de Gaulle's June 1944 call to all French men to defend the nation certainly underscores this concept of masculine duty. De Gaulle's words resounded on an *affiche* posted throughout the country: "For the sons of France, wherever they are, whatever they are, the simple and sacred duty is to fight by all means possible." He described France as a "nation that fights, linked through fists and feet." And finally, he assured French men of the nobility of the performance of their duty: "Behind the heavy cloud of our blood and our tears this is the sun of our grandeur."[61] A physical masculinity which belied a strong commitment to the nation would restore France to the glory of yesteryear. Even in his speech at the Liberation of Paris, in which he claimed Paris as a "martyred" city, de Gaulle also said this: "This duty of war, all the men who are here and all those who hear us in France know that it demands national unity. We, who have lived the greatest hours of our History, we have nothing else to wish than to show ourselves, up to the end, worthy of France. Long live

France!" It was the men who would restore France's greatness, even if they had to die doing it, and their sacrifice was for an honorable purpose, rather than a solemn tragedy.

In stark contrast to the values of modesty, humility, and duty that garnered praise for female victims, their male counterparts often received large public commemorations. As Megan Koreman notes:

> Memorial services overwhelmingly honored men, in part because they drew on the gestural and rhetorical tradition that conceptualized patriotism as the military endeavors of men . . .; and in part because men were usually the victims in most Resistance deaths that fit the military model of patriotic tradition and Gaullist myth, either because they died in battle or because the Germans generally executed men but deported women to a slower, more obscure end.[62]

The image of a solitary *male* Resistance hero ingrained itself in popular memory through rites such as these, and male victimhood was actively constructed as patriotically heroic. In turn, the public nature of the memorials served to teach the French populace the Resistance myth, albeit a gendered version, in which men were the sole heroic actors for France. Men would also rebuild France, and women were to stand in support roles.

The artist Paul Colin's immediate postwar work again serves as a visual representation of the gender-heavy imagery of memory. In 1944, he produced a poster for the newspaper *Libération*, which, three months after the Liberation of Paris, organized an exhibition at the Palais de Chaillot to pay "homage" to the resistors who freed Paris, described as "patriots who risked their lives each day to sabotage the enemy's efforts."[63] For this piece, which unlike his earlier work *Libération* was commissioned, he envisioned the resistor as a solitary man, wearing the Cross of Lorraine (the symbol of de Gaulle's Free France), armed and kneeling in front of Paris. The city remains in the resistor's protective shadow, as he stares resolutely ahead at an unseen enemy. When Charles de Gaulle intoned at the Liberation of Paris that all men were ready to do the ultimate duty for France, this image is the visual representation of his statement. The Colin's *affiche* reinforced the notion that the actual resistor was male and powerful, while the experience of war was remembered as female and victimized.[64]

While there were undoubtedly many men who died for France, like Léo Lagrange, Robert B., and those men who received public memorials, the living public representation of them often took female forms. In one example of this, during a 1952 trial of torturers, a judge read a letter from the daughter of one of the victims, a Mlle Mandel, who pleaded that she was too young to testify, she

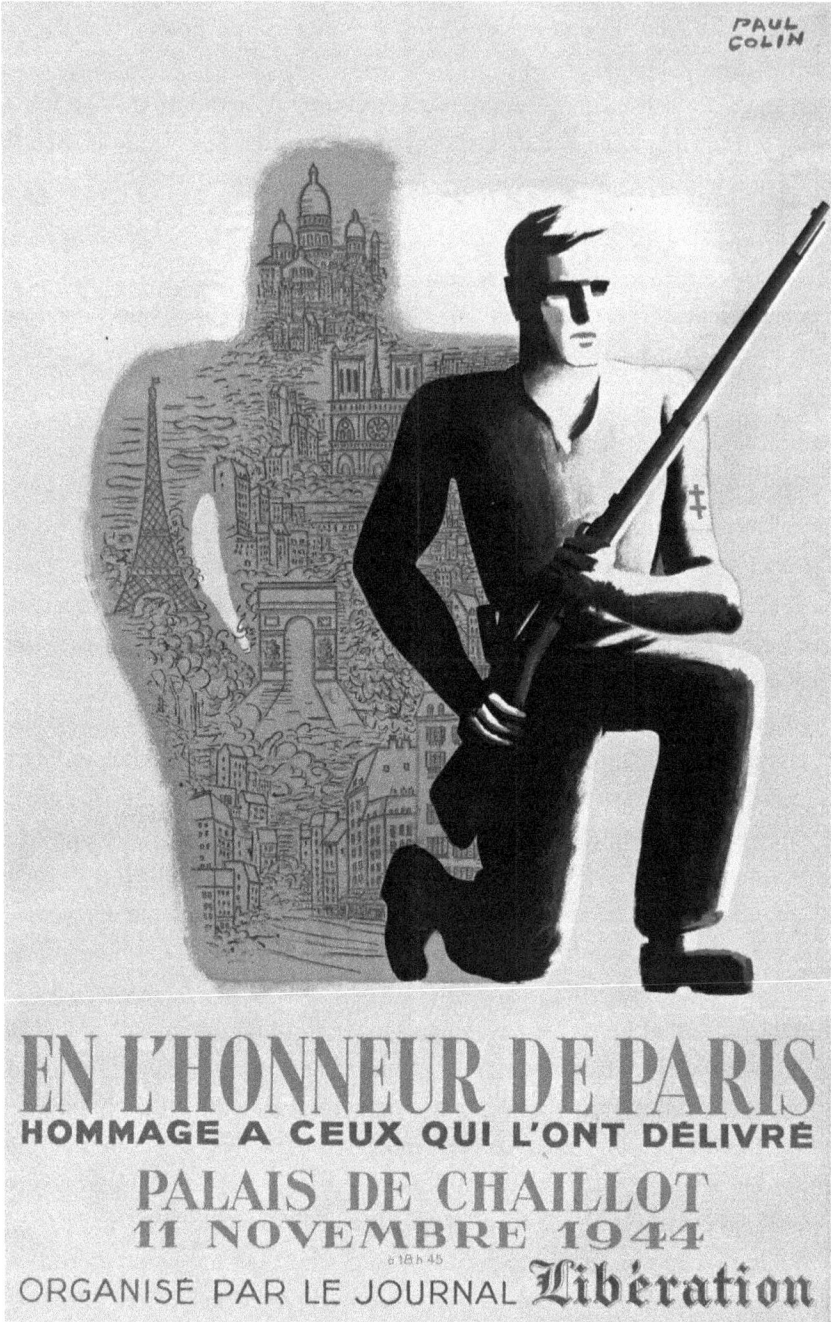

Figure 3   En l'honneur de Paris.

did not have the strength to come and stand "before the person who so made my father suffer that I would only be able to cry. Today, I am simply an orphan girl."[65] The male victim here is represented by those he left behind—his symbolic power is embodied by his daughter, a fifteen-year-old girl. Women were allowed in public if there was a symbolic man justifying their presence there.

Similarly, widowhood, the image of the woman as representative for a fallen husband, became a public identity for women in postwar France.[66] Rosane begins her memoir by referring to her train of female deportees as "widows or mothers of shot patriots, hostages too, arrested in place of a husband, a brother or a son in England."[67] In all likelihood, these women were also resistors, active in their own right, and yet Rosane describes them as placeholders for men. Additionally, in the case cited above of Léo Lagrange, the former minister of sport in the Third Republic, Bernard Busson reprinted a letter Lagrange's wife received upon his death from another soldier in his unit. The soldier wrote: "Cry for him, Madame, but hold your head up high. Be proud of him. Lieutenant Lagrange was a brave man, he was a leader, he proved this in front of the enemy, which many of our politicians have never had the courage to do."[68] Busson's article publicly emphasizes both the honorable masculinity of Lieutenant Lagrange and the widow who will have to be strong and carry on in his memory. Even female victims could define themselves by the men in their lives.

Widowhood as an identity was more than a way to mourn male victims, however; just as female victims were lauded for their wartime action and often their postwar testimony, widows were able to step out into the public sphere and not face criticism for transgressing the prescribed boundaries of femininity. In November 1945, *Elle* magazine ran a story entitled, "They Have Taken up the Torch." The article highlighted the new female members of the National Assembly, several of whom were widows of former politicians. They included Mme Mathilde Gabriel-Péri, whose husband (and fellow communist) was shot during the Occupation, and Mme Raymonde-Nedelec, the widow of a deputy from Bouches-du-Rhône, who died while being tortured by the Gestapo. (Raymonde-Nedelec was herself imprisoned at Ravensbrück, the women's prison in Germany, during the war.) The article stressed that these women were acting well within the boundaries of proper French female behavior by serving as deputies, despite what postwar appearances may have necessitated. The magazine assured its readers that "None of these women—who were dignified companions of their husbands—can be called 'veuve abusive' [abusive widow]."[69] As long as they conducted themselves with propriety (both during their marriages and in their newfound roles), widows could stake a claim to the public sphere in postwar France. However, they would not operate fully independently of their husbands in their new roles. As Joan Scott posits, " The choice of widows [as candidates] for these first elections suggests . . . those who formulated the decree granting citizenship to women wanted to continue to consider them as members of families or of collectives with a particular interest to defend" rather than as individual political actors.[70] In describing politically public women, cultural productions such as women's magazines emphasized their identities as the former wives of male victims.

Motherhood also resurfaced in discussions of male victims as a method of understanding the sacrifice of children (and consequently France's sacrifice of "her" children) during the war. In January 1946, *Elle* published, "She Would Have Given Everything," the fictional story of a woman who is attending a ceremony. According to the piece, the woman feels tired, and she wished she would not cry; her son would be cross with her for crying. She had not seen her son in this form for so long—smiling, ready to walk around. She just wanted to go hug him, and for one second she thought it was possible. But it was just a bronze statue that she was there to help inaugurate.[71] In this story, the memory of the fallen soldier is embodied and nearly alive again because of the thoughts and regrets of his mother. This fictional piece reflects the reality that Koreman describes, of a number of public commemorations of male victims. Here, the reader sees the commemoration through the eyes of the victim's mother, a woman. Here she serves as a foil to enhance the solemnity associated with the death of a French hero.

The kiss became a symbolic gesture associated with the male victims, and once again, a woman was left behind to symbolize the loss embodied in that gesture.[72] This time, though, instead of the motherhood described above, the kiss came to represent the sense of virility associated with male victimhood. This stands in direct contrast to the tragedy associated with the losses of French women, especially mothers, whose deaths take on extra depth because of their potential to give life and provide virility to France and French men. This solemn virility is certainly on display in "The Kiss," a story published in *Elle* in January 1946. In this piece, the young, famous French aviator from the First World War, Georges Guynemer, stops by the Ministry of Foreign Affairs. While there, he meets up with Daniélou, and they encounter a pretty young typist, who is extremely excited to meet the storied Guynemer. He tells her he would like to give her a kiss, pleading: "I am leaving. Perhaps I will not come back. This is our personal destiny, air combatants, and maybe I will not have the chance to kiss any woman other than you." The young girl threw her arms around his neck and kissed him, crying with the emotion of the moment. The very next day, word reached the Ministry that Guynemer's plane had disappeared and there was no sign of him. Daniélou sees the young woman who had kissed the young pilot. She is sitting at her desk, head in her hands, sobbing.[73] Here, the kiss embodies the power of French femininity, as well as the loss of a man in his prime. French women could represent the nation for the doomed man through their kisses. The kiss, although laden with transcendental symbolism, still has a sexualized aspect to it—notice that Guynemer asks a young, attractive woman for a kiss. In this way, French female sexuality is intimately—literally—tied to the good of the nation.

In another example of the symbolic and sexual power of the victim's kiss, the Bordelaise teacher Manon Cormier was able to tell her head Resistance chief, Michel, a message from her regional Resistance chief, Philippe, who, along with Manon, was deported to Germany and later died there. Philippe said, "I will be shot tomorrow, if you see Michel again, tell him that I died a good Frenchman." Here, Philippe displays the heroic sense of masculine duty common to male victims. According to the memoir, Cormier told her sister that she and Philippe were in a car together when this happened, on their way back from an interrogation. After he said these words, Manon "kissed him so that, before he died, he might have the kiss of a French woman."[74] In each case, the French woman's kiss bears transcendent powers. As noted in the anecdote about Guynemer, the kiss is still sexual, but it also carries with it the values that are both "eternal" to France and that must be constructed in this moment: purity, beauty, and youth. Philippe is off to his death, but in a sign that he is still attractive to French women, Manon kisses him; in this moment, it was also as though the nation embraced Philippe. A French woman conveyed a pure, sexualized nationalism through her embrace. She would heal French men, using her kiss to restore his virility.[75]

A poem by Philippe Fauquet, a leader in the Brittany Resistance, about French men's love for France, exemplifies both the transcendental and sexual aspects of the kiss. Additionally, just as in Colin's *affiche* or Fresneau's poem, in Fauquet's poem France is again a symbolic female entity, but instead of being a victim, France is a sexualized healer:

We are, very far inside ourselves,
With France in our arms;
Each believes himself alone with her
And thinks no one can see him.

Everyone is full of awkwardness
Before such a precious being . . .
Is this really la Patrie,
This body with the face of the heavens? . . .

Each holds her in his own way
In an immeasurable embrace . . .

[Fauquet adds:] "In the measureless embrace of eternity, each tortured patriot holds, in effect, between his tightened, shattered or deformed arms, France who makes one body with him."[76] In this poem, France is sacred, so precious that it has "the face of the heavens." But it is also all too real, as Fauquet describes French men's quest—and ability—to possess France sexually. In keeping with the need to reaffirm masculinity of the time, the poem portrays the concept that it is through a sexual embrace which reinforces the virility of both parties that man and France are healed. But this equation is an exclusive one: a woman cannot know France in this sexual way—the poem has no sense of that possibility. According to Fauquet's poem, the new French nation must embody this healing femininity, which can be transmitted through the transcendental, sexual nature of the female embrace, in its reconstruction in order to be rehabilitated. The end result, though, is a potent, masculine populace.

Conclusion

During the Liberation, both male and female victims became emblematic of larger societal trends. Women victims were allowed into public, an extraordinary turn in this particular context, but only to relay their stories of victimization, as well as the stories of male and female loved ones who gave their lives for the nation. Because this behavior—women out publicizing their uncommon wartime activities, activities which would normally challenge male authority— was so extraordinary, the messages ingrained within their stories were meant to be exemplary for the French people.

Ultimately, the evocative image of female victims as a symbol of France at the Liberation did not translate into an open, powerful, and public stance for either the many women who actually had been active members of the Resistance, or the majority of French women who had simply existed during the war.[77] Such messages of victimization reinforced a domestic, private vision of French female identity. For men, conversely, death in the name of France was a duty to be born out in a time of crisis. They were heroes for their nation, and their images reflected the sense of strength and duty that calls for postwar masculinity demanded. For women, on the other hand, their deaths for France were tragedies, ways to measure the depth of the enemy's evil. But within such stories, it is possible to discern patterns of behavior that promote a stabilizing vision of femininity that served this need for a strong masculinity in postwar France. Women's wartime activities were temporary forays into the public sphere. They sought no recognition for them, and would downplay them when queried. In this way, postwar femininity was modest and, most importantly, was happy to return to the private sphere, rather than challenge postwar patriarchy embodied in phenomena such as the Resistance myth.

If victimhood was tied to women, it could take on essentially female qualities and could even become an identity which would limit the scope of women's lives. Women, even public women, were subjected—and restricted themselves—to a more traditional role, one which would not challenge the prevailing mores of the time. This vision of moral femininity was especially potent during the Vichy regime with its insistence on women as the moral base of society through their roles as mothers. As Miranda Pollard notes, during the Vichy years, "Women were imagined inextricably enmeshed in a social pyramid, a network of virtue and duty, of beauty and femininity, which constituted 'the real'. . . . The real represented order and harmony, calm and reassuring . . . opposed to disorder and anarchy, threatening and destabilizing."[78] Women under Vichy were meant to serve as agents of protection against the outside and to stabilize society through morality within the home.

After the war and the Occupation in France, women had to stand in as the symbolic national body, as seen in the Colin's *affiche*, as well as their own physical body.[79] Women could not afford to subvert the dominant vision of femininity in any way—or perhaps more importantly, France could not afford for women to act outside of the norm. In this time of confusion, when stability and the projection of a positive image for France was so important, women's comportment, especially as it related to their bodies, stood as a measure of the health of France itself. Any attacks on their person, symbolic or otherwise, held deeply felt consequences for the idea of the nation.

3

The War for Love

Introduction

By many measures, French women's war did not end in May 1945. Materially, daily life in postwar France was undeniably difficult, with strict rations, bad weather, and shortages among the many hardships. Metaphorically, as this chapter emphasizes, women were engaged in new battles for love and romance. Success in these areas meant finding and retaining a man, which cultural sources like women's magazines painted as the ultimate goal of the postwar period. If women failed, magazines implied, they were personally lacking. This chapter will detail the role of women's magazines in postwar life, and it will examine how their discourses about love and marriage addressed both single and married women, all with the ultimate goal of promoting a specific vision of domestic love. Just as discourses of victimization served to delineate the boundaries of female propriety, so visions of love and romance articulated to women the acceptable lifestyles of the postwar years: marry, have children, and protect your family. The consequences of remaining single were dire: complete solitude and social isolation.

Establishing "normalcy" was an obsession during the postwar years.[1] The quest for stability was partly an understandable response to the chaotic nature of war. The very definition of normalcy, though, was historically specific and influenced by gender: France would be stabilized by the heteronormative family. In its ideal form, this family included a man who was a virile Resistance alumnus and a woman who cared for little but retaining this stability, as well as many children who would repopulate France. It was women's work to attain this ideal of normalcy and to retain it in coming years. This was their new battle, and the theater for the war was love.[2]

In his study of twentieth-century Britain, Marcus Collins argues that the postwar period there witnessed the birth of new vision of love, one based on what he terms "mutuality." He defines mutuality as "an intimate equality [that] should be established between men and women through mixing, companionate marriage and shared sexual pleasure," and he paints it as the driving ethos of love during that time.[3] He argues that such a sense especially crystallized in the years immediately after the Second World War, which he refers to as the "zenith" of mutuality.[4]

Unlike in Britain, "mutuality" in France after the Second World War was neither a stated nor an unstated goal of marriage. Through a reading of contemporary women's magazines, themselves a cultural juggernaut, it emerges that love existed solely where a man found his wife pleasing. Finding and fostering coupledom, with the hope that love would eventually emerge, rested solely on the shoulders of women. In order to establish a romantic relationship, magazines encouraged women to sacrifice individuality, not savor it. This chapter will first introduce the major women's magazines of the postwar period, and then it will turn to an analysis of how these magazines promoted love and marriage to single and married women. It will then look at magazines' actively pronatalist stances, which coincided with fears of homosexuality. Ultimately, love in the postwar period was women's responsibility; women had to make men happy in order to have families and avoid social ostracism, and magazines worked to help them achieve this fulfillment.

Magazines—a woman's best weapon

In postwar France, magazines constructed love and marriage as women's ultimate goal—and responsibility. The breadth of influence of such images should not be understated in this endeavor. As Francesca Cancian and Steven Gordon have argued with respect to American women's magazines, this type of periodical can construct the "emotional norms" of a given society.[5] In the case of postwar France, the nuclear family, anchored by a virile man and a bewitching, yet devoted, mother, was the bedrock of an imagined nation. A caveat: It is not possible to know exactly what women took away from women's magazines. Perhaps many readers disregarded the advice. Some may well have focused on the articles addressing women's political participation or work lives. Far more common numerically, however, was the emphasis on women as soldiers in a new war for love. The desperation that women's magazines attributed to the quest for finding and retaining a mate was unmistakable; their popularity reveals their resonance with postwar women's lives.

This book cites several examples of the feminine press and the mainstream print media, but it heavily utilizes two particular women's magazines: *Elle* and *Marie-France*.[6] This is true for several reasons. First, these were both newly published magazines, meaning they were not tainted by any association with Vichy and the less palatable sides of the war (unlike *Marie-Claire*, for example, which ceased publication in 1942 and did not recommence publishing until 1954[7]). Second, they both began publishing right in the immediate aftermath of the war—*Elle* in 1944 and *Marie-France* in 1945 (unlike *Vogue* or *Nous deux*, for example). In the relatively limited chronological scope of this book, their steadiness is both unique and important for establishing a narrative. Third, rather than limiting themselves to one aspect of women's lives, like fashion, for example, they took a holistic view of their role, addressing areas from marriage to fashion to work—and beyond, making them a one-stop-shop for advice and counsel about postwar femininity. Fourth, their readership numbers were remarkably high: with 110,000 subscribers in 1944, 340,000 in 1948, and 500,000 in 1950.[8] By the end of this book's scope, their combined circulation was above 600,000, quite a coup in a time of major paper restrictions and an overall population of 40 million. In addition to official numbers, there was plausibly a more casual and immeasurable readership—people lending magazines to friends and family with regularity, for example.[9] In 1952, a fashion trade journal, expressing satisfaction at the immense influence of *Elle* and its ad buy therein, wrote "When one knows that this magazine publishes 600,000 copies, and it is read by over a million and a half women, one can imagine that women will be talking about what we do in days to come."[10] Attesting to the pervasiveness of these magazines, the phrase "si elle lit, elle lit *Elle*" (which loosely translates to: if she reads at all, she reads *Elle* magazine) had become commonplace by the 1960s, a mere fifteen years later.[11] As of 1955, one in six French women read *Elle*; its influence was, according to journalists Samra-Martine Bonvoisin and Michèle Maignien, "unequaled."[12] Finally, the magazines were designed to appeal to middle-class women of different ages—*Elle* to young women, *Marie-France* to those "of a certain age"—and so they reflect a broad swath of mainstream society for women at this time.[13] Steve Zdatny recognized this influence when he called them crucial to the "growth of a [female] mass market" in France.[14]

In articles, advice, and fiction during the postwar period in France, writers worried that women were not fulfilling their life roles and finding love. For them, the effects of war were a particular concern. In the case of postwar France, if war was an impediment to romance, magazines and mass media worked to soften that blow, providing advice as to how to find a love that would eventually lead to marriage. While the forms of the pieces analyzed here differed, the overarching message—of gender norm adhesion—displayed striking continuities.

While this chapter largely deals with defining proper femininity in France with respect to love, it is, as always, impossible to separate this analysis from that of postwar French masculinity.[15] This interconnectivity becomes more evident in considering why marriage roles became so conservative at this time. One reason is certainly the postwar period's emphasis on stability, which was both a reaction to the chaos of the previous decade and a justification for France's inclusion as a Great Power. Recovering France's reputation was an obsession for France's immediate postwar leader, Charles de Gaulle.[16] Such efforts existed within the metropole, in the colonies, and in international politics. Sarah Farmer writes, "In this [postwar] atmosphere of uncertainty, President de Gaulle decided that his physical presence, as the head of state, would promote the cause of order around the country and, by eliciting massive popular support, would convince the Allies of the provisional government's claims to legitimacy."[17]

The attempt to reestablish order took place on both the macro and micro levels, and the postwar notion of order has much to do with reasserting French power and masculinity. As Julian Jackson has noted, there was a "strong emphasis in the rhetoric of the Resistance on the values of masculinity and virility: France, prostrate and enfeebled for four years, must show herself to be vigorous again."[18] If, as George Mosse and Luc Capdevila have argued, the trench soldier became the very image of manhood during the interwar years, the contrast between that image and the one of frightened men cowering at the edge of France, waiting for an airlift, could hardly be starker.[19] French masculinity and virility had been compromised by the events of the war, and reestablishing a vision of docile femininity was absolutely essential to their restoration.

The trend of female domesticity and its inherent focus on the home and family in the late 1940s and 1950s is not unique to France; many nations of the West, especially Great Britain and the United States, also experienced this cultural phenomenon.[20] What makes France distinct, however, is the especially intense context in which this call to femininity took place and the functions that it served. The embarrassingly quick collapse of the French military at the outset of the Second World War led to a long occupation by Germany (long a source of fear for the French) and Italy for the duration of war.[21] During the war, the leader of the authoritarian Vichy regime, Maréchal Pétain, attempted to situate himself as the "father" to the French people,[22] a role which de Gaulle would later distort and then co-opt at the Liberation. And at the end of the war, the French created a new government that they hoped would address the concerns from the Third Republic while whitewashing the realities of Vichy.

France's embrace of the liberal democratic heteronormative family, as well as its definitions of femininity and masculinity, takes on new meaning in the face of this context.[23] The French under de Gaulle adopted gender roles as politicized choices because the confinement of possibilities for femininity served France's interests at both the national and international levels.

The remainder of this chapter will examine how women's magazines, which exploded culturally and numerically in the postwar period, acted as a guide for women. This was particularly true in the realm of love; this chapter will analyze stories and columns in the feminine press which emphasized how women needed to attract and retain a man at any cost. In doing so, they defined fulfillment for women quite narrowly: a heteronormative family in which the man's happiness dominated the family dynamic, and the wife's role was to keep him happy. The pieces, from fiction to nonfiction to advice columns to surveys, take individually different forms, but they remain remarkably consistent when it comes to constructing the boundaries of proper behavior. The price for straying from their narrow vision was severe: total social isolation.

The amount of responsibility a French woman bore on a day-to-day basis seems exhausting: everything about her life had to be ordered and perfect in order to support her man. Physical spaces needed to be pristine and tasteful, mental unpleasantness (depression, for example, or even just a bad mood) needed to be pushed aside in favor of a sunny disposition, the people in her life needed to be expertly educated and fed, as well as happy, and the woman herself needed to be proper, sexy, stylish, youthful, and always attentive for any sign of a disturbance to her orderly world. An ad for Jil lingerie in *Elle* in November 1947, one of many which appeared in women's magazines during these years, exemplifies the gender tightrope women had to walk in the postwar era. The ad featured three drawings of women. The first was labeled "ni garçonnière" [not a garçonne, or an overly masculine woman], and showed a young woman standing with legs apart, wearing rolled up trousers, with short hair, hands in pockets, smoking a cigarette. The second drawing, "ni oie blanche" [nor a "white goose," an overly reticent and shy woman] depicted a girl staring primly down at the ground, legs together, wearing a very feminine dress, seeming quite modest. Finally, the "mais feminine" [but feminine] drawing portrayed a woman in slim fitting blouse and skirt, with hair done up in feminine bun.

The advertisement summed up the drawings, saying "do not imitate men, do not stay a child forever, attire your feminine grace in a branded practical, solid, and comfortable lingerie."[24] Women's roles in postwar France were razor-thin in terms of acceptability—they had to be alluring and noticeable enough to attract men, but not too bold, lest someone think them mannish, or even lesbians. How would they ever be able to navigate such a treacherous atmosphere successfully?

A woman was not alone in this quest, however; magazines such as the extremely popular *Elle* and *Marie-France* promised to be there to help guide her in her never-ending search for improvement. While overt demographical statistics about readers are difficult to come by (the OJD, Office de justification de la diffusion, which officially counts media circulation in France, did no demographic analysis), it is clear that magazines like *Elle* did not necessarily direct their articles solely at parisiennes. Françoise Giroud later remembered that "the reader envisioned by the staff at *Elle* was most likely young, between twenty-five and thirty-five . . . and she lived in Angoulême [not far from Bordeaux]."[25] She was a universal creation, the "femme au foyer . . . flanked by her refrigerator or laundry basket."[26] And feminist scholar Evelyne Sullerot describes Hélène Gordon-Lazareff's vision: "In the miserably heroic atmosphere of the era, she sought to give women an improved vision of themselves: to surprise, even arouse, to offer luxury."[27] Whether or not these images of the reader reflected reality is not always clear, although Jean-Pierre Rioux claims that the feminine press of the Fourth Republic touched "all the popular social classes."[28] What is clear is that *Elle*'s editors expressly intended for their magazine to appeal to people across the nation.

The magazines did provide useful information about dealing with problems and issues that women regularly encountered in their work as postwar wives and mothers. For example, the winters of 1945 and 1946 were exceedingly cold, and made more difficult by gas rations, as well as a lack of firewood and other staples. *Marie-France* tried to lessen the sense of hardship by publishing statistics about far colder winters, such as when the entire Rhône River froze in 1822.[29] Also, in January 1946, *Elle* published an article about how to make nightgowns warmer, so that women would not be so cold at night.[30] Additionally, the harvest of 1945 was so bad because of the cold that, according to historian Jean-Pierre Rioux, "a one-third shortfall of bread, meat, butter, and milk could thus be expected" for the coming year.[31] At this time, rations were such that the average adult was only consuming 900 calories per day in August of 1944, and ingredients were so rare that people could expect to wait in line for long periods for basic food.[32] In fact, in March 1946 the famous American socialite Susan Mary Alsop, in Paris with her diplomat husband, complained, "Our food is getting worse. We are so lucky to have the pork chops and the tuna fish and the chicken, but oh, the chicken is so tough, and I am sick of tuna fish with sauce creamed with Klim [powdered milk used in army rations] or cold with canned mayonnaise."[33] As the wife of a diplomat Alsop was indeed "lucky," especially since she and her husband had access to the American Embassy's commissary, yet still the monotony and difficulties of the rations obviously wore on her.

Magazines attempted to alleviate the stresses of prolonged rationing upon women, urging them to be more creative with the limited ingredients they did have. In the magazine's very first issue in November 1945, *Elle* published, "Don't avoid powdered eggs!" in which it printed many recipes for readers that used the comparatively plentiful ingredient. In the same issue, *Elle* also published "Verdict on elegance," an article which told women that it was all right to wear a three-year-old dress out on the streets and still call oneself elegant. This must have been a relief in a time of textile rations and aesthetic pressures.[34] In some sense such magazines could be a true comfort to women with advice during the difficulties of the Liberation.

At other moments, such magazines distorted their "older sister" role, instead specializing in telling women how to think and behave, even teaching women about their own experiences and normalizing the vagaries of postwar life.[35] For example, in preparing for summer vacations in 1946, *Marie-France* advised its readers to practice swimming well before the start of vacation so that they would look like "mermaids" in the pool. Swim on your side, the magazine counseled, as that stroke is not too taxing and people will not think you are struggling.[36] Indeed the editors of the two main periodicals that this book emphasizes, *Elle* and *Marie-France*, had explicit goals for how they wanted women to read and interpret them. Remembering her time spent working with Hélène Lazareff to start up *Elle*, Françoise Giroud wrote, "We were small, but we had a grand vision." In her description of laboring in a small office and brainstorming about what *Elle* might be, she recalled that at the end of the war people were tired of bleakness. Giroud and Lazareff recognized this fatigue: "We were oversaturated with tragedy. Long live life! [In this spirit], *Elle* opens its wings."[37]

There was tension over the conflicting role magazines were to play in a woman's life: confidante or general. *Elle* defined as its purpose to serve and designate the needs of the average French woman, which largely involved pleasing her man. In fact, *Elle* billed itself as "Le journal des femmes que les hommes regardent." This sentence has two meanings in the French language. First, it can be "the women's magazine that men also read." Or, it can mean "the magazine of women that men look at."[38] In both cases, *Elle* presented itself as a magazine for women who wanted to please men. Either their men were reading the same material as they were, or their men were taking notice of the changes *Elle* was advocating in its readers. In order to attract and retain a man, women's most important postwar task, *Elle* painted itself to be an indispensable weapon.

Elle was extremely successful in terms of numbers, in no small part because Lazareff caught on to the current mood in France in terms of gender and stability, and she created her magazine around it. As Giroud notes, Lazareff "went with the tide instead of trying to go against it."[39] Sentiments of the need for gender stability were already in the air; women's magazines simply needed to seize upon these, heighten them, and make their role in the new culture indispensable.

The very first issue of *Marie-France* was more explicit than *Elle* in defining its purpose in the lives of postwar women. It even devoted a full page to the editorialization of its importance:

> We all dream of being: . . . "complete" women, cultivated, naturally elegant and "chic," and beautiful in moral and physical health; . . . women "with great hearts," generous, always ready to help others, creating around them, and first in their family, an atmosphere of love and of union; . . . practical and ingenious women, knowing how to make their home a "house of happiness"; . . . women who are truly "French," aware of important historical events and of the essential problems of today, proud of those who went before them, courageous in facing the future, ready for their patriotic and social role. This is the idea that *MARIE-FRANCE* proposes.[40]

In this article *Marie-France* was actually articulating the role and spirit that French women were meant to embody: they needed to be adaptable, friendly, attractive, intelligent, and brave, all in the name being "truly 'French.'" The usage of "we" creates a relationship not only between the magazine and the reader, but also among all the readers, that they all have the same thoughts and same agenda. It is a homogenization of women's past experiences, current realities, and future goals.

The *Marie-France* article went on to exhort all French women to embody the two names of the magazine, Marie and France: "one name from the sky, one name from the Earth." The construction of the phrase, in parallel terms, equates the weight of Mary and France. Women were thus supposed to act as the ultimate model of pious, maternal, devoted womanhood, Mary. This was consequently the same as acting in the name of France. The magazine also promised to attempt to live up to its two names and make France "a humane land," which it would accomplish only with the help of women. The editorial noted:

> One often says that women are the soul of the house. It is also true to affirm that they must be the soul of the nation, and that, without them, without their ardent and devoted support, tomorrow France could no longer respond to her eternal vocation. France is counting on us, more than she has ever done at any time in her history. To help you in this difficult and magnificent task, you can count on your friend MARIE-FRANCE.[41]

Thus *Marie-France* placed an enormous responsibility on women's plates: through their roles as guardians of the home, women became caretakers of the nation and its soul. Without women's strong moral guidance, the country, eternal yet tenuous, according to *Marie-France*, would surely fail.

Magazines such as *Elle* and *Marie-France* acted as both friend and enemy to French women during the Liberation, guiding them along the path toward a constricted definition of self and happiness, all while constructing the ideal woman. Their role was to steer women to make sure that they kept their homes happy, their marriages strong, and the spirit of France true to its eternal self. Magazines in effect created voids which only they could fill. They gave women a certain burden, and then placed themselves in the role of necessary confidante and mentor.

Love in a time of (post)war

The tension-filled role of women's magazines is especially evident in their promotion of romance, love, and marriage. In fact, *Elle*'s editor Hélène Lazareff believed that women's entire purpose for existing was to attract and seduce men:

> [She] used to say that women who understand how men look at them will spend all their life sipping champagne on sunny terraces. And indeed, ELLE, the smart-looking, weekly fashion magazine she created in Paris in 1945, showed war-weary French readers how to be that fantasy creature—the attractive and sympathetic woman men dream of meeting on the terrace of a chic resort hotel.[42]

Lazareff's *Elle* became a sort of tactical aid in the new war women were to wage in order to attract and meet men. Co-editor Françoise Giroud described her in exactly these terms: "To hold a man, or several men, was for [Hélène] the epitome of female gamesmanship, the only thing that made life meaningful. *What war is to men.*"[43] [emphasis mine] The magazine emphasized that the war had not ended for women, who had to fight in order to find a man and consequently retain a proper French identity through heteronormativity.

The issue of how to reestablish romantic relationships or to deal with the havoc the war wrought on romance and marriage was a stressful one during the Liberation. Women's magazines assumed that a stable marriage was women's ultimate goal, and they created conceptualizations of love and romance to go along with this. These conceptualizations traversed the array of types of articles in magazines, from advice columns to surveys to fictional pieces and all the vagaries in between. Despite the diversity in kinds of pieces, the stability of the message is astonishing. Love and romance were functional entities in the postwar period. In order for the "juggernaut" of marriage to exist, the qualities that drove such a movement had to work in the interest of a higher authority. In the case of postwar France, this authority was the state, with all of its national and international goals. Just as women's magazines normalized women's experiences of war, so they did the same with postwar love.

To promote romantic relationships, women's magazines cast the new quest for love as a war, and they positioned themselves as readers' ablest weapons. For example, in December 1945, *Elle* magazine printed Rosemary Dujardin's fictional piece, "He Preferred Cinderella." In the story, the protagonist, Simone, is wracked with fears and anxiety over the return of her old boyfriend, Jacques, who has been off fighting in the war and is just now returning to France. They have not seen each other since he enlisted two years ago, when she was fifteen and he was a few years older. She worries that Jacques will no longer be interested in her, that he will have found someone else during his time away: "Fifteen to seventeen—a lot of changes can happen!" Her older, more coquettish sister, Jacqueline, tells her that she must look impressive for Jacques, and she dresses the normally more practically attired Simone in trendy fashions, even adorning her hair with a brooch. She is so done up that when Jacques arrives to escort Simone out for the evening, he does not recognize her. They go to a popular dance club on the Champs-Élysées at Simone's suggestion, where they have an awful time. Simone feels like she cannot even speak to Jacques anymore, that there is a distance between them. She asks him to take her home, and once there she goes to her bedroom and cries. After a while, she adopts a new positive attitude: "Everything will be better tomorrow, she thought, *taking a lesson learned from her favorite fashion magazine.*" [emphasis mine] The next morning, having sobbed herself to sleep, Simone gets up to an empty house, and while breakfasting tries to resign herself to the idea that her life will go on without Jacques. Then the doorbell rings—it is Jacques, coming to talk to Simone about the previous night. He asks why she had dressed up so much; when he had remembered her during his time fighting for France, she was wearing her normal dresses and they were biking to the milk-bar to play ping-pong. She said, "That's how I remembered you, too! But Jacqueline said . . ." Immediately, Jacques interrupted, "Ah, I should have known!" The young couple reconciles with a kiss and heads off on their bikes to the milk-bar, reclaiming their love and ready for the future. Simone's desire to seem more worldly, to impress her returning soldier, actually created a divide between her and Jacques.

The story's message is that it is neither necessary nor even advisable to be anything other than what you were before the war; if you try to put on airs and be too worldly—if you have changed too much, your brave Frenchman will be unimpressed, and you may indeed lose him—the worst of all possible fates. Jacques "preferred Cinderella," a humble, hardworking French woman, to her more coquettish manifestation, the older sister Jacqueline, here associated—in an extrapolation of the Cinderella story—with the evil stepsister.[44] Simone needs to be wary of the woman who will lead her astray. In the end, Simone's simple goodness wins him back, and she presumably gains a stable harmony through her romantic coupling. Simone is an example of the good soldier in the new war for love.

The story of Simone exemplifies the difficulties women had in navigating postwar gender exigencies. Women had to be coquettish enough and yet simultaneously humble and domestic enough to remain attractive to their men without challenging masculinity or virility. And they must perform womanhood without complaint or difficulty, for sources constructed it as their natural role. Women's magazines purported to be women's allies in this pursuit.

In addressing the problem of postwar romantic instability, however, such stories in women's magazines also created a post facto experience of war to which their audiences could—or rather should—relate: that all French men had been involved with war and were heroes, and that all French women needed to welcome them home and treat their men with the care and respect they deserved. Their universalization of wartime experience thereby mobilized the Resistance myth and the Gaullist agenda.[45] Sarah Fishman highlighted this trend among war prisoners' wives, stating that for prisoners' wives, the "most important" part of prisoners' return was that these women "had to prepare themselves to let their husbands resume the position of head of the family."[46] In this case, one's femininity had to be at its peak—but it was a specific construction of femininity that would not challenge existing male authority.

In the context of concerted calls for order in the wake of war's tumult, the issue of how to deal with the problems associated with love and the war inspired women's magazines to devote huge amounts of space to the issue of postwar romance. As Kristin Ross argues, "A new ideology of love and conjugality was necessary if the state natalist policy . . . was to meet with any success."[47] To that end, women's magazines mobilized the need for gender stability and family. Between May and July 1946, *Elle* magazine published an entire series of articles by André Lang, a fairly well-known writer and journalist of the time, called "Did the War Kill Love?" about romance and love in postwar life. Each appearance of the series featured two different yet purportedly representative women's stories. After each story, Lang would give his opinion on the situation. He would then offer the woman's situation up for debate, asking *Elle*'s readers what they thought. *Elle* then printed certain exemplary reader reactions in the next issue. The section "Did the War Kill Love?" highlighted this series of romantic issues that were common to the postwar period—a soldier's return and wartime indiscretions, for example—in a way that rendered these problems universal to a French public. The universality of the problems meant that they could have universal solutions. The opinions of Lang were then presented as near-truths for readers to absorb.[48]

In the first article of the series, Lang posed a series of critiques about postwar French society: it was selfish, greedy, and even cruel. He wondered whether something as fragile and special as love could survive in such a volatile environment. The vignettes that Lang chose to highlight serve more as responses than as evidence for the reader to evaluate. Indeed, Lang offered critical commentary in his articles, giving his advice to women across France within the case studies. Through a deeper reading, it is clear that the column operated more as an advice column than as one that demanded or even necessitated a reader response. Lang, like many other writers of the immediate postwar period, argued for marriage and a commitment to a nuclear family to rebuild this broken society. In order to achieve this heteronormative ideal, articles showed that women may need to sacrifice their wishes and needs for a greater good.

In the first installment of "Did the War Kill Love?," which appeared in May 1946, Lang recounted the story of a young woman named Geneviève, using the title: "Geneviève, who, since the man who loved her in silence died [during the war, now] believes that she does not have the right to marry." Geneviève's life as an "intelligent and athletic" student from a proper, well-to-do family was thrown into turmoil by the advent of war. Her first crush, Jean S., who "inspired in her a violent, passionate love," joined the Resistance and left the university. While he was gone, she met Albert D., a more level-headed "recently repatriated prisoner," who proposed to Geneviève, and she accepted, as they made a perfectly nice couple. Just before the wedding, though, she received word that Jean S. had been killed by the Germans, and she decided that she could not marry Albert D. In fact, she decides never to marry, and instead to choose a career as a doctor. According to Lang, Geneviève's story had been submitted to *Elle* by her friend, Marianne, who worried about Geneviève and her questionable choices. In his commentary, Lang turned to the audience with deeper concerns regarding Geneviève: "This sad adventure, which became more dramatic during the war, but which could have happened in a time of peace, will it prevent Geneviève from becoming an accomplished wife and mother? What do you think?"[49] In this way, Geneviève's story, her "sad adventure," is first presented, and then judged by Lang, and only then thrown to the reader for her own evaluation. Lang's underlying assumption here was that Geneviève, in renouncing a more practical, less passionate marriage for a career, had committed a grievous error. The question, "What do you think?" which was posed to the readers at the end of the article was not necessarily a serious appeal for reflection on Geneviève's particular situation. It was rather a call for them to make sure that they themselves were not foolishly forsaking marriage and abandoning their quest for love.

Women's magazines portrayed themselves as central to the postwar quest of landing a man and protecting a marriage. An analysis of their related messages also disputes the position that "mutuality" was the goal of love in the postwar period. Instead, magazines subverted the individualism of the woman in order to please the man and promote the formation of couples.

Unmarried women

As the commentary on Geneviève's case suggests, finding a man was the first objective of any single woman in the postwar period. There was no possibility of being a fulfilled single woman. Instead, magazines promoted the idea that it was crucial for young women to damp down their expectations of men and marriage in order to increase overall marriage numbers. As *Marie-France* opined in a 1951 advice column by "Francine," "There are no longer very many young girls who are naïve enough to believe that they will meet a Prince Charming." There are always drawbacks to every man, Francine continued, stating that she often received the question: "What is it better to do without in a husband: appearance, fortune, family, health, intelligence? Because perfection cannot be (alas!) demanded, what is the quality to which you should attach the least importance?" Francine went on to say that anyone who claims to have "everything" is not being honest. One cannot, according to Francine, predict the "sacrifice" one will inevitably have to make in choosing a partner. To a certain extent, she goes on, that "depends on our own generosity" and tastes. "When you truly love," Francine says, "you do not consider the lacking in your partner to be important." The article presents as fact that women are not going to meet their absolutely ideal spouse, and it even names the specific characteristics that a young woman might have to abandon in favor of having a man in her life. In this way, the magazine explicitly tells women to give up their romantic notions—everyone settles in the end.[50]

Francine's advice implied that for unmarried couples who were dating, marriage was almost always the assumed goal of the relationship, and indeed of women's larger war for love. Hardships encountered along the way were usually considered to be temporary obstacles to an enduring and romantic end. In this struggle, women had to remain confident in victory. When a woman felt unsure about her decision or her man's commitment, the doubt reflected poorly on her own character. No matter the situation, contemporary advice columnists' counsel was similar: do not break up your home, do not disrupt your future happiness, and do not give up your man. In 1946, *Elle* magazine printed a new advice column, "Elle and You." In each issue, there was one highlighted letter. The first issue featured a letter from a woman named Raymonde, whose fiancé, Jacques, seemed more interested in her best friend than in her. Should she step aside? she wondered. The response from *Elle* was unequivocal: "If you have to ask advice about how to sacrifice, Raymonde, you are not a woman who sacrifices herself. This is a question of temperament. Some cede. Others fight. The former know the whole time that they will give up. You hesitate, so resist."[51] This advice made clear that Raymonde was to preserve the sanctity of her union with her fiancé no matter what. If necessary, she must even deny her natural female tendency to put others before herself. According to *Elle*, Raymonde must participate actively in French women's new war: finding and keeping a man.

Like disciplinary officers, magazines chastened those who wavered in this quest for love. For example, in early 1947, the "Elle and You" columnist responded to a young woman who was not in love with her fiancé. "Unlucky," as she signed her letter, was already twenty-seven years old, however, and had no other prospects. She was thus seeking counsel about whether or not to continue with marriage plans. She asked *Elle*, "Do you think that I will still be happy with my future husband? He is, as they say, very nice in every respect." *Elle*'s advice columnist responded to "Unlucky" by telling her that she had to want to be happy, and that her past experiences with love, all failed, seemed to be a sign that "you refuse happiness and you seek out suffering." If "Unlucky" did not take the opportunity to marry this perfectly nice-sounding young man and make an attempt to be happy in her marriage, she would drive away yet another man and continue on her path of misery.[52] The anxious feelings of the young woman are afforded little to no validity in the eyes of the columnist. She was to marry, and then force herself to be pleasant, all the while ensuring the contentment of her husband. The woman was presumed to be able to control whether or not she loved her husband. By this definition, love is a functional entity—it can be used to create happiness, and it is not something that is more organically engendered. A woman who does not respond to the offer of stability through partnership with an acceptable man is flawed. The potential marriage—and the stability it would create—was more important than any feelings surrounding its undertaking.

At times the actual men seem incidental to a young woman's quest for marriage; it was more important to have a husband than to quibble about his personality traits. In November 1944, *Marie-France* printed a fictional piece by Simone Cantineau, which detailed the travails of a woman who was trying to choose her future spouse from two very different suitors—even though neither had proposed. The first, René, was a very serious student who hoped to become a successful professor; he had not yet committed to being with her forever. The other, Michel, was more adventurous and had a reputation for being a playboy. Michel had, however, told her that she was the only one for him. The young woman is utterly confused: "René? Michel? Which of these two? *Might I still hope that marriage will stabilize this finicky heart?*"[53] [emphasis mine] This last lament reveals that for the young woman, marriage is the ultimate goal, the promise that will bring stability to her life and to her "heart." Here, the men—and the hopefully resultant love—function as a means to that stable end, despite any reservations the woman might have.

All tactics were on the table in this war: magazines even advocated using methods of dissimulation, men's ultimate fear of public women's natures, provided the objective was acquiring or maintaining a relationship with a man. Dissimulation was the opposite of transparency, and it stipulated that women would lie and cajole and manipulate if given a public role. Fears of dissimulation attached themselves to public women in the time of the French Revolution, particularly women in power, like Marie Antoinette. It was in many ways the opposite of republican motherhood, in which women nurtured republican values in their families in the private sphere.[54] Thus it must have been crucial for women to find a partner if dissimulation was an acceptable tactic at this time, when France had just come through a period when it was not immediately evident who had collaborated or resisted, and reprisals were severe. In *Elle*'s first issue in November 1945, the magazine published the fictional piece, "Vous Ici!" In the story, a young woman, Simone Disieux, encounters a man in a hotel who says he is an old friend of one of her brothers. They go for a walk down the Champs-Élysées, and he gets a bit choked up, as he has not seen it in years, but he dreamed of it while he was in Italy and Germany, fighting for France, just as all French men did during the war. Simone and Jacques have a wonderful evening dancing and walking around, and then later in the night, Simone tells Jacques that she has to make a confession. She has never met him before in her life. Jacques counters by admitting to Simone that he made the whole story up just to approach her.[55] In this story, the dissimulation of the woman is acceptable for two reasons: first, because the objective is to establish a relationship with a man, and second because Jacques is ultimately aware of the entire situation and in control. It is a wartime guerilla tactic. As long as the goal is a stable relationship and the man holds control in the end, the act of dissimulation is less severe.

All of these methods of finding a man were certainly preferable to the vision of solitude presented by Marcelle Segal in *Elle* in 1948:

> Six o'clock in the evening. The cheerful crowds descend at top speed into the Metro. Couples in love hug. Husbands and wives find one another. You are alone. You make your purchases. Those who have right of way pass before you. The shopkeepers treat you like a negligible quantity. Such a little client. You are alone. You go home. In the stairway, you encounter busy neighbors, children who laugh. You go up without haste. Nobody waits for you. You are alone. Down. You go to the cinema. In the shadows, in front of you, two heads nearing one another hide the screen from you. Next to you, lovers whisper and prevent you from hearing. On the screen, they laugh, they hug, they give each other infinite kisses. You are alone . . . Eleven o'clock. The crowd leaves the cinema, families—Dad, Mom, children—or by two, one arm on top of the other's arm. You are cold. You are alone.[56]

Segal—and *Elle*—presented a fearful picture of a lonely life, one which a single woman could prevail against with the help of her magazines. The confinement of possibilities for women worked by not only promoting their active searches for a stable family, but also by painting the frightening image of her solitary counterpart.

Married women

Married women were not immune from the instability and romantic crises of the postwar period—magazines constructed the retention of a man as just as difficult as the winning of him had been. Women would have to work and sacrifice to retain the sanctity and stability of their homes. It was time for them to preserve the peace. In this vein, rather than emphasizing marriage as a complementary partnership, stories and articles associated marital bliss solely with making the husband happy. Magazines could be even more direct in challenging women's devotion to their marriages and husbands. For example, in 1946, *Elle* published a quiz entitled, "Five years have gone by since you married," in which they asked women to take honest stock of their marriages and see if their efforts had been sufficient. The article posed questions like: "Do you no longer want to have a baby with him?" or "When you eat chicken that you have received from the country, have you stopped pretending that you prefer the wing because you know he likes the breast?" or "Are you tired of hearing him tell of his exploits in the Resistance?" or even "Right when you go to bed, do you often tell him that you have a migraine headache?"[57] The quiz mobilized the normalcy of postwar experiences—including the idea that all men had resisted. It also challenged women to keep their marriages fresh. Postwar love was designed to increase the number of marriages France produced, as well as to solidify notions of gender. Images of romance and courtship existed in the service of producing more stable, permanent unions, often at the expense of the couple's own feelings and potential happiness.

The theme of sacrifice for the peacetime retention of a marriage is evident in André Lang's vignette about Sonia, a young woman from a Russian immigrant family, which appeared in *Elle*'s "Did the War Kill Love?" series in July 1946. Sonia's father disappeared soon after the family arrived in France in 1920, and so Sonia and her sister helped her mother as best they could. Still, Sonia kept her spirits high; as Lang notes, "Her letter breathes frankness and simplicity." Here, Lang is constructing the particulars of a French woman (frankness and simplicity), even in the midst of a discussion about the larger concepts of marriage, love, and stability. When Sonia was nineteen, she met a nice man from a good family, and they married soon after they met. They got along quite well, but then he went off to war in 1939. "He was so nervous to leave me on my own without much money," Sonia remembered, "I really could see that I hadn't seen just how much he loved me. I promised to wait for him and to stay faithful." Sonia's husband was imprisoned in Germany for three years, during which time she struggled in Paris and eventually joined a Resistance movement. The head of the Resistance movement was a man named Philippe, and the two of them soon fell in love, although Sonia did her best to "[fight] against it." Circumstances ultimately forced them to be in closer and closer contact, and she fell for Philippe fully in a way she had never loved her husband. Despite Philippe's repeated entreaties, Sonia would not break it off with her husband, as he "relied on me for hope." She recounted to Lang the story of his homecoming:

> Then, the liberation. I saw my husband, and he was changed—thinner, older-seeming. He looked at me with eyes full of adoration, and I lost my nerve. He could tell I had changed as well—I blamed it on the six long, hard years. Philippe pressed me to tell him so we could marry. I went to my husband and told him almost everything except for the fact that I had already cheated. He told me that he had thought this might happen and that he had planned out his response: he understood, he still loved me, he would forgive me and forget everything, and we would start anew. So, I broke up with Philippe, my true love, and I am trying to start over with my husband. I hope I can have a baby soon; if I do, maybe I will be redeemed. You ask if the war killed love? As for me, it introduced me to love, a marvelous love that makes us infinitely happy and infinitely unhappy. Also, I don't regret anything. I am sad only for my husband, who I will live with without loving, and for Philippe, who I will never see again.

At the end of Sonia's story, Lang comments on how proud he is of Sonia, for her ability to fight the unauthorized love within her and stay with her husband, a good man: "She decided to kill the love in her, to renounce happiness to follow her duty as a wife. What a perilous route she undertakes! May her strength not betray her! May she be compensated for it!"[58] Here, Sonia's lie of omission to her husband is less important because she ultimately chose stability. The illicit love that a woman feels must be suppressed in order to do her postwar duty: to seek out marriage and hence stability, and even, in the case of Sonia, to have a baby in order to cement it and to reward Sonia's choice of duty and stability over passionate love with motherhood.

Just as unmarried women were responsible for their own regrettable situations as single people, married women, according to "Did the War Kill

Love?," could behave in a manner that would drive their husbands away from them. In June 1946, Lang presented the case of Suzanne, a perfectly wonderful French woman, "lovely, intelligent, cultured." He asked, "Is it the war that broke up Suzanne's marriage or is she not her own worst enemy?" In women's ongoing war, the reader already knew that Suzanne was pitted against herself. Suzanne should, Lang wrote, be "enjoying the security of her age (emotional security, as material security is unimportant)." Note here Lang's emphasis on stability through marriage rather than financial stability, again damping down women's expectations of their partners—and themselves. Suzanne's main problem, according to Lang, was her complete lack of self-confidence. She is thirty-nine years old, has a daughter, and is in her second marriage, after her first husband proved to be only after her money and social position. She met Jacques, an old childhood friend who had also just been through a divorce for similar reasons; the one black mark on their newfound happiness was Suzanne's tendency toward depression. Still, in December 1941, they married and moved to Lyon—"a marriage built on love and not passion." One day, they ran into Thérèse, another old friend, and her child. Thérèse had a bit of a bad reputation, but she was trying to rehabilitate herself. Jacques proposed to allow Thérèse and her daughter to stay with him and Suzanne, a gesture that was "de rigueur in a period like that one." Suzanne was a bit nervous, especially given Thérèse's reputation, "to leave Jacques to the demons of promiscuity, which the exode and the bombardment had so imprudently favored." Eventually, she relented, and she even began to enjoy having Thérèse around. Her worst fears came true when she discovered that Jacques and Thérèse were having an affair, and she left and moved to Paris. She did refuse to divorce Jacques, "the one manifestation of her will." Now Suzanne feels like she will never lead a happy life.

Lang came down heavily against Suzanne in his evaluation, blaming the end of her marriage on her own poor attitude and moodiness. He acknowledged that the war played a role in bringing Thérèse and Jacques together, but he notes that the war also brought Suzanne and Jacques together. The real question for Lang is: "During peacetime, would Suzanne have known how to keep Jacques?" Lang then asked if it was the nature of certain women that they do not attract men to give them "confidence and joy." According to Lang's analysis, women could not simply blame the war for their romantic misfortunes; rather they must look inward, and see how their own foibles caused the demise of their relationships.[59] Here, male virility and sexual license were unquestioned facts of French masculinity. Given that, the uncoupled woman in the postwar period had only herself to blame for her deficiencies in love.

A case such as Suzanne's also made it clear that a wife had to be sure to behave in a manner which would please her husband. Otherwise, magazines warned, she could lose him, a frightening thought during an era that so stridently celebrated marriage and order and painted unmarried women as flawed. In January 1945, author A. Rastoul de Mongeot's fictional piece, "New Beginning," appeared in *Marie-France*. The story featured a couple, Arlette and Henri, who had been perfectly happy, in the postwar androcentric definition of love-related happiness: "Arlette and Henri always had a great life; Arlette knew exactly how to calm Henri down and make him feel better after a long, hard day." After a while, though, Arlette became depressed, and Henri could barely bear to go home at night. Then, Arlette left him; when she announces this, all Henri says is "Oh," and Arlette cannot believe his lack of response. They decide to try a trial separation, but while they are apart, war breaks out, and Henri is imprisoned by the Germans. They are barely in contact, but one day, the priest comes to see Arlette with a letter saying that Henri's health is failing, and he calls out for her in his sleep every night. Arlette rushes to his side, "feeling nothing but guilty over the way she behaved. She arrives at the hospital, and Henri hears her voice, and they reunite, talking all about their future together."[60] In this story, Arlette's depression, or perhaps unhappiness in her marriage, where the husband's needs are constantly primary, is portrayed as selfish and unreasonable. Arlette feels guilty because she has driven her husband away with her concern only for herself; she almost lost him in her egoism, and she is lucky she did not destroy her marriage completely. These stories crystallized the idea that even once married, a woman could not let down her guard and relax about the stability of her home; she needed to remain vigilant and cater to the needs of those around her that they might be content. Through their contentment, it was possible that a woman would find happiness; if not, the fault was her own.

While a long, stable marriage was the ultimate goal for women in postwar France, infidelity and divorce were realities for many French people of the time.[61] Women's magazines stepped in to offer counsel as to how to handle these difficult situations. Demographically, many men were still away, but there were also plenty around for a woman to choose (or rather be chosen by). As in the above case of Sonia, however, it was clear that a woman's duty was to stay faithful to her husband or boyfriend. And, as evidenced by the case of Suzanne, it was often considered a woman's own fault when her husband strayed. In fact, as Sarah Fishman has noted, during the postwar period, "Not only forgivable, a husband's infidelity could be the fault of the wife herself."[62] France was a nation full of virile men, and their sexual prowess was to be expected and withstood.

In July 1946, *Ève* magazine's advice column printed a letter that dealt with infidelity, this time from the perspective of the jilted wife who called herself, "An Isolated Mom." "AIM" wrote about her unhappy home life, saying she had been married for six years, with an "adorable" three-year-old child, when her husband met another woman "who does everything to make him leave his home." She is worried about the future, she reports, and her husband is no longer affectionate with her. "I cry endlessly," she writes, "I am sick from the pain; I don't deserve what is happening to me, and I want to keep my child and my beloved husband." The response from the magazine partially blames the woman for losing her cool and displaying "a terrible edginess, a sort of mental turmoil." The columnist advises her to take care of her mental health so that she can "wage war and triumph" in this difficult situation. If you want your husband back, the article counseled, "It does not do to always show him a face of perpetual reproach." Instead, "AIM" was told to pretend not to see what is going on, to hold herself with dignity, and her husband would begin to admire her resolve. She must compliment him, to show him the depth of her caring, and that way her rival would not be able to take advantage of her in that way. This happens all the time, the magazine reports, and in the vast majority of cases, the "crisis" is resolved fairly quickly, and the home returns to being a place of pure happiness.[63] If "AIM" would just adopt a happy, warm, domestic exterior, and ignore any problems at home, most likely, the magazine advised, she would again enjoy domestic tranquility. The woman's responsibility in this case was to ignore her own needs and wants and issues, and instead concentrate on besting her rival and restoring a sense of stability to her home.

A woman's infidelity, however, was a different matter altogether, especially if she was the proverbial "other woman." *Ève* magazine's advice column reinforced this notion in October 1945, when it published a letter from "She who waits." "She" wrote in, asking *Ève* to help her: "She" has loved a man for years, but this man is married and has children, and does not think it right to leave his wife and children alone. However, "She" knew that while the man was imprisoned in Germany, his wife had cheated on him; in this case, she asks, "Doesn't he have the right to free himself in order to marry me?" *Ève* responded cautiously, asking if "She" had any proof that the wife had cheated. And in fact, the magazine continued, "She" and the man had been unfaithful to begin with, and they were thus guiltier than the wife, if she had in fact cheated. Most importantly, the magazine emphasized, "She" must not lose sight of the children: "In the case of a divorce, they would be the sacrificial lambs, and that must not be. Your ardent, selfish passions happen above their heads. It is just, it is necessary that you do not forget them."[64] In this case, the love of the other woman was far less important than the stability of the home and the health of the children.

While infidelity on the part of the husband was not a justifiable reason for the dissolution of a marriage, betrayal on a larger scale, between man and France, was intolerable. In June 1946, André Lang's "Did the War Kill Love?" profiled Germaine, a young mother and wife who found herself in a problematic situation. She had married for love, ten years before the war "would make a nightmare out of her dream." She met her future husband, Gilbert, when she was sixteen and he twenty-six, after "he fell off of his bike in front of her and she took him home and nursed him," like any innately nurturing French women would do. Germaine and Gilbert married a year later, to the great joy of all around them. They had two children fairly quickly, and then Gilbert began to have numerous affairs. At first Germaine was distraught, then jealous, and then she even began to become coquettish, but eventually she realized that Gilbert did love her, and she accepted the situation. When the war came, Gilbert enlisted and was sent to the Maginot Line. He was taken prisoner by the Germans, and then "GENEROUSLY" liberated, and returned home. At that point, he became an ardent supporter of Pétain. Germaine could not deal with this national betrayal which was so much worse than his personal betrayal of her, and so she left and went to live with her parents. Later, Gilbert repented and became a strong supporter of the Allies, and he and Germaine reconciled. "He even wanted to join the Resistance," Lang recounted, "which Germaine forbade, but he did anyway, becoming a captain in the FFI." In September 1944, Gilbert was denounced and imprisoned at Fresnes because of his past. Germaine has had no word on what will happen to him, but she reports to Lang that she believes in him and in their love, and she vows to take him away from all of the politics which has caused them and their union such pain. Germaine tells Lang: "He needs to be steered. He needs to be steered. He will be! I will save him, hear me, I will save him, and our children won't have to be ashamed of their father and of their name!" Germaine sacrifices in the name of her husband and her children, and the heteronormative ideal that results from that sacrifice earns her laudatory praise in Lang's piece. However, this ideal cannot come at the price of loyalty to France, a fact Germaine understands and performs well.

Lang went on to state that this case of wartime infidelity was exemplary of so many postwar situations, where the ambiguities of war distorted normal realities of guilt and innocence. Lang remained optimistic about Germaine and Gilbert's situation, though. He noted that Germaine's story "is, in my opinion, revealing about the nature of the healing power of love. Germaine is sure in her belief that Gilbert will be acquitted. But, even if she's wrong, she will have avoided the worst, because love will have made her a missionary and given her life meaning."[65] [original emphasis] Here again, infidelity was an essential characteristic of the virile French man, one which women must expect and tolerate. In terms of a more macro view of infidelity, it is clear that through stability and love, and ultimately marriage, women could heal the wartime wounds of the nation.

In this context of marriage as a juggernaut, divorce rates declined during the 1950s, a nearly uniform trend across the board in the West.[66] This drop occurred even though divorce laws became more lenient in the postwar period, especially when compared with those of the Vichy regime.[67] However, right after the war, France experienced an immediate jump in divorce rates.[68] Between 1945 and 1946, for example, divorce rates nearly doubled, from 4,960 in 1945 to 8,484 in 1946.[69] Claire Duchen argues that this was most likely "due to postponed divorce after the lifting of restrictions imposed by the Vichy government, but must also have been due to the separations of the war years."[70] By 1953, according to Rebecca Pulju, the number had become relatively steady at 35,000.[71]

Certainly, magazines and writers did not consider this jump in divorces to be a positive change in the postwar climate of heteronormative stability. If a man's flaws were to be disregarded when searching for a potential mate, they should not then become a reason for postnuptial marital dissolution. In a 1945 article, *Elle* magazine attributed the increase in divorce rates not to demographics but rather to women becoming emboldened by their war service and consequent entry into public life. Both magazines and the state discouraged women from pressing their divorce claims. Often, *Elle* reported, when unhappy couples went to the courts to have their cases settled, they were told to go home and try to work things out there, as there was no guarantee of either future happiness or even a court audience, tribunals were so overloaded with divorce cases.[72] Despite this initial jump, the generally low occurrence of divorce was a phenomenon that allowed France to sing its praises on an international level, asserting its dominance over the United States in at least one area. As *Marie-France* wrote in 1952, "No, marriage is not in danger in *our house!*"[73] [emphasis mine] Ironically, the magazine went on to note that only 15 percent of French people were actually happy in their marriages, perhaps unsurprising given the French emphasis on stability rather than mutual satisfaction, as well as the number of stories telling women to hide or mask their problems, lest they upset their husbands. According to the magazine, the crucial piece was that couples were staying together.

Magazines also warned women to consider the consequences of divorce through the fiction they printed. In June 1946, "He only knows me," a short story by Alain Mercier, appeared in *Elle*. In the story, a divorced woman, Gisèle, brings her son to the train station to meet his father for a two-month vacation. They had split a year and a half earlier, when Guy was only five, and he does not know what his father looks like. Jean-Louis arrives late and introduces Arlette, his new wife. Gisèle thinks, "typical Jean-Louis." Guy is a little shy at first, but he quickly warms to Arlette, who gives him a harmonica and tells him about the pool that they have and their rabbits that he can feed. Guy happily goes off with Arlette toward the train, and Jean-Louis tells Gisèle not to worry, that two months will fly by and he will be just fine. Gisèle is teary now because Guy barely even says good-bye and barely even looks out the window at her as the train pulls out of the station. Now Gisèle has lost her status as a mother and a wife, and she sees herself being replaced by her husband's new wife.[74] A woman's whole purpose and identity were tied to this heteronormative ideal, as women had to be wary of this type of situation if they were thinking of divorcing their husbands.

Natalism

Clearly romance, marriage, and love were highly important in the postwar context, but their ultimate aim was to create normalized nuclear families. It was from these families that a new generation of French citizens, raised in an era of stability and ready to restore France's greatness, would grow. In order for this to happen, women needed to have babies and raise them in a way which would cement these children's French identity. Motherhood was, as Julian Jackson characterized it, "a civic obligation" during this time, in which women engaged in a fight for the next generation.[75]

Natalism was a concrete manifestation of the importance of the family, along with France's need to repopulate the nation in order to compete on a world stage after the demographic devastation wrought by two world wars.[76] The Vichy regime acted to reverse this slowing birthrate, which officials painted as a result of women's selfishness.[77] Interestingly, many of these pronatalist trends continued in the postwar period when, postwar official government policies again supported large families. Indeed historians "have described this as the golden age of family policy in France."[78] For example, in August 1947, just as rations were ending on milk and bread, the government in the Seine department enacted an increase in family allowances, from 5,650 francs to 7,000 francs. They also sanctioned large bonuses for pregnancies and prenatal care.[79] Simultaneously, contraception remained illegal until 1967, abortion until 1974, and denunciations for violators of the abortion ban initially went up from the time of Vichy.[80] While cultural media attempted to smooth over uncomfortable continuities in pronatalist policies, the government continued to view the low birth rate as a problem for the nation. For a nation vigorously asserting its own virility on the national and international scales, a rising birthrate would, at least demographically, provide useful evidence.

French people certainly responded to these calls for large numbers of children. According to Robert Gildea, the birth rate in France went "from 14.6 per 1000 population in 1938 to 21.4 per 1000 in 1946, and still at 18.1 per 1000 in 1964. Whereas on average women had two children in 1935, between 1942 and 1964 they had three. This baby boom was in no sense unique to France, but France had a long demographic history of a low birth rate which was now dramatically reversed."[81] Additionally, Tony Judt notes, "Between the first post-war census of 1946 and the end of the sixties, the French population grew by almost 30 percent—the fastest rate of increase ever recorded there." In fact, as Judt goes on to note, much of this growth happened immediately following the war: "In 1949 869,000 babies were born in France, compared to just 612,000 in 1939 . . . by 1967, in France, one person in three was under twenty."[82] Perhaps most striking is the statistic that four percent of France's GNP was spent on natalist policies under the Fourth Republic.[83] Yet where historians like Judt have attributed much of this postwar population growth to better medical care and a resulting lower infant mortality rate, it is also crucial to consider the effects of French people's acceptance of cultural gender norms.[84]

Much media of the time fully embraced Charles de Gaulle's famous call for "twelve million beautiful babies."[85] In 1945, for example, the rightist magazine *Questions actuelles* (which became *Écrits de Paris* in 1947) published an extended article devoted to the depopulation of France, calling it "the only" problem France had, the one from which all others, including the war and defeat, stemmed. The magazine placed the burden of responsibility for countering this trend on couples: "Refusing children, is, on the part of a people, surrendering." In fact, the magazine advocated that couples have at least four children, each with a different purpose behind their birth. The first child was a couple's responsibility to repay God for giving humanity life. The second child was so that a couple could replace themselves. The third child was a hedging of bets—hopefully no harm would come the way of the first or second child, but "experience, alas! has taught us that sickness and accidents wreak havoc amongst young lives." Finally, the fourth child was to be the result of optimism and idealism in the face of war: "One must consider, especially after a hideous war, these numerous young girls who will not have spouses at all, these mutilated and sick men who will never be able to set up a home, these households that, for various reasons will remain sterile; who will replace, as they disappear, these beings without posterity? Whence the law of solidarity: fourth child." The French must be willing to fight this problem using "every possible means at once," the magazine advocated, for the "decadence" and "selfishness" of the French people was too much to conquer by any slow or moderated action. The article even proposed revamping and strengthening the Napoleonic Code, hardly a model of liberated thinking, in order to boost the birth rate.[86]

Less than a year later, Henry Bordeaux, the writer and member of the Académie française, echoed these pro-family sentiments and fears of depopulation—for which he was well known—in an article for the same journal. "Wars are never favorable to the home when they are prolonged," he wrote, "for the isolated man breaks away through reflection, illusion, deception or distraction, and the single woman becomes accustomed to an independence that she will never consent to renounce." The state needed to do more, he argued, to preserve traditional life in France. By this Bordeaux was really saying that traditional gender roles needed to be safeguarded. A woman in postwar France had many opportunities that took her away from her home and children, an unnatural turn of events. He argued that women's natural tendencies and proclivities were suited for the home; as evidence he pointed to little girls playing with dolls and exhibiting maternal and housekeeping instincts. Once she went to school, Bordeaux argued, a girl was automatically steered into public life, with the thought that she needed to earn a living. A woman can earn this living, Bordeaux noted, practicing careers that are much more suited to her natural talents: "housework, fashion, minding children. No more governesses, no more couturiers, no more cooks, nothing but employees, typists, salesgirls." The long-term result of female employment, he argued, was "eating charcuterie at the last minute or going to a restaurant, outfits look like wrecks and children are seen as an annoyance." The primary matter of national exigency, according to Bordeaux, was to return women to the home, whether or not they wanted it.[87]

Advocates for stronger, larger families emerged not solely from political figures and organs. Women's magazines of this era also dutifully called for more children. In 1947, *Marie-France* even printed a whole checklist that expectant mothers ought to follow before birth, including the social allowances that they

were owed, and in 1948, *Ève* answered readers' questions about the intricacies
of the new natalist government policies.[88] Perhaps predictably, multiple births
were cause for great celebration in the natalist postwar era. For example, in
1948, the birth of quadruplets to a French woman in La Celle-Saint-Cloud, a
town not far from Paris, made front-page news in *Le Figaro*.[89] *Elle* also feted the
newborns' arrival, even appointing itself to be a "deliriously happy" godmother
to the children. *Elle* reported that *France-Soir* (the newspaper edited by Hélène
Gordon-Lazareff's husband, Pierre, making them a media power couple in
postwar France) would be the godfather, and it detailed all of the gifts it had
given to the new mother.[90] The government even got in on the act, allocating
two tons of coal—a rationed good—to the clinic to make sure the babies were
warm enough, and the prefect of Seine-et-Oise visited the mother and babies to
congratulate her. The mother of the quadruplets received 84,000 francs for the
four births. With two children already at home, she would receive an allowance
of 26,250 francs per month.[91] This was a substantial amount of money for this
time, when the average salary of an office worker in 1945 (admittedly three years
earlier) was 2,000 francs per month.[92] The publicity surrounding the births and
the attention to the financial and immeasurable celebrity benefits of multiple
births are striking in their intensity. Both the state and the mass media were
sharing in the merriment of new babies for France, and they were consciously
inviting readers to get caught up in the celebrations.

Women's magazines also portrayed motherhood as a weapon to combat the
kind of selfishness and greed that cultural critics bemoaned at this time. In 1945,
Claude Mouthiez published a short story in *Marie-France* about a young wife at
the moment of Liberation, and her transformation through motherhood. The
main character, Gisèle, had always been privileged: she was the only child of
wealthy and indulgent parents. Now she is married to Jean-Louis, a successful
surgeon. Sadly, they are unable to have children, but Gisèle is almost relieved
by this—she would have had to sacrifice so much for them. During the war, the
couple had faced some difficulties, but nothing too harsh. As the Allies marched
toward Paris, Jean-Louis called to tell Gisèle that he would not be home that
night, that he had to stay at the hospital, and that "my darling doll" should stay
home and avoid danger. The next day, when she still had not heard from Jean-
Louis, Gisèle set off for the hospital to find him. Along the way, she heard shots
and even saw a man fall. Once at the hospital, she watched the hardworking
nurses admiringly. Then she heard two doctors talking about Jean-Louis's
bravery from the night before; when she finally found him, he confessed that

he had been a Resistance organizer, but he had not wanted to tell her because: "You would never have been able to make yourself useful, you don't know how to do anything." At that moment, Gisèle decided to become the kind of woman Jean-Louis wanted; the next day, she went off in a convoy for Normandy, where she brought all sorts of aid. At one point she came across a young mother with many children whose husband had been killed. Gisèle found herself drawn to the youngest, a beautiful one-year-old girl. The woman said she was an orphan, the only survivor of a bomb that had hit her house. Gisèle brought the girl home as "her final whim," and she was nervous about what Jean-Louis would say. Jean-Louis was ecstatic, and he turned to Gisèle and said, "my darling doll." He noticed Gisèle was unhappy with this, and he said, "my darling wife."[93] Gisèle's reward for her sudden desire to make herself useful—in the service of France, as a public woman, and in the guise of pleasing her man—is a beautiful baby and the newfound respect of her husband. The subtext of the story also shows that just because natural childbirth might not be possible for a couple, that did not exclude them from their familial—and national—duties, and it did not take away a woman's essential maternal nature.

The experience of motherhood and the influence a woman wielded in her guise as a mother were not limited to the actual birth of the child in postwar France. Much as in the vein of republican motherhood, a mother was to imbue her progeny with particular national values.[94] Most importantly, both boys and girls were to carry a deep love of France in their hearts, and a mother needed to train them to bear out this love for the nation in a gender-specific way. This training extended to official pressure from the French government. According to Kristin Childers, "One family association from the Côtes-du-Nord highlighted this [continued postwar] focus on the family and the child in a letter to the Provisional Government":

> Just as a child is living in the womb of its mother, and only joins the family after a long period of gestation, during which it is impossible to separate it from her, so is that child a citizen, as soon as he is born, and only joins the national community after a long period of education in the bosom of the family.[95]

In this way, the home itself became a womb in which a mother could grow her children into French citizens.

Celebrations of the mother and her importance to France as such, especially the *Fête des Mères*, were central to the Vichy program, but many of these traditions–and the relevant policies—continued after the war was over, despite the postwar regime's desire to distance itself.[96] Miranda Pollard distills

Vichy philosophy on women into one simple equation: "woman became mother."[97] At the Liberation, Pollard argues, across the political spectrum, family policy saw a "reworking—not a repudiation."[98] This Vichy/postwar continuity seems incongruous at first glance: Why would the aggressively republican sentiments of the Liberation allow for the continuation of such a Vichy-associated holiday? In January 1945, *Marie-France* called for people to remember Mother's Day. The magazine argued that the retention of what they called "la journée des mères" was "good. Because it illuminates the devotion of mothers who, even though silent, are no less often heroic and always admirable. Also because this custom contributes to restoring France's familial climate."[99] *Marie-France*'s article seems to ignore the fact that one of the major policies of the Vichy regime was indeed to prop up "France's familial climate" in order to repopulate France and restore the country to its former greatness.[100] This uncomfortable continuity, while not directly addressed in the article, could be smoothed over using rhetoric about the need for a new kind of family to support a new France.

The French mother's task was pointedly sex-specific: she was to teach her daughters how to be domestic women and she was to teach her sons how to be strong men. A girl needed to know the domestic arts, inasmuch as they were related to pleasing men. A January 1950 article in *Marie-France* asked readers if their 1949 had been successful. It then offered a series of examples that readers might be able to identify with in determining whether or not their year had proven worthwhile. One such example dealt with the clothes a mother had made for herself: "The pretty dress that you made yourself with the help of your daughter proves that you are not forgetting the duty a woman has to be beautiful and to 'bring honor' to her husband by her charm and elegance."[101] The inclusion of the daughter is telling in lieu of the fact that the entire purpose of the work of making a dress lies in the pleasure of her husband. Here, the daughter is supposed to help the mother in sewing, a task which is deemed successful only if it is pleasing to a man, thereby teaching her daughter some of the concrete and abstract skills necessary to attract and retain a man.

A French mother also had to be sure that her daughters would be ready to marry and perpetuate the stability so important to the future of France. If a mother raised a single daughter, magazines told her she had only herself to blame. In 1948, a *Marie-France* article, "Some recipes for not staying an 'old maid'," urged mothers to follow certain important rules to ensure that this solitary fate would not befall their daughters. Tips included: "Do not fear seeing your daughters grow up," "Do not fear marrying them off," and "Help them to get married." Mothers had to act concertedly in order to accomplish their task of marrying their daughters. They had to be wary of statements such as, "She'll only ever be happy here with us." and "He's not good enough for her." Instead, the magazine urged mothers in postwar France to encourage marriage actively. They could even be matchmakers, hosting groups of young people in their homes and taking their daughters on vacation so that they would meet people of their own age and perhaps find a match. Finally, the article also included advice for single women who were looking to marry: "He'll marry you if . . ." and "He won't marry you if . . ." For example, a man would marry a woman if she said, "I'm not at all a suffragette. I just don't understand feminists." He would not marry a woman who did "not apply makeup to his tastes."[102] Thus, an unmarried woman had to walk a tightrope to catch a man. She needed to be wary of seeming too independent or frivolous, but she also needed to be as beautiful and pleasing as possible. Her man needed to know that he would be the focus of her life, and her mother was responsible for teaching her how to attract and retain him. Single status was social anathema in the postwar period in France, and a mother could be responsible for the social pathology of an unmarried older child.

The responsibilities of women's maternal pedagogy even extended to the French Empire. De Gaulle actively promoted a vision of a France that was unified throughout the Empire: "From one end of the Empire to the other, just as in each city and in each village of the metropole, there is only one more wish: to liberate the nation and return it to its rank. One hundred million men make up today's France."[103] The Empire was intrinsic to de Gaulle's construction of French identity and France's international status. It was at least partially up to women to reinforce this imperial identity in their children. In December 1945, *Elle* magazine encouraged women to buy sets of educational dishes. These dishes would be printed with little pictures and facts about the various places in the French Empire, and would serve as a great conversational piece, "especially [for] our children."[104] At meals which a mother prepared and served, she could also multitask by stressing the importance of the French Empire through her china choices. In this way, women, through consumption and motherhood, were responsible for promoting and thereby sustaining the French Empire. As the de Gaulle quote suggests, this coincides with a time when France's empire became discursively essential to reestablishing France's greatness in an international context. A mother's role was not only to inculcate the glories of the French Empire in her children; according to an anonymous article in the rightist journal *Questions actuelles*, she was also responsible for repopulating it and hence maintaining its status. The empire, the article stated, dearly needed colonists, soldiers, and civil servants, or it would wither away: "No hope can be founded on a depopulating nation."[105] Because of France's pressing need to show itself as a major power to the world, Jean-Pierre Rioux argues, "The imperial mystique was carried to a level rarely equaled in the history of French colonialism."[106] Women's magazines once again mobilized state and national interests through cultural discourses of motherhood; a woman's national duty manifested itself through her activities in the private sphere.

Homosexuality

Within this pro-marriage climate, fears of homosexuality did appear, often in the form of scorn for those who did not conform to the call for a masculine, heteronormative virility. As historian Stephanie Coontz writes, after the Second World War, "The cultural consensus [in the United States and Western Europe] that everyone should marry and form a male breadwinner family was like a steamroller that crushed every alternative view."[107] In this climate of aggressive heteronormativity, homosexuality was perceived as a particular threat to French claims of virility.[108] Additionally, according to Julian Jackson, "At least as far as the specific laws affecting them were concerned, for gay men 1945 was certainly no Liberation." In postwar France, where people celebrated the Resistance, homosexuality was even equated with collaboration. Jackson goes on to state that "the fact that several high-profile homosexual literary figures had collaborated was noted by several observers, and Sartre wrote a famous article about the psychology of the collaborator which he linked to passivity and homosexuality."[109] At a time when the ideal French man was an active, honorable, and virile Resistor, this portrayal of gay men negated their ability to belong to the French nation.

Lesbians did not escape this critical attention; their role in the apparently pervasive depletion of masculinity was to take young women out of the pool of potential mates.[110] In the satirical magazine *Le Crapouillot*, the journalist and author Elisabeth Porquerol wrote that the only reason women became lesbians, or *garçons manqués*, was because they were frustrated at their general inequality within society. In a misguided expression of power, Porquerol continued, they preyed on other women, usurping a role normally associated with men and virility. Porquerol saw evidence for this inversion even in lesbians' physical bodies, "which became more manly," she wrote, as they "were meant to express this search for power, consciously or unconsciously."[111] In his *Forbidden Senses*, the pseudonymous writer Paul Reboux, famous for his ironic pastiches, even warned young straight women to watch out for predatory older lesbians. Reboux noted that such women were ugly and no longer interested men, so they would try to seduce younger girls by drugging them. Reboux even painted the scene of dastardly seduction: "the poison, little by little, gets into the bloodstream of the young woman, while the evil genius [the older lesbian], with the pale claret of languid lamps, on deep pillows pregnant with scents, watches out for the instant when both will go bad together in the delights of a deadly paradise."[112]

A mother's maternal responsibilities at this time also included ensuring that her children would be heterosexual for France. Homosexuality inspired fierce critiques during this time, and the consequences of ignoring a son's masculinity could be dire. In his postwar book on homosexuality, the writer Paul Reboux was especially concerned with the negative effect mothers could have in the "desexualization" of their sons. For Reboux, the preservation of male virility was particularly important. He warned women not to be so jealous at the thought of another woman entering their sons' lives that they preferred them to be "disordered" rather than face a "rival" for their affections. The mother was to teach her children "normalcy" in gender so as not to endanger the masculinity and virility of French boys, French men, and ultimately, France itself.[113]

These examples merely skim the surface of the immediate postwar history of images of homosexuality and their relationship to an atmosphere of persecution in a climate of confined gender norms. This history is rich for potential analysis, as it represents a part of society that did not conform to heteronormativity at a time when such policy was at its most aggressive.[114] The consequences to those who did not adhere to heteronormative standards were humiliation and ridicule, at best. In this context, the amount of energy a "normal" French woman had to spend on keeping up appearances in a variety of spheres took on added importance.

Conclusion

In postwar France, the social pressure to marry and have a "normal" family life was intense, as evidenced by the mass media's castigations of those who rejected such conventions either by choice or by circumstance. Magazines could certainly help women navigate the postwar tumult in practical matters. In fact, women's magazines explicitly constructed themselves as women's friends and mentors. However, these kinds of pragmatic articles grew rarer and less necessary as the war receded into history, and even within them it is clear that women's roles in the postwar period were defined solely in the service of men and masculinity. In both describing and constructing postwar "problems," women's magazines cast themselves as an essential friend and confidante as well as a force which shaped and normalized French women's experiences.

In terms of love and marriage, the two most important goals of postwar women according to the magazines, French cultural productions did not embrace Britain's marital "mutuality." Rather, French women bore the brunt of responsibility for attracting men and keeping their interest; magazines even used military language to describe women's war for love. To win that war, magazines promoted a functional definition of love in which women's expectations of their romantic partners were not so high as to preclude them from making matches. Once married, women could not rest on their laurels. Magazines urged them to work hard at remaining alluring and attentive to their husbands' needs. This promotion of love and marriage served the interests of the national government, which actively sponsored pronatalist policies that rewarded large families. Postwar French motherhood involved much more than the act of birth, however. It comprised the transmission of a set of culturally gendered imperatives, such as virility for boys and domesticity for girls, repeating the cycle for the following generation.

4

Looks

In November 1947, *Elle* magazine printed "*Elle*'s Great Search: Look How Men Like You," a survey of 1,200 men who responded to various questions about women's appearances as well as diverse skills and behaviors. *Elle* justified this as a useful deployment of the magazine's resources by saying, "Before telling you that men like this or men don't like that, we thought we'd simply go ask them." *Elle*'s staff thereby defined the existence of the magazine in relation not its female readers, but to men. And what did men want, according to the magazine? Aside from more predictable desires for good cooks and surprise gifts, the men surveyed asserted that they wanted their women to be looked at in the street, to stop wearing dresses that the men did not care for, and never to wear hair curlers in the morning. One of the most vehement responses (with 1105 in favor) was that men firmly wanted women to change dresses and styles more often.[1] In this article, *Elle* is crafting the ideal French woman for its readers: she has a beautiful, extensive wardrobe, despite the fact that cloth was still under rations; a husband happy at home with delicious gourmet meals, despite the fact that any luxury foods (not to mention staples like butter) were quite rare; and a beauty who makes her husband the envy of all other men when she goes out for the evening. *Elle*'s ideal woman had to contain her goals to fit within strict parameters. If she did not, the consequences were harsh.

Magazines would help French women live within these postwar bounds, even while simultaneously contributing to such bounds' construction. Postwar French women's responsibility to be constantly pleasing extended outward from love and romance into the realms of aesthetics. In her *Second Sex*, published in 1949, Simone de Beauvoir refers to this female requirement of unending beauty as a "social duty, 'to make a good showing,'" again emphasizing the necessary publicness of a woman's commitment to femininity.[2] There were two main components to the demands of aesthetics in the postwar period: pleasing a man and conforming to national expectations of femininity.

The expectations of conformity were high. In the article, "You could be as pretty as ELLE," the magazine asks if the reader knows how to put on her makeup well, or if she just throws it on haphazardly. Springtime is coming, the article continued, and there is a new palette to master. The article then points to a photo of a pretty young woman on the page, saying "the ravishing young woman you see is following these 'rules of the game' and notice the results are rather good . . ."[3] Even the title of the article suggests that the feat of applying beautiful makeup would be difficult, perhaps impossible, without the help of *Elle* magazine. More interesting, though, is the subtext that a woman was always on display, that she had to know the web of cultural expectations placed on her, "the rules of the game," and follow them.

There are two components of this gendered delineation of aesthetics that shaped postwar norms: cultural arbiters, those who determine acceptability, and cultural consumers, those who accept and perform acceptability. Pierre Bourdieu has argued that the determination of the value of an aesthetic must take into account the receptiveness of the audience. He describes the process of creating "art"—not beauty, but certainly a related field—as one that involves multiple levels of socialization. Most relatedly for this subject, Bourdieu posits that there are complex processes of preparation for reception by cultural arbiters, who instruct the people about the art. This preparation, in turn, is how art is imbued with value.[4] In the case of postwar France, women's magazines acted as arbiters of aesthetics, preparing women to perform their postwar femininity.

Appearance, theorists have argued, is intricately linked with the construction of cultural belonging. According to the anthropologist Christine Arzaroli, identity as a concept takes its meaning in relation to others, "Thus the signs of artifice contribute to [identity] because they signify adhesion to a culture or a society."[5] For women in postwar France, wearing the correct clothing, welcoming guests into a "tasteful" home, or following the latest beauty trends signified their acceptance of social expectations. Beauty was a critical way to assess a woman's adherence to the postwar gender norms. Fields like beauty can be sites of power-related dialogue, or even resistance, as scholars have argued.[6] This book takes as its subject the confinement of women and the creation of an ideal type of femininity, and as such resistance was far less important—and rarer—than adherence, as examples will demonstrate.

This chapter will examine the arenas of beauty, home, and fashion to determine how each realm shaped notions of proper femininity in the postwar period, contributing to the quest for normalcy and ultimately the war for love.

Each arena acted separately and in concert to shape an ideal type of feminine behavior, one which confined women to specific vision of acceptability. If a woman did not conform, she faced social shaming from her peers and from cultural authorities like magazines.

Beauty

A woman's physical appearance was a crucial weapon in the war she waged to find and retain a man. Claire Duchen has argued that "in the Liberation years as in the Occupation, women had permission *not* to worry about their appearance, *not* to spend time and money working to be a 'Real Woman.'"[7] On the contrary, this project exposes how façades of happiness, clothing, attitude, and home all contributed to putting on a front which would conform to tightly construed postwar norms. A postwar French woman had to avoid any sort of questioning of her femininity; depictions of lesbians and chastisements of unkempt women served to reinforce these constructs.[8] It had little to do with the needs and desires of the women themselves.

Beauty culture and beauty arbitration are not unique to France after the Second World War. Even in the earliest throes of the modern period, commentators concerned themselves with women's appearances and their relationship to civil society.[9] In the interwar period, beauty rules proliferated, and contradicting them was, according to historian Dominique Veillon, akin to "contravening the rules of good manners that governed female conventions."[10] Even women who rejected the "rules" in the interwar period, like the infamous—albeit relatively rare—figure of *la garçonne* embraced a beauty and an exploding beauty industry that emphasized her youth and daring, straddling the line between "'just audacious enough', very chic, and 'too audacious', verging on vulgarity but still fascinating."[11] All women had a code to follow. During the Second World War, women made do with the clothing they had, dealing with massive scarcities during the war using strategies like newspapers in shoes, and cultural sources encouraged them to remain wedded to some sort of beauty standard, however difficult it might have been.[12] After the Second World War, the beauty landscape shifted again, and French women now performed a version of femininity that emphasized an older, traditional womanliness.

In the postwar period, all the parts of a woman's body were fodder for public discourse about her upkeep. In January 1946, *Elle* featured an article entitled,

"Let's Look at Your Neck . . ." The article tapped into women's anxieties about both their physicality and how they appeared to others, asking, "Is [your neck] pretty? People are looking at it. So take care of it as well as you do your face."[13] Women had to be on constant notice that when in public, they would be on display, and every inch of their person had to be perfect. The ideal a woman's entire body had to reach in order to be publicly acceptable in the postwar period was quite difficult to attain, and trends came and went quickly.[14] A woman had to be on top of her physicality, lest she fall behind and perhaps miss out on her chance for happiness and marriage, and her magazine would help her with this. In January 1947, *Marie-France* published an article telling women how to attain physical perfection along the lines of statues and paintings. Four exercises accompanied the article, one for round shoulders, one for a slender shape, one for a flat stomach, and one for thin and shapely legs.[15] Each of these elements was necessary to complete the prescribed package of a beautiful body. A few months earlier, in August 1946, *Elle* printed, "Do you deserve people's critiques on the beach?" just in time for women's annual vacations. The article advocated that women follow a checklist to make sure that they were not objects of ridicule at the beach under "the rays of the ardent sun." One of the points the article stressed was that women could absolutely not wear a bikini, "even a pretty one, if [they] have so much as a hint of a belly."[16] Women, it seems, were always to be on the lookout for someone else's gaze. Less than one month later, in September 1946, *Elle* printed, "This winter, you should be pale," an article which told women that "porcelain" skin would be the style for winter. The article stated, "Returned from Cannes or Deauville with a diligently acquired tan despite the sun's defection, [the Parisian woman] comes back to find (and she will find quickly) the whiteness of porcelain and the fragility of keepsakes." Despite the fact that summer vacations had recently ended, *Elle* would keep women abreast of the latest trends and the ways to adopt them quickly. In the article, *Elle* reported that it was monitoring chemical labs, where scientists were feverishly working to ensure that women would not have to walk around in public with tanned skin, in order to attract wanted attention and avoid harmful and hurtful critiques.[17] This frenzy of advice points to how magazines acted as an essential tool to keep a woman up to date on the latest trends, which would in turn endear her more to her man, her ultimate goal.

During a time when France was attempting to justify its place at the table of the Great Powers, women's beauty standards even came into play as a measure of France's international worthiness. Advertisers in women's magazines used the label "American" to emphasize the superiority of their products: for example, the nail product manufacturer Cutex explicitly referred to itself as "the American nail polish" in its advertising.[18] To some extent, the French could retain satisfaction in their own national products. In September 1948, *Marie-France* published an advertisement for Carignan nail polish and lipstick which carried a bold headline: "*My American Friend* Envies *My Nails!*" [original emphasis] Even though American women had many quality goods to choose from, the advertisement continued, they were still jealous of Carignan beauty aids, which were "incomparable."[19] Such advertisements in women's magazines from the era reflect a sense of anxiety that French women were not keeping up with their American counterparts aesthetically.[20] In this way, women's appearances and beauty regimes in postwar France could have international implications.

Within France, the pursuit of beauty ultimately centered upon luring and retaining a man. In the short fiction piece, "I am leaving my wife," by André de Richard, a young man and an old man are traveling together in a train compartment. The older man is a bit disheveled, and he seems like he wants to tell the younger man something. He starts talking about how he has just left his wife, how he has been trying to work up the courage for five years, and about how miserable she made him: wanting his attention constantly; never letting him write his novels; not allowing him to pursue his interests. The younger man wonders why he stays with her: because she is so pretty, the older man responds. They pull into the train station and the man blanches, then smiles. His wife is there waiting for the train. "She even missed lunch to come for me, he says." The wife smiles at the younger man with an air of victory, and then invites him to accompany them to the cinema.[21] The retention of a man is a woman's ultimate triumph, and this goal becomes all the easier when she takes appropriate care of her appearance.[22]

Here again, a woman could utilize dissimulation to make herself more beautiful using makeup, if it meant attracting male attention. The cultural anthropologist Christine Arzaroli has argued that makeup represents the gendered codes of a society writ large on women's faces. "With makeup," she writes, "the exterior world, through its codes and criticisms, penetrates the skin and is to a certain extent absorbed by it."[23] To that end, women's magazines stepped in to ensure that women would follow the new "rules of the game" properly with respect to cosmetics. In March 1945, *Marie-France* printed an extensive guide for women that dealt with how to properly apply makeup. According to the magazine, a woman's makeup should not be obvious or loud. Instead, it should highlight her best features in order to work to her advantage. The magazine advised, "In order to be tasteful, one's makeup must be discreet . . . a well made up woman must not seem like she is wearing any."[24] This is different from notions of aesthetic beauty during Vichy, when, according to Dominique Veillon, women were encouraged to embrace their "true nature," without the artifices of too much makeup.[25] During Vichy, makeup was meant only to reflect the reality of a woman's face, the simplicity within her. In the postwar era, makeup could *create* that artifice of simplicity and reveal it to those she was trying to attract. *Marie-France* echoed the theme of acceptable aesthetic dissimulation in July 1946, when, in an effort to help readers with the meager material situation of the Liberation, the magazine featured an article that showed women how to make one dress appear to be four.[26] In the postwar era, a woman could use dissimulating tactics to convince others that she had a complete, fashionable wardrobe.

Dissimulation and other methods of fortifying one's appearance in the hopes of finding and retaining a man became less urgent in the event that a woman was a mother. Beauty, according to the magazines, came naturally with motherhood. When motherhood itself was the goal, beauty could be the reward. In June 1946, in André Lang's "Did the War Kill Love?" series, he recounted a friend's tale about a woman named Louise, an unattractive spinster who eschewed all politics and judged other people's behavior quite harshly. After her mother died, Louise had to take over running the household. She did with severity, even alienating her siblings, but she seemed not to care. Rather, "she was happy to be congratulated for [her sacrifice] at Sunday mass." During the war, Louise finally married, and she and her new husband "moved to a small apartment and passed the war in relative ease. Louise submitted to the orders of Vichy and the Germans without question, and kept a picture of Pétain up until she replaced it with one of de Gaulle on August 25. The only thing that really bothered her was the sight of people having a good time." Louise had little interest in politics; she was only concerned with her own priggish sense of piety. And this, according to the piece, helped to render her quite ugly. This was the case up until she experienced the joys of motherhood. After that point, Lang writes:

> But my friend saw her last month. She had just had a boy, her firstborn.
> –Maternity has touched her like a blessing, he told me. She is already less ugly.
> —Without a doubt, that's because she truly loves something for the first time in her life, [Lang] told him. There are no ugly women. There are only women with love, ideals, or faith.

Lang went on to argue that women like Louise deserve "sympathy" rather than condemnations. If motherhood could soften a woman who was as ugly and undeservingly self-righteous as Louise, and even make her *slightly* attractive, imagine what it could do for other French women.[27]

While motherhood might suffice to make even an ugly woman beautiful, this did not mean that married women had the luxury of relaxing about the solidity of their unions. A woman could never allow herself to grow too comfortable about her marriage or relationship; she constantly had to be on guard, making sure her husband was happy and would not leave her, and her beauty was to play a large role in this ongoing endeavor. In November 1946, *Elle* printed the article, "Even more beautiful when it's just for him," in which it cautioned its readers about taking a night off from being gorgeous and charming, even if their husbands felt like spending the evening at home:

> You're beautiful and your husband loves you. Don't take advantage of that by letting yourself go in his presence. Don't forget that if he found you attractive, it is without a doubt because you are charming, intelligent, and prudent, but also because that day you were particularly beautiful, well made-up, clean, polished, with combed, shiny, luscious hair, a fresh, smiling mouth, and brilliant eyes. **Don't forget that you have to earn his happiness every day, that nothing is a given, and nothing comes from indifference or negligence. . . . Yes, men are repulsed by unkempt women.**[28] [emphasis mine]

A few pages earlier in the same issue, another article, "He doesn't want to go out tonight," echoed this sentiment. Here, the reader was exhorted to make an evening spent in a special one for her husband. She would accomplish this by wearing her most wonderful house dress, doing her hair and makeup only for him, and generally creating a warm and tender environment.[29]

Women's inattention to their beauty had consequences for their husbands' sexual interests as well. A 1952 article in *Elle* by editor Françoise Giroud told women that their inattention to appearances alienated their husbands. Giroud cited the example of Christine, a wife who was not taking care to make herself constantly beautiful in front of her man:

> Each time Christine has shown herself with dirty hair or an old housecoat, each time she has diminished herself physically, she has simultaneously diminished the importance of the object of her husband's desire, she has devalued herself. And each time she struts around with cream on her face, it's a way of saying to him: "Just for you, it's not worth the effort." Acting like this, she humiliates him. Now, nothing kills desire more certainly or rapidly than humiliation for a normal man.[30]

This article paints a woman's sexuality as a weapon in retaining her man. Her beauty could serve to attract or repulse the one she wanted to retain. While perhaps the franker writing about sex signified a discursive shift,[31] the message remained the same: always look beautiful for your man. These examples highlight how a woman could never take her situation for granted; at every opportunity she had to ensure the happiness and comfort of her husband. By focusing on remaining beautiful for him, she would ensure the stability of her marriage.[32]

Fiction in women's magazines reiterated that women needed to be careful to make sure they were beautiful in order to keep their husbands. In Georges Keyer's "She wasn't jealous," for example, two couples, Louise and Raoul and Madeleine and Francis, are away on vacation. One night, Madeleine and Louise are off having a chat about how happy their marriages are. Louise realizes that she has never really thought about whether her marriage was particularly happy; even considering it makes her nervous. Perhaps the initial passion has cooled, she reasons, but she still loves Raoul. As they go to find their husbands, they hear them talking. They hide in the bushes and listen, and it becomes clear that Raoul is talking about a woman named Mathilde, whom he has loved for twenty years. Francis says, "My compliments! . . . At least you are faithful in your infidelities!" Louise trembles with anger and hurt. She thinks about her life with Raoul and all the time spent caring for him and their children:

> [Louise] does not have the time to be like his lover probably is, going to trendy clubs and having her hair done all the time. In the past, when she felt her love threatened, she always took the time to cultivate it ceaselessly. And then a sort of numbness took over her. Her confidence in her husband, her certainty in having him all for herself for always, made her forget the constant combat that is love.

The next day, her husband's laughing awoke her. "You thought I was having an affair with Mathilde de la Mole!" [from Stendhal's *Le rouge et le noir*] he said. At that point, Louise felt relieved, but she also knew she would always doubt.[33] In this case, the story intimates that Louise's husband (potentially) strayed because she no longer took the time to beautify herself and do other, similar little things to make sure that her marriage remained strong. These "little things" consisted of paying attention to her husband by doing what he wanted to do, and also spending the time on herself with the goal of becoming beautiful enough to sustain his interest. Louise's own personal esteem played no role in her aesthetics.

These stories and vignettes about postwar feminine beauty represent a powerful concerted pedagogy about the role of women in French society during the long Liberation. It taught women that they were to focus on themselves, but only in the context of pleasing their husbands. If their husbands were satisfied, they were successful as French women.

Fashion

The display of femininity traversed the porous lines of the beauty and fashion worlds. Both milieus encouraged an aesthetic that would emphasize hyper-femininity for the benefit of spectators, at a time when it was imperative that women showcase their femininity as a language of belonging to the French nation. Any boon women received from their efforts would come only peripherally, from the contentedness of their husbands or boyfriends. In *Ève* magazine in 1945, for example, there was an article entitled, "To be pleasing to him," which dealt with the latest fashions. The article highlighted particular trends and styles of the time with photographs of models wearing them. Behind the models, however, were drawings of male gazers, who were staring at the women with smiles on their faces.[34] In order to be pleasing to one's man and limit public criticism, a woman had to look a certain way. Simone de Beauvoir highlighted this concept in her *Second Sex*, writing, "The purpose of the fashions to which [woman] is enslaved is not to reveal her as an independent individual, but rather to cut her off from her transcendence in order to offer her as prey to male desires."[35] A woman's aesthetic existed for the edification of others.

The fashions of the postwar period largely encapsulate in a visual package the various gender trends of controlled beauty and domesticity—as well as the disconnect between reality and fantasy of the time—and the meaning that they held. These fashions were explicitly meant for public consumption. Much in the same way that women in department stores in the late nineteenth century were subject to the politics of looking and display, after the Second World War fashion remained a cultural marker meant for women to wear and others to consume.[36] For example, an *Elle* magazine article from November 1945 encouraged women to wear pants in their homes because it was so cold. However, the magazine cautioned, this behavior was unacceptable in public, where a woman would face public disapproval for her unfeminine ways. According to the article, it was only allowed "in the privacy of your own home, [where] nobody will even know about it!"[37] Here it is clear that fashion acted as a language through which women could communicate their hyper-femininity and acceptance of "proper" styles, taking care not to violate any rules of acceptable behavior.

Where the scholar Gilles Lipovetsky characterizes fashion as being an individualizing agent within liberal democracies, evidence from the postwar time suggests that fashion can also be a homogenizing agent, a language which reflects and indeed defines social and cultural trends.[38] As cultural studies scholar Rebecca Arnold posits, "Fashion displays the promise and threat of the future, tempting the consumer with new identities that shift with the season and expressing the fragmented moralities of . . . social uncertainty."[39] Therefore, a context of social anxiety such as the one of post–Second World War France could, in turn, beget a collection that hearkens back to a time of perceived peace and tranquility.

French women's physical attributes and their ability to wear high fashion again played a role in illuminating larger French anxieties about the nation's role in the postwar world on the national and international stages. When there was a shortage of fashion models for the 1946 couture collections, magazines and newspapers portrayed it as a source of national shame. *Elle* magazine reported on the lack of suitable candidates, saying:

> Nobody went to these calls [for models] by the grand designers. Is it because there are no pretty girls in France who fit this bill? Certainly not! It is true that this profession has never really tempted French girls—since 1918, Russian girls have been the main fashion models. Then the Slavs also came and became models. Then the Americans. Today, it is hard to travel abroad; the French Work Commission doesn't permit visas simply for exotic beauties. But why can't French girls present the creations made in France? Young French girls, aren't you a little tempted? The most elegant toilettes in the world await you.[40]

Elle thereby turned the beauty of French women into a marker of international standing, but one whose judging took place largely within France and affected French women. Surely there was no reason, the magazine suggested, why French women should have to watch their Russian or American counterparts model French creations. Consequently, *Elle* issued a challenge to French women to be beautiful enough to beat out non-French models. International pride was at stake, and magazines called upon French women to model French clothing in the name of France.

The need for elegant beauty in postwar models was quite different from the requirements for immediate prewar and wartime models, who, according to Nigel Cawthorne, "had to look like they drove jeeps rather than were chauffeured around in limousines."[41] Now, France was cultivating supermodels like Capucine and Bettina, who would soon become avidly watched celebrities, ambassadors of the best French femininity had to offer the nation and the world.[42] After Dior launched his New Look in 1947, modeling scholar Patrìcia Soley-Beltran writes, he was able to define the standards of the modeling industry: "a worldly-wise, sophisticated, self-assured-looking woman in her mid-thirties . . . [with] haughty eyebrows and glossy, groomed hair." The top models in the world conformed to Dior's vision of beauty, making him dominant in two main areas of appearance: fashion and beauty.[43]

Modeling—and conforming to Dior's vision of aesthetic perfection—was a way to garner fame and attention in postwar France. By 1950, the French supermodel Fabienne was famous enough to merit a feature in *Marie-France*, in which readers, through a series of photos, watched her over the course of a day, following her simplest activities.[44] Appeals to the beauty of French women during the "long Liberation" became a pathway toward the reestablishment of French women's superiority. Models for haute couture, the prestigious, influential milieu of Paris fashion at the time, were beautiful and sophisticated, not approachable or earthy, like a Brigitte Bardot.[45] Unlike their British and American counterparts, French designers sought runway models, not photographic ones, women who could walk and display their creations in motion.[46] A dearth of suitable models meant there was a dearth of women who could achieve a living femme-fleur status. And French women responded, at least to *Elle*'s call for French models to wear French couture in the shows. So many wrote to *Elle* in hopes of becoming famous models that the magazine had to discourage them from getting their hopes of a famous modeling career too high: "remember! In couture as in heaven, there are many candidates but few elected!"[47] France's ability to produce internationally recognized women was a source of anxiety in a time when the country was trying to prove itself as a liberal democratic player on an international stage.

Relatedly, if a woman of any nationality wanted to obtain a Dior original (or a Fath or Balenciaga one, for that matter), she needed to adopt high financial and beauty standards. Arriving in style to the couturier's house was a must; American magazines advised their readers to book a Rolls Royce, "after having reserved a seat for the collection through the hotel concierge." Magazines then counseled their readers to look "haughty" and rich so that they could obtain "an incomparable dress that will be immediately recognizable back home as an authentic Paris model." The trappings of arrogant wealth would still not suffice to obtain a first-run piece, though. A woman had to make sure she could actually fit the sample that the couturier produced, so being as close as possible to French model size was crucial, but, magazines counseled, "worth it."[48] For French couture, establishing physical and financial requirements established an unequal relationship with foreign buyers, who had to conform to French ideals in order to access French couture. In creating that rigid paradigm of near-unattainability internationally, French couture established itself as a cultural force.

Within France, every French woman, model or not, couture-clad or not, had to maintain a perfectly kempt appearance at all moments of her life. In fact, magazines dictated that there was a specific fashion geared for every event a woman might ever attend. In late November 1948, *Elle* published the article, "The time to be beautiful is approaching," which consisted of a guide to what to wear to eight types of events that a woman might reasonably expect to attend during the upcoming holiday season. Just as conceptions of beauty were tied up in pleasing a man, each event (and clothing choice) was linked with what a man would want. The events included going out with a childhood friend ("he'll love this pleated dress in silk muslin"), being seen with an important father ("he'll appreciate the style of this outfit in taffeta with a very low-cut corset and with a very full skirt"), or even going to a dance with a husband ("he will find you very becoming in this fine gown of moiré whose neckline shows off your shoulders").[49] The article's wording reinforces that the importance of fashion lay in attracting and pleasing a man.

A woman could not escape the responsibility of being pleasing at any moment; her clothes always had to be correct for the benefit of others. Magazines published articles about what a woman should wear to the beach, skiing, and gardening, among other activities.[50] Even pregnancy was no excuse for a woman to neglect her clothing. In 1950, the maternity wear company Materna published an ad in *Elle* magazine that told "future mommies" to "be in fashion" by buying Materna. A photo of a woman who did not at all appear pregnant accompanied the ad.[51] No circumstance should prevent a French woman from constantly looking her best.

Dior and the New Look

In 1947, to the astonishment of the fashion world, Christian Dior launched his legendary New Look, a collection meant explicitly to revolutionize how women dressed. When the collection debuted, the "ecstatic" crowd gasped, and people cried out, "'*bravo!*' '*ravissant!*' and '*magnifique!*'"[52] Anticipation about Dior and the new fashion house had run high prior to the new collection: Jacques Roüet, the first director of the House of Dior, recalled that "invitations for the presentation . . . were sold on the black market."[53] Editor Bettina Ballard of *Vogue* recalled how she felt during the collection:

> I was conscious of an electric tension that I had never felt before in the couture. Suddenly, all the confusion subsided, everyone was seated and there was a moment of hush that made my skin prickle. The first girl came out, stepping fast, switching with a provocative swinging movement, whirling in the close-packed room, knocking over ashtrays with the strong flare of her pleated skirt. . . .We were witnesses to a revolution in fashion.[54]

The New Look achieved a stunning success: the Dior couture house underwent a massive expansion almost immediately after he first presented the collection. In fact, Dior opened two extra workrooms in order to deal with the demand the New Look created, going from three rooms to five.[55] By the end of 1947, Dior "began to make room for [a] seven-storey extension."[56]

As anecdotes about calls for models suggest, the fashion industry had strong ties to national images of superiority and dominance.[57] During the Second World War, Paris, the fashion center of the world, had exported very little, in large part because Germans severely rationed textiles.[58] Many major houses shut down or moved to New York, and it was unclear whether people and ideas would return. There were some immediate postwar efforts at collections, including the Théâtre de la Mode in March 1945, an event in which major designers presented their collections in luxuriously detailed miniature, using dolls as models, because of the restrictions on items like textiles and leather.[59]

It was the arrival of the collection from Christian Dior in 1947, though, that solidly reestablished Paris as the fashion capitol of the world. While the fashion world came nowhere near the burgeoning French auto industry in terms of profit, nothing could touch French couture in terms of prestige, and Dior almost single-handedly put French designs back on the international map.[60] He proved that new ideas could come out of Paris, considered a beleaguered, war-torn city. Crucially, he attracted American interest and money at a time when the United States had become the economic and political power center of the West.[61] The stakes were high for Dior and for France: Françoise Giroud wrote later that "he saved the supremacy of French couture at the very moment when people ceased to believe in it."[62] This sentiment was echoed by others inside and outside of the fashion industry, from the influential editor of *Harper's Bazaar*, Carmel Snow, to the American socialite Susan Mary Alsop.[63] In 1948, at Dior's second collection, Americans came in droves to see what he would do. In fact, he had become one of the most famous French people in the United States, behind only

Sartre, de Gaulle, and Picasso.[64] Through the movement of American fashion attention away from New York and back to Paris, Dior had reestablished France as the fashion capital of the world.[65] Emphasizing the national and international importance the French placed upon this feat, the honors afforded to Dior for this feat even included the Legion of Honor, which he was awarded in 1950.

The New Look was Dior's direct reaction to the gender-neutralizing trends of war. Bored and uninspired by the military-style masculine garb of the war, Dior sought a return to femininity and a feeling of good times, to "liberate all women from a poverty-stricken era."[66] He wanted the New Look to reflect his optimism at the end of the war, which, he said, "enabled me to temporarily forget that we were still living in the aftermath of a terrible war. Traces of it were all around me—damaged buildings, devastated countrysides, rations, the black market, and less serious but of more interest to me, hideous fashions."[67] And the New Look certainly delivered—it was a luxurious vision of France's glorious past, presented at a time when the country was making a play for a return to world prominence, and fashion would be at the front lines.

Dior promoted a very specific standard of femininity for women; as he said, he attempted to make "woman-flowers," visions of womanhood that would conform to the idea that being female was both intimately tied to one's body and yet seemingly effortless, like a flower in bloom. In regarding a flower in bloom, gazers do not see the complex processes at work; instead, they note only the outward beauty. Similarly, for the man who gazed upon the New Look, femininity was sunshine, ease, confidence. Gone were the dowdy, drab wartime clothes: Dior presented an image of conscious confidence in France's future. In fact Dior himself affirmed fashion's escapist role: "Fashion comes from dream and the dream is an escape from reality."[68] As Diana de Marly writes:

> *Harper's Bazaar* greeted his first collections as "a sensational success." *Elle* declared that the name which shone was Dior. He launched two new lines, the Corolla and the Figure of Eight, and in his programme notes wrote that the first was a dancing line, dressed up with petticoats, with a moulded bust and narrow waist, and the second was a very shaped and clear cut line, with the bust underlined, the waist narrow, and the hips accentuated. He actually used the term excavated to describe the waist—thinking of women as building sites. In *Elle* Chamine wrote that the Corolla was a bustline which then opened out into a supple bell composed of regular or irregular pleats, suggestive of the dance, and youthful paces.[69]

These characteristics are evident in the picture of one of the original pieces from Dior's 1947 collection. Note the extremely cinched waist and accentuated hips and bustline in the design, as well as the generally unnatural pose of the model, especially evident in the positioning of her ankles. She resembles an inanimate store mannequin who has been posed along the banks of the Seine, more a vessel for the image the clothes are conveying than a real woman who is wearing them.

Dior's relationship with the model Renée, pictured here, further reinforces the idea of the woman as an inanimate object, as a vessel for messages about gender. He described Renée as bringing "fabric to life so exquisitely that her face is lost. As she shows her clothes, distant, aloof, it seems as if her very life centres around the folds of the material."[70] Renée, fashion scholar Ilya Parkins argues, transforms into a "commodity" rather than a woman in that moment.[71]

Figure 4 A 'femme-fleur', 1945.

The woman wearing the clothes, in this instance, became less important than the clothing itself. If the message transmitted by the clothing was a transformation of women into "woman-flowers," the dehumanization of the wearer takes on extra significance. The woman is not an individual, but rather a vessel for a message about aesthetics.

As Dior's financial success suggests, the look was wildly popular with French women. Dior himself stated that the primary reason for his designs, and ultimately his success, was that his penultimate goal was women's happiness, which he thought could be achieved through beauty: "My first creations had names like 'Love', 'Tenderness', and 'Happiness.'"[72] However, these are not fixed concepts. As seen above, love at this time was rooted in a quest to please men. In that sense, Dior's "Happiness" and "Love" dresses fit nicely into the larger cultural context. In 1947, Dior noted, "Fashion was weary of catering to painters and poets and wanted to revert to its true function: enhancing feminine beauty."[73] But the question of what exactly constituted the specifics of this beauty is not obvious; Dior was *creating* notions of beauty, not simply channeling them.

A particular quality associated with the New Look is its hearkening back to the *belle époque*, when women mechanically reshaped their bodies. In the 1920s, women began to dress in more free-flowing, even masculine styles, and the corset was discarded. Perhaps the most famous example of this is seen in the designs of Coco Chanel, who, according to Mary Louise Roberts, "tried to create a look for the modern woman that was comfortable, practical, and compatible with an 'active' life."[74] Even women's bodies had to change in order to support the New Look, whose constraints, as noted above, stood in marked contrast to the freeing, loose-fitting fashions of Chanel and Paul Poiret in the 1920s. Dior later responded to general criticism about bodies somewhat pithily, saying, "War had passed out of sight and there were no others on the horizon. What did the weight of my sumptuous materials, my heavy velvets and brocades matter? When hearts were light, mere fabrics could not weigh the body down."[75] In 1949, a writer from *Elle* magazine described for women the ideal body they would have to try to attain in order to best wear Dior's designs: "refined, slender, very elegant to see."[76] Here again it is important to note that a woman's body was not her own; it existed in order to be pleasing to those who would gaze at it.

The fashion contrast between the 1920s and the Liberation period could hardly be greater. Where after the Great War, fashions became "boyish" and masculine, in the aftermath of the Second World War, women were freely electing to adopt a cosseted public existence.[77] As Steven de Pietri and Melissa Leventon argue in *New Look to Now*:

> That women chose to adopt these fashions, after very small resistance, to corset themselves and pad their busts and rumps as they had not done since the 1900s, says far more about the desire for change and need to express and aesthetic ideal than it does about the public's thoughts of progress or comfort. Chanel stated, with great vehemence, that it had taken her a lifetime to simplify and modernize women's clothes and that, within a couple of months, this man Dior had undone everything. For a number of reasons, nobody listened to Chanel at that moment.[78]

[Certainly first among these reasons was that Chanel had been in a relationship with a German officer, and French anger at her was still fresh. In 1944, *Le Canard enchaîné* printed an article about how while France was occupied by Germany, Chanel was "personally occupied" by a Gestapo officer.[79]]

Despite this financial success, it is important to point out another considerable irony associated with the design: the New Look starkly contrasted with the economic realities of postwar life in France. While the government had recently lifted rations on fabrics, the country was experiencing a major fiscal crisis. In fact, the government was near a financial disaster because of the rising dollar and the falling franc. In 1947, Paris-based *New Yorker* correspondent Janet Flanner described the sense of economic and general depression among Parisians (and Europeans in general): "For the past two months . . . there has been a climate of indubitable and growing malaise in Paris . . . as if the French people . . . expected something to happen, or, worse, expected nothing to happen."[80] On a more personal scale, as Jean-Pierre Rioux shows, French household incomes rose by only 2.4 percent from 1938 to 1950, and most people hardly had the money to spend on one of Dior's dresses, which cost around 40,000 francs.[81] The New Look's aggressive emotional happiness and luxury contrast markedly with the economic and emotional actuality of postwar existence in France.

There was also some backlash against the New Look, particularly among the working classes. One revealing anecdote from 1947 reveals just how frustrated people were when faced with the sight of this luxury and extravagance, particularly when they continued to struggle with privations. Apparently, the couture house set up photoshoots for the New Look in "typically" Parisian settings, one of which was Montmartre, staunchly a workers' neighborhood. When the model, dressed in her Dior attire, emerged for the session, two women attacked her "with a shriek of outrage . . . in a very short time clothes and models were heading back to the safety of [the couture house on] Avenue Montaigne."[82]

Anti-Dior protests were not limited to the metropole. When Dior traveled to the United States that same year, he was again met with protests over the new fashions, with one Los Angeles garage owner even threatening "to tear Dior apart because the New Look had made his wife look like a Civil War-era stuffed doll"[83] and women in Chicago yelling "We abhor Dior!"[84] The cultural studies scholar Angela Partington has also noted that working-class women in Britain attempted to negotiate Utility clothing (left over from the war) and the New Look through their own interpretations of the new fashions, rejecting the discomfort and immobility of the New Look but adopting some of its essential qualities. These women argued that their "style was 'free' and comfortable rather than restrictive and ornamental, allowing it to be worn in an 'everyday' way rather than for evenings or special occasions."[85] In doing so, these women created some agency for themselves within a bourgeois couture identity. However, to the extent that working-class women modeled their own clothes after his designs at all, Dior certainly permeated their fashion consciousness as well. As fashion historian Valerie Steele writes, "Ultimately, the women of the world *chose* to adopt the New Look," and in doing so, they ascribed a high level of prestige to Paris fashion.[86]

The vast majority of middle- and upper-class women, the targets of Dior's campaigns, adored his fashions. As socialite Susan Mary Alsop wrote, "It is impossible to exaggerate the prettiness of the 'The New Look'. We are saved, becoming clothes are back, gone the stern padded shoulders, *in* are soft rounded shoulders without padding, nipped-in waists, wide, wide skirts about four inches below the knee."[87] And writer Marie Bertherat argues that women were "crazy over this new style which permits them to reject the clothes of the war and to regain a form of femininity characteristic of a time when a woman was a fragile being that a man owed it to himself to protect."[88] Either way, the New Look was a juggernaut, and "opting out was not much of a possibility" if you wanted to be fashionably mainstream.[89] It accounted for three quarters of France's fashion exports in 1947.[90] Dior tapped into deep anxieties and pedagogies about gender with his New Look, and as such, among his target audience, he was a hit.

The New Look and the return of couture designs demanded a newfound focus on fashion on the part of women that they must understand and conform to the new "rules of the game." This was another responsibility women would have to assume in order to achieve aesthetic feminine perfection, and women's magazines again stepped in to act as guides for the French populace in navigating high fashion. In the early months following war, magazines had at times advocated for using the same dress from previous seasons. For example, in January 1946, *Elle* published "How to make one dress look like ten!"[91] In July 1946, *Marie-France* printed an article, "I have only one dress," which told women how to make that one dress look like four.[92] And even as recently as December 1946, *Elle* had printed the article, "So many invitations and only one dress!" which included advice on how to stretch that dress to fit with various social and domestic obligations.[93] Now, however, in March 1947, as seen in the article "Hello New Fashion," *Elle* put forth a new vision of fashion's role in a woman's life. The stakes were high, according to the article: "One is well obliged to admit that fashion is a tyrant whom it is impossible not to obey, under penalty of losing confidence in oneself."[94] The next article in the same issue was "You will be fashionable if . . ." This consisted of a list of seventeen new rules a woman had to follow if she wanted to look all right in public. If not, how could she have "confidence" in herself?[95] In fact, just two years after the appearance of the New Look, *Elle* presented itself as an indispensable guide for women to use in navigating postwar clothing trends. The article, "ELLE presents to you FASHION 1949," presented women's confusion about fashion as a problem only *Elle* could resolve:

> You have, like us, anxiously tested the arrays of cloth, felt the woolens, measured the intensity of a blue. And you went away hesitant. . . . NOW YOU ARE GOING TO KNOW EVERYTHING and will no longer be able to make a mistake. We have, for your information and your pleasure, studied as we do two times a year, the new collections of the great creators of Paris. With thousands of people coming from all over the world to quench their thirst at these sources of talent, we have seen for you, understood for you, chosen for you that which Paris brings that is new, charming, desirable. Just now, we said, "We are in year II of the new Fashion." And here you are, reassured, for you have already understood: YOU ARE NOT STARTING FROM ZERO. NO![96]

Now a woman could feel slightly more at ease in a sea of new trends, none of which came with labels to tell her what she could actually wear out in public, what would be in good taste, and what would be irreproachable in a climate of anxiety about heteronormative appearance. As long as she had *Elle*, she would know what to buy, what to wear, and what generally was appropriate for an acceptable postwar woman. Whereas previously a woman might have thought it prudent simply to spruce up her old clothing, now it was clear she needed a whole new wardrobe, one which would aggressively assert her femininity and conformity with gender norms.[97] She could not accomplish this without magazines' guidance.

Magazines also took up the torch in urging women to adopt certain standards of physical beauty in order to look their best in the appropriate clothes. Discussion of a woman's proper body went down to the most intimate details. In 1950, for example, Alice Chavane of *Elle* wrote an article about the aesthetics of women's breasts, which were more and more on display in the new fashions. Chavane, who later helped Dior with his autobiography, wrote that "naturally, this fashion is only 'devilishly sexy' as long as one has the chest of a goddess. So you want a pretty bust? Here are the fourteen questions you should ask yourself." Chavane then went into great depth about the ideal form of a breast, detailing its perfect size, shape, general position, and height. She even gave four exercises that women ought to do to improve their breast aesthetics.[98] Advertisers in women's magazines also focused a large amount of attention on women's chests in the wake of the New Look. In November 1948, *Marie-France* published an advertisement from Star-Sein, a breast enhancing cream. The copy of the ad argued that a woman's breasts, the "seductive expression of [her] femininity, remarkably emphasized by current fashion, **have the right to as much care as [her] face.**"[99] [original emphasis] After the arrival of the New Look, corporal beautification became more geared toward emphasizing the very aggressive femininity that Dior's designs embraced. The new aesthetic of womanhood focused on a small, corseted waist, a large bust, and round hips, rather than strength or functionality. It reflected a more confined sense of femininity that, as in conceptualizations of love and beauty, saw women's primary roles confined to pleasing others.

Like beauty, fashion acted as a discursive language on two levels. First, women could dress in a way that signified their acceptance of postwar gender norms. These norms were, in fact, communicated through clothing like Dior's New Look. Second, fashion projected a vision of French superiority to the world. French couture would once again dictate the world's tastes and make France an international player. Women's magazines acted as cultural arbiters throughout this process, designating to women the limits of acceptable femininity.

Home

Like beauty and clothing, the aesthetics of a woman's house played a significant role in the retention of her man and her general acceptance of postwar gender norms. Magazines portrayed a woman's homemaking skills as key to the contentment of her husband—and, consequently, to the preservation of a happy marriage—as well as a cultural signifier of her belonging to the French nation and her acceptance of the "rules of the game."[100]

The privileging of the home and concerns about its aesthetic importance were not new to postwar France; in fact they were major foci of the Vichy regime. Housekeeping, historians have argued, symbolized the entirety of women's role under Vichy. All education and official training for girls focused on making them efficient managers and domestic scientists.[101] After the war, with the enfranchisement of women, it is striking that the home remained a place of retrenchment for women, and it raises questions about how postwar processes of confinement represent continuities between the authoritarian Vichy system and republican postwar one.

In many ways, the home itself was a metaphor for all of postwar French life in the sense that order must prevail there. If women controlled the home and ran it well, then the citizens of France would know stability. In 1946, Alice Roche wrote an article in *Elle* magazine entitled, "Four out of Five French Women Don't Know How to Organize Their Work—Be the Fifth." She wrote that women needed to be highly functional and have everything they needed exactly where it should be. In fact, she made a list of questions that women were to ask themselves at each task, including: "Am I settled in well enough? Do I have everything I need? Are my work instruments in a good state? Is everything I need at my fingertips? Is this work useful?"[102] In early 1947, the magazine *Marie-France* echoed *Elle's* call for domestic order, publishing a list of twenty questions, each with an assigned point value. The reader was supposed to take the quiz, and her total would tell her whether or not she was "orderly" enough. The questions included: "Do you write down all of your expenditures?" "Are your drawers so orderly that they never jam?" "When you get undressed, do you immediately hang your clothes up in your closet?" "Do your keys have labels indicating the lock to which they belong?" The article did note that a woman could go too far in organizing her life; however it also cautioned the least organized readers that "if you do not change your home will be in danger."[103] Each of these articles strongly emphasizes the theme of a woman's control over herself and her immediate environment.

Magazines depicted the desire to "make a home," and a tasteful one at that, as innate to a French woman. Even in the least likely situations, French women would find a way to improve conditions in order to maximize the comfort of those around them. In June 1946, *Ève* magazine printed a fictional letter from a woman to a good friend, in which she described her summer vacation. The woman, her husband, and another couple went on a camping trip; she thought she would hate camping, but she turned out to love it. Each woman, she relates, has set up a little "apartment" under a tree. Every day the men take care of supplying food, and the women, who take turns being hostesses, prepare the food the men gather. In this way, it is as though they are replicating a hunter-gatherer society, and it comes so naturally to them.[104] The joy that the woman feels during her vacation is related to this order, this stability and routine, which *Ève* depicts as eternal. A woman can take even the most chaotic environment, read the privations of the Liberation, and with her innate feminine touch, it will become a happy home.

Magazines' emphasis on domestic skills and taste resonated especially loudly in the kitchen. In November 1946, *Elle* published the article, "Good Care Makes Good Husbands," which highlighted women's responsibility to hold their husbands' attention through inventive and attentive cuisine. The article advised women: "Each husband has his own personality. It is for you to know him well enough to choose your menus. A good recipe has as much seductive power as a pretty dress."[105] The article again emphasizes that it was a woman's natural duty to hold her husband's interest in a variety of ways. In order to do so, she needed to become an expert in fashion, cooking, and her husband's specific culinary palate. Thus even a single meal took on extra importance in the context of the Liberation, for each dining experience had to remind a husband that he was indeed content with his marriage choice.

The appearance of a woman's home became another cultural signifier that represented both her own vision of herself and her family's willingness to conform to the postwar standards of taste. The magazines worked hard to make sure that women knew tacky from elegant, tasteful from kitschy. In February 1946, *Elle* magazine published a quiz, "Do you know how to tell the ugly from the beautiful?" The magazine posted several photos of different rooms, and the reader was supposed to act as an arbiter of taste. Rather than being a way to construct an idea about a country's prominence, this was more a way to universalize the concept of French taste. Just as Leora Auslander has shown that taste was a historically contingent category, and she and Lisa Tiersten have articulated how women's sense of taste became a source of anxiety in the context of mass production, now French women's taste would be a way of cohering French national identity.[106] In 1945, in the fashion magazine *Album de la mode du Figaro*, André Siegfried, geographer, writer, and member of the *Académie française* raised the stakes for women, writing, "It is in the quality that we [French] must seek out the true expression of the most profound, the most personal within us."[107] Here, Siegfried places the responsibility of preserving the essential character of the French nation on women's shoulders. French women would do so not through physical or mental acuity, but rather through an ability to choose the most appropriate aesthetic accoutrements for daily life.

As a letter to *Elle* from a desperate reader, C.R.L, in November 1949 demonstrates, the stakes surrounding French women's ability to be tasteful were high. She wrote: "I am over 35 years old and my budget is limited. However, I hope that it is not too late to . . . educate my tastes in order to keep my husband and please my children. How do I do this?" The response from *Elle* reflected a sense of self-importance: "Read *Elle*. From the first page to the last, we do nothing else but help you in this direction."[108] Internationally as well, the promotion of French taste and craftsmanship was so important that, in 1946, *Le Monde* fashion writer Marian Roland-Marcel encouraged women to accept lesser versions of couture accoutrements in order to send the real items overseas to display French fashion superiority.[109] Women's taste in home furnishing would both signal their adherence to codes of femininity and secure France's place as a great nation.

Work

It was important for women to maintain high aesthetic and behavioral standards even if they had to work outside the home. The amount of work—innate or otherwise—that women did inside the home was quite substantial, but work outside the home was also a reality for many women in postwar France. This is especially the case considering the deprivations of daily life and continued absence of four million French workers in Germany. To a certain extent, the government recognized this necessity and even made it possible and equitable for women workers. As Sarah Fishman notes, "The provisional government . . . endorsed the provision of equal pay for equal work. The French Economic Planning Commission even recommended recruiting female labor by providing more training facilities, access to higher positions, and day-care centers."[110] Despite these incentives and need, the number of women working outside of the home in France lagged far behind American and British women in the postwar period. According to Robert Gildea, "Women had taken themselves out of the labour market after the war. Only 35 per cent of the working population was women in 1954, and the figure remained the same in 1968."[111] These statistics point to the pervasiveness of the heteronormative domestic ideal in France, even relative to other nations with strong rhetoric about domesticity. How would women continue to perform femininity while simultaneously meeting the material demands of postwar life?

Attempts to reconcile the realities of work and the imposition of strict gender norms occurred again in women's magazines. An examination of their pages exposes the tension between the practical need for work and money and France's less tangible need for confining the potential energy inherent in that work. For example, even if the shortages of postwar life demanded that women work, magazines and cultural critics demanded that women should certainly preserve their essential feminine character, especially in terms of the content of that work. *Marie-France* brought some of these anxieties to light in February 1945, when it printed an article entitled, "Remain true women." The article was written by Elisabeth Masson, and it had actually been reprinted from *Forces Nouvelles*, a new weekly put out by the MRP, the postwar Christian democratic party. Masson recognized the reality that, with the lack of men around, women were going to have to work, but she called upon women not to let that work change their essential characters. "Work with courage," she wrote, "but wish for a prompt return to the home; [be] women who unlock for victory, but especially for peace; women who think above and beyond the war, knowing that they will be the artisans of peace, that [their work] will help to maintain it."[112] This article shows how women's work in the immediate postwar period was constructed as temporary, with the idea that women ought to know that their essential natures—as perceived by society at the time—made them best suited for the home. This is interesting given the male student whom Simone de Beauvoir quotes in her *Second Sex*, published in 1949, as writing in to a student newspaper to say, "Every woman student who goes into medicine or law robs us of a job."[113] Here, just when magazines were pushing women to stay home, focus on being pretty, and remain true to themselves, a man expressed anxiety that women would take his job, which he considered his right.

Similarly, in 1946, *Elle* published an article about the British movie star Ann Todd, who had recently given up her international career and fame to stay at home with her children and be a mother, all while promoting the arts in Britain. The article lauded Todd for the attention she paid to her husband, writing, "She is a good homemaker, an attentive mother. One of her greatest joys is to put on a veil and an old hat and to take her own children for a walk in a nearby park. In the evening, she often sends her maids home, makes dinner herself, and dines with her husband."[114] In the eyes of *Elle*, Ann Todd became a picture of domesticity, a woman for all to admire, not for her public achievements, but simply because of the attention she paid to her family at the expense of her career.[115]

When women did have to work outside the home, they were to do so in jobs that emphasized their innate qualities—nurturing and love for France and the French, as well as a realization of their need to sacrifice for the country. In November 1946, for example, *Marie-France* called for French women to fill the national need for nurses. The magazine presented the qualifications necessary, and it also had a rather frank discussion of the hardships involved in nursing, especially the low salary and the lack of supplies. However, *Marie-France* argued that women ought to look at nursing as a call to duty, and that they must remember to "smile" through the difficulties, "for your smile . . . it is sun to the ill person and you cannot deprive him of it." The magazine then exerted a kind of peer pressure on women to answer the need for new nurses, asking, "Are you really surprised that there are still many woman coming forward who have as their ideals the gift of self, the desire to alleviate suffering, women in whose eyes the notion of profit disappears and who are happy living on 4000 francs per month."[116] The magazine ignored the harsh realities of postwar life, instead using guilt to appeal to women, saying that they were needed and that they should be happy in hardship. The story of Gisèle, the privileged woman who, in the midst of the Liberation, joined a nursing corps, adopted a baby, and found happiness, takes on new meaning in light of this. Acceptable work outside the home was constructed to be an expression of women's innate natures, and, if so, it could be a pathway to happiness inside the home.[117] Financial considerations were to be secondary to this. The great irony of the situation was that, while the material situation of France did improve, albeit slowly, most French people were still in dire need of supplies.[118] Thus there seems to be a disconnect between what the magazines were offering and everyday life.

Conclusion

The call for a new ethos of environmental and personal beauty combined with the "war for love" to present a dominant vision of "normal" female behavior. This vision emphasized the limits of women's public role in postwar France, while simultaneously imbuing them with an enormous amount of responsibility for the actualities of daily private sphere life. Women could literally be trapped in the domestic arena by their clothing and the demands of their homes. Women's magazines acted as cultural arbiters during this time, both delineating the new "rules of the game" and telling women how best to meet postwar demands on their gender.

Discourses about proper femininity became prominent during this moment when notions of power and propriety were in flux across the board. It was uncertain whether Charles de Gaulle was the official leader of France—the United States did not even recognize his government until two months after the Liberation of Paris; it was uncertain who had collaborated and resisted and what these even meant; and it was uncertain whether or not there would be enough food to feed one's family at the end of the day. A quick and efficacious stability was of the essence, so that people could start the business of rebuilding France nationally and internationally.

Magazines helped with the process of rebuilding a gendered French identity through creating a sense of normalcy within the society. They showed that it was normal to wear certain clothing and makeup; it was normal to train children to be proper, heterosexual citizens of France; it was normal to provide delicious meals; it was normal for a woman to keep a smile on her face no matter what; it was normal to sublimate any personal demands or feelings in the interest of family preservation. When issues arose within women's lives, magazines advised women on how to deal with them: above all, women needed to keep their husbands happy and always remember their place as a subordinate female. Additionally, fashion, beauty, and taste acted as visual and discursive articulations of feminine propriety at this time. A woman's clothing and appearance—as well as the appearance of her home—served to transmit her acceptance of cultural norms articulated in the feminine press. These normalizations of daily life were essentially constructions rather than realities. They created an idealized identity in which women and femininity were to serve as rehabilitators for French men and masculinity after the tumult of war.

Confined articulations of gender benefited the French populace both nationally and internationally. Nationally, this worked in the sense that France could stabilize around new conceptualizations of eternal gender norms. In turn, these gender norms helped to bring France into conformity with other Western nations. In this context, it was crucial for women to communicate that they were indeed appropriate and productive citizens of the *patrie*. As the next chapter will show, the consequences of nonconformity included ostracizing, humiliation, or worse.

Disreputable Women

betrayal?

Introduction

If the confinement of definitions of femininity was fundamental to reconstructing France after the Second World War, women who strayed from those norms presented serious challenges to the state and society. Negative imagery of femininity played an important role in delineating the boundaries of acceptable femininity as imagery of a proper, private, unflinchingly feminine French woman. Luc Capdevila has argued that the Second World War had been a time of "suffering and frustration" for French men, putting them in "a situation of denial of their virility"[1] because of their embarrassing defeat and the subsequent German Occupation. Fabrice Virgili's extensive documentation of the *femmes tondues* and the complex gender meanings behind the shavings complements the scholarship on postwar French masculine frustration and anxiety.[2] Given that, then those who threatened that masculinity, such as powerful women who subverted the prescribed norms of femininity, had to be put in their place. The publicizing of these punishments through memoirs, newspapers, and the dispersal of images showed all French women the limits of acceptable behavior in the postwar period.

This chapter will examine two main negative images of femininity: female torturers and spies. Their stories work on two levels. First, they demonstrate how the postwar media and state portrayal of these women's stories took shape in ways that painted them as utterly unnatural and anti-feminine. Given the weight placed on being a "normal" woman in postwar France, depicting a woman as masculine or duplicitous or generally "other" was a harsh course of action. The stories also describe a harsh discipline meted out by the state and society, one which was often disproportionate when compared with similar cases of male criminals and perpetrators. Combined, this dual purpose worked to articulate both the boundaries of female propriety and the perils of nonconformity.

Many of the women and men discussed in this chapter committed violent, harmful acts during the war and beyond. They violated human rights and caused immeasurable pain and suffering for the many people they affected. They are still difficult to read so many years later, and their realities must be acknowledged. However, this project focuses less on the actualities of the crimes and transgressions than on how these actions, and the people who committed them, were construed in the postwar context and then mobilized to make an argument about the place of men and women in French society.

Female torturers

The antipathy toward female torturers grounded itself in a basic gender assumption: women do not harm the physical body, whether or not they are acting in times of war. For a woman to torture, she not only contradicted laws of humanity, but also contradicted assumptions about women's natures. Even today, women who torture are not culturally categorized as simply "*bad*," as political theorists Caron E. Gentry and Laura Sjoberg have put it, they are "*bad women*."[3] [original emphasis] The assumption is predicated on inequity in gender; women can learn science and run marathons not because they are extraordinary women, but because people do these things. Similarly, women do not torture because they are somehow flawed in their womanhood; rather, they torture for the same reasons that other human beings torture because they are also human beings.[4] In the postwar period, assignations of female and male characteristics worked to stabilize the society and promote the nuclear family. In that context, a woman who physically threatened French bodies presented a frightening threat, but she also undermined the differentiation between the sexes that was so crucial to postwar reconstruction.

While men's wartime violence ultimately cleansed the nation, ridding it of external and internal violators, women's killing was anti-normative. Female torturers in postwar France had transgressed traditional gender boundaries to the point where they began to take on characteristics traditionally associated with men and virility. These transgressions did not go unnoticed by the general population or the government, for whom the reestablishment of this virility was so crucial. Their punishment, then, had to reflect their gross impropriety. Public humiliation of such women, whether physical or rhetorical, "taught" the French populace how to behave.

Newspaper coverage, personal memoirs, and photographic and other visual evidence, rhetorically defeminized female torturers. These sources combined to delineate the proper place in French society for men and especially women who had harmed French bodies. The female torturer had subverted traditional power structures by *physically* controlling male bodies through torture. She was different from male torturers; her body bore extra symbolism precisely because of her apparent rejection of the prescribed femininity of the postwar period.

The public punishment of women served a purpose that is not necessarily immediately self-evident. Female torturers had not only abnegated their femininity, they had also usurped male roles or threatened and humiliated French masculinity. The sources portray women as sexual pursuers; it was women who delighted in having physical power not only over other women, but also over men. Women menaced men physically, women gawked at male—and female—nude bodies, and within their general disrespect for humanity, such women showed their disdain for the sanctity of masculinity. Their punishments hence needed to restore—or construct—a sense of gender balance in which masculinity was tied to physical dominance and virility.

The section on female torturers focuses on three main iterations of that figure. First, it will examine how French women prisoners portrayed the German and Eastern European women who exercised control over them in their time in camps. In doing so, memoirists particularly delineated the German woman as "other" than the morally upright French woman, adding to the idea that France itself was a moral nation, despite its wartime actions. It will then turn back to French soil with a look at newspaper coverage of the 1952 trial of a Gestapo cell, which portrayed Denise Delfau, the cell stenographer, as the antithesis of a normal postwar woman, despite her relative impotence within cell activities. Finally, it will examine the extraordinary figure of Violette Morris, who went from controversial national sports hero in the interwar period to postwar national symbol of female monstrosity.

In the camps

Female torturers received considerable attention in women's memoirs about their time in the Resistance and concentration camps. There, the torturers were often Germans or Eastern Europeans, so the trials and punishments of these women did not receive much coverage in postwar testimony or press in France.

Still, the memoirists used similar descriptive tropes to describe the women in charge of them in the camps. Descriptions of the prison guards in Germany often became distorted echoes of the gender normalizing trends of the time. They acted to define camp guards as "other" in relation to French femininity and French identity itself, while simultaneously shoring up certain qualities—attractiveness, good fashion sense, nurturing—as inherent to a French woman, as well as a narrative of honorable national behavior. Camp guards, to use Gentry and Sjoberg's categorization, were indeed "bad women."

Memoirists portrayed female torturers as antithetical to proper French femininity in the areas most central to a French woman's national role. For example, in France, women have a long tradition of being associated with the nurturing comforts of a specific kind of food, *cuisine de femmes* (decidedly different from the masculine realms of haute cuisine).[5] Where one of the most important tasks a French woman accomplished over the course of her day was providing varied and nutritious food for her family, thereby keeping her husband interested in and attracted to her, the female guards treated food as a weapon, denying prisoners their basic rights and rejecting the nurturing qualities that were supposed to be so intrinsic to French femininity. Marie Jeanne Bouteille-Garagnon described how one of the guards in the Ravensbrück camp in Germany, a woman called Frieda, would consistently stand in front of the group of hungry French women and eat a delicious-looking snack "out of thoughtlessness or sadism."[6] Also in Ravensbrück, Germaine Mornand described the woman she called the worst of the prison guards, Frau Mauser. According to Mornand, the detainees referred to Mauser as Méphisto, in reference to the Christian demon Mephistopheles, who since the Middle Ages has been associated with the devil and the founding of hell. Mornand wrote that Méphisto stole the women's belongings and starved them. Mornand depicted the usual scene around lunchtime in the camp:

> A bit before noon, the daily ration of bread was distributed. They threw it at [the women] sometimes like at beasts. It was the guard Méphisto who took pleasure from this cruel game. Avoiding as they could, and when they could, being hit on the face, the detainees tried to adroitly seize on the fly the bread that was launched at them like a new insult![7]

This scene, particularly the behavior of Méphisto and the other female guards, stands in marked contrast to the one Mornand went on to describe, in which the French women prisoners gathered together and shared their meager rations with one another. Indeed Germaine Tillion took pride in the fact that the French block was the only one "where a crust of bread could be left around without disappearing instantly."[8] It also is highly different from the vision posited by many postwar cultural sources which called upon women to nourish their children and their husbands, for in doing so they would make France strong and proud. In contrast, sometimes the guards actually used food as a physical weapon. Rosane remembered one German "throwing boiling coffee at our faces," or rewarding other cell blocks with extra soup "because we were talking."[9] If the definition of true French femininity included a nurturing aspect that manifested itself through food, then the behavior of the guards was presented as this definition's antithesis.

Memoirs and other sources portrayed the appearance of female prison guards as sloppy or masculine, a direct contrast to the norm of a beautiful, well-kempt French woman. In her *An Ordinary Camp*, for example, Micheline Maurel, a deportee who had been a professor in Lyon before joining the Resistance and was later imprisoned in Germany, described the prison guards in the Neubrandenburg camp, where she spent part of the war, as hideous in appearance. This was especially true of her block supervisor, Frau Schuppe, who, according to Maurel, possessed "legs shaped like enormous bottles, a large rump—though her face was angular and sharp—gray wisps of hair and burning eyes, a diabolical smirk, always armed with the leg of a stool (the favorite tool of the *blokova*, who was not given guns or other weapons) and ever poised to use it—this was Frau Schuppe."[10]

It was not simply the guards' physical characteristics that rendered them unattractive in French memoirists' depictions; their outer trappings also added to their portrayals as ugly and unfeminine. Germaine Tillion caustically described the guards as "fat [and] well-dressed,"[11] a derogation possibly owing to their better supplied and fed status as well. In her memoir, Simone Saint-Clair describes parading around the camp with the German prison guards, "horribly attired in their reseda-green [a grayish green] uniform." Once the prison guards passed by, the French women would "giggle" behind their backs at the Germans' appearance: "'How ugly they are!' is a unanimous echo."[12] In her memoir, Rosane sarcastically expressed disgust at the Germans' laundry habits: "Let's talk again about great German hygiene!"[13] For example, Marie Jeanne Bouteille-Garagnon portrayed the woman who would be in charge of her group of French prisoners as jealous of them and their possessions. The woman coldly hurried her charges along, according to Bouteille-Garagnon, and during this march she "squinted at the fur coat of my companion with the face of a *phtisique* [consumptive]."[14] In another scene from Bouteille-Garagnon's work, she describes a scene in which a "pretty" French woman is forced to strip off all of her clothing at the orders of a "dumpy" blond German woman. The guard and her friend then go through all of the French woman's belongings as though they were pigs "in lard" [*en saindoux*], taking all of her possessions.[15] Rosane remembered the guards rifling through the goods from new convoys, stealing French "clothing and provisions; they gave themselves the most beautiful goods."[16] These dismissive or critical reactions were no doubt an important part of survival for women in the camps, but they also worked to sharpen distinctions between fashionable French women and ugly Germans, as well as between France and Germany more generally, thereby intensifying *résistancialisme*.

Given that at this time, fashion and beauty became points of national pride, the construction of German prison guards as jealous of French women and ugly and poorly dressed themselves was a way for French women to hold a certain level of superiority over them. When a group of French women was assigned to a moving squad in Ravensbrück and given a task within the guards' barracks, they "took delight in ransacking the German women's possessions by opening cupboards and throwing the contents—'common clothes and cheap perfume'— all over the floor."[17] Even when German female guards tried to improve their appearances, memoirists emphasized how they did not possess French women's innate talent for self-beautification. Sabine Hoisne recalled seeing a German prison secretary wearing makeup—a rarity in and of itself—and commented upon its poor application. "God! She was wearing a lot of makeup," Hoisne wrote. "A thick layer of red covered her lips, her cheeks were in ochre, and her hair was dyed the color of an overripe carrot."[18] Similarly, Rosane remembered the guards as oversized "cowherders" with "poorly curled wigs."[19] This was not limited to the camps; in her *Les lettres françaises,* the Surrealist Lise Deharne described German women in Paris during the war as "fat . . . overgrown trouts packaged in gray."[20] These negative observations likely reflected the massive deprivations the French women faced in the camps and in France, but they articulated them aesthetically, in a way that dehumanized and defeminized the Germans. In the postwar context, the aesthetic superiority of the well-attired French women set her apart from the frumpiness of the Germans. Such memoirs aided in tying French women's national identity to their appearances.

In contrast to a "normal" French woman, who sacrificed her own safety in order to protect her children and family, the female guards destroyed humanity and generally had no respect for the sanctity of life. Germaine Tillion recalled one assistant Oberaufseherin, Dorothea Binz, who in her words was pure "evil." Binz, according to Tillion, would walk the ranks of the prisoners, "her crop behind her back, searching with menacing little eyes for the weakest or most frightened woman, simply to beat her black and blue."[21] Tillion referenced one particularly galling incident when, having beaten a prisoner to death (or close), Binz stepped on the prisoner's bloody, unmoving legs, "her two heels on one leg, toes of her boots on another. Binz balanced herself there for a while, rocking her weight from heel to toe."[22] Another deportee, Suzanne Busson, also recalled Binz as particularly "sadistic, she fed off of our sufferings, smacked as hard as she could with her whip, her iron fists, her booted feet, happy once blood flowed."[23] Binz also made appearances in the memoirs of Rosane, who was warned about her cruelty by a fellow prisoner: "Binz kills [prisoners] with an axe after weeks of starvation, [gives] 25, 50, or 75 [blows] to the backside . . . without shame."[24] Yet in her disregard for humanity, the notorious Binz was certainly not alone. Charlotte Delbo even recalled her Blockova, Magda, urging women to volunteer to die to meet her quotas.[25] Rosane depicted another prison guard as "rigid, glacial, with an evil, hateful air."[26]

In other moments, female guards actively relished pain, and sources often depicted them as inhuman and "hysterical,"[27] with nicknames like the "furies," "panther," "hyena," and "tigress."[28] They were "brutal" and "animalistic," recalled the prisoner Suzanne Busson, "veritable sadists in front of our sufferings!"[29] Rosane called the guards "wolves nipping at our heels, menacing and ferocious."[30] Not only had camp guards ceased to follow the aesthetic graces of French women, but also they had gone past the point of simple ugliness to an animal state.

Female medical professionals in the camps, trained to nurse and care for the sick and dying, behaved no better than prison guards. Marie Jeanne Bouteille-Garagnon described visiting the Ravensbrück dentist, portraying her as a sadistic woman: "The cattle dentist [*dentiste pour bétail*] grabbed with her pliers, pressed down with all her weight, forced, extracted, threw the bloody and still white tooth in a bucket that was already half-full, plunged her pliers in a formalin liquid which rid it of the slivers of bone, and [said] to the next woman . . . *Schnell*! [fast!]"[31] This is one of the tamer episodes of physical pain from the camp, yet it still highlights the dentist's detachment from any maternal femininity. She does not show caring to the women, takes no interest in them or their physical pain, instead she systematically moves on to her next patient. Rosane described another female doctor, Kurt, as "neither man nor woman . . . [but] butcher."[32] Toward the end of her time in the camps, she remembered nurses forcing sick women to consume a "white powder; those who had resisted at the cost of all their energy, those women who, in France maybe would not be dead, those who wanted to see their children again, who sensed the [approach of a] victory for which they had sacrificed themselves, there they are stiff on their straw mattresses."[33] This stood as the opposite of the palliative caring expected from a nurse, or really any woman at the time.

While Dorothea Binz and the Ravensbrück dentist displayed no emotion in the face of extreme pain, writings about the camps also portrayed women who actively delighted in causing physical hurt. Germaine Tillion estimated that about one half of all female guards took "visible pleasure in striking and terrorizing their prisoners."[34] Similarly, Charlotte Delbo recounted an incident when she was forced to carry a friend's freshly beaten dead body, while the female kapo danced and joked next to her.[35] In her memoir, Simone Saint-Clair described a visit to the infirmary at the Ravensbrück camp where Ranya, a Danish female medical assistant, seemed to take pleasure in the possibility of the pain she could cause: "While I was stretched out on the table, [she] let out [*égrena*] a sardonic laugh while saying: 'How we have been able to amuse ourselves, the *doctoresse* and me!'" Ranya goes to operate on a Polish woman, whose pain Saint-Clair describes as horrific, so much so that Saint-Clair thought she herself might die from hearing it and empathizing. Yet despite the shrieks of pain and the contortions of the patient, Ranya "continued to laugh, the vile creature."[36] For Saint-Clair, Ranya has lost her humanity and become a "creature," taking pleasure from pain.

In memoirists' accounts, a female torturer's animalistic murderousness was not at all separate from considerations about her sexuality. Instead, this penchant for violence was often highly linked to her insatiable lustfulness. A "normal" French woman carefully saved her sexuality for the process of attracting and retaining her husband. In the camps, by contrast, writers and witnesses of female torturers portrayed them as sexually excited by the very sight and act of torturing others. Female torturers were the actors, and those who were tortured remained in more passive roles. Where postwar depictions of female sexuality implied that women's desires should only to be used to augment the French population within marriage, the torturers' sexuality was unbounded and dangerous. Memoirists also portrayed the female camp guards in Germany as sadistically violent to the point of ecstasy; this rhetorical linking of uncontrolled sex and violence suggests that the two are inextricable. Micheline Maurel, for example, recalled Frau Schuppe's obvious delight when she was beating the French women who were under her charge: "When she flailed us it was with obvious joy. When she knocked a Frenchwoman down to trample her, her eyes flashed, she smiled, she rejoiced. Her hindquarters quivered with eagerness as she frenziedly wielded the stool leg [her weapon]."[37] In this case,

Schuppe's usage of a stand-in weapon—evidently a phallic symbol and a further defeminization of Schuppe—that made her "quiver" when wielding it points to the notion that she is sexually satisfied through torture. Similarly, in *For France*, Suzanne Wilborts describes one German prison guard and her dog during the inspections prisoners endured at the end of the day to establish their work output:

> If a woman falls from fatigue they punch and kick her; she doesn't get off the ground, she is half dead: they set the dog on her, he makes some cruel bites, but the woman is so weak she can no longer get off the ground. Furious, the <u>German woman</u> picks up the spade and hits her in the stomach until the poor woman is mortally injured. . . . It's over, the brute calls her dog and caresses him. She will be congratulated tonight. Oh! Binz, oh! Lehman and Binder, will you pay one day for your crimes?[38] [original emphasis]

In this case, woman and beast have become one, with both performing the same physically violent tasks, and both receiving some sort of satisfaction for it: the dog in caresses from its owner, the German woman in felicitations from her colleagues. There is an evident sexual aspect to this violent scene: the German woman uses a spade to repeatedly hit the woman in her stomach, and the dog is rewarded for his physical attacks with caresses. It is as though both the dog and the German woman are sexually assaulting the woman, and they both ultimately receive pleasure from it. In these portrayals it is clear that the guards are so out of the norm in their fantastical homoeroticism that they have become violent, sexually deviant animals.

Jacqueline Richet, in her memoir, portrays another case of prison guards' sexualization through violence. She describes a time when she saw a group of German women beating two fellow prisoners: "In effect these women—*should one give them this name?*—excite themselves with this infernal game. They make themselves breathless in their murderous effort; their eyes have glimmers of joy and their faces, with each blow brought, betray a bestial pleasure."[39] [emphasis mine] The language Richet uses to describe the Germans' reactions to the beatings is highly sexualized; they are "breathless" and their violence begets reactions of "joy" and "pleasure." These women are acting out their dangerous sexual fantasies upon their French victims. Their active sexuality is threatening both in the sense that it is masculine (the man as sexual actor and predator) and in the sense that it presents a homoerotic/masculine vision of femininity, one which would have to be erased to conform to gender norms in the postwar period. Indeed the author wonders if they are women at all.

In her memoir, Germaine Tillion attributed some of the guards' acts of violence to sexual frustration. She stated that the nurses in the Ravensbrück camp, the Schwester (*sisters*), were essentially like nuns. The Oberschwester, their head, "a square-faced, hard-eyed woman" named Elisabeth Marschall, was like a Mother Superior. Her band of nuns, Tillion argued, were "old and full of hatred." Tillion specifically referenced a woman called Schwester Lisa, whom she described as "mean-tempered and cadaverous, soured by spinsterhood, looking like a scratchy, dried-up tree root."[40] In this example, the lack of normal sexual contact served to embitter—and embolden—the Schwester. Similarly, Rosane recalled an incident of sexual frustration from Dorothea Binz involving a young American soldier, a parachutist who landed "near Furstenberg, an athlete so beautiful that Binz wanted to take him as her lover, and then kill him by her own hands."[41]

It is often not possible to separate the guards' suggested lesbianism from the sexual delight through physical and emotional abuse memoirists ascribed to them. Rosane remembered one guard as a "sleazy person, she felt the need to pervert [us]. She took 'favorites' whom she rewarded with extra food; an atmosphere of debauchery pleased her."[42] Later, in describing a Binz attack, Rosane states "Binz strikes, in rage, imperious and contemptuous. She roars, gets excited, chafes, becomes glacial again, confident in her omnipotence."[43] Clearly, in Rosane's telling, Binz's attacks are a sexual experience for her. Or in Richet's account, for example, the women are both lesbians and inhumane in their sexuality, as their sexuality is directed at women, but in a manner reminiscent of animals.[44] Here again, when Richet questions whether or not these women could fairly be labeled as such, it is clear that for her, the answer is no. Instead they are crazed lesbians who exist outside of the bounds of society. When lesbianism, as noted earlier, inspired fear in postwar society for their inversion of traditional sexuality and threat to heteronormative families, leveling the moniker of lesbian upon anyone signified their extreme outsider status.

German women in the camps did not necessarily need to be the active torturers to derive joy and pleasure from physical violence. Germaine Tillion also recalled Dorothea Binz being the lover of the Schutzhaftlagerführer, Edmund Bräuning, whom Tillion described as a "huge and brutal man." When Bräuning engaged in beatings, Binz, whom Tillion described as "a blond young flirt who would have been pretty if her face had not always been literally contorted with hate," made a point of being present. Clearly Binz enjoyed the beatings, according to Tillion, for she attended "without any official need . . . and they were often seen in a passionate embrace during or after this 'ceremony.'"[45] In French memoirs, sex and violence served to dehumanize and defeminize German women.

Depictions of female prison guards portray them as less than human, and they embody the opposite of the qualities of a French woman. It is important to remember that these are French memoirs written for a French audience, and they must be analyzed in this capacity. They are not for a German audience, which would potentially render them a cultural indictment in German for Germans. Certainly they depict many of the guards in a less than positive light, but this rhetoric performs an important function in the postwar period. They highlight the heroism of French women, but they also show the deprivation of character of the female prison guards. These two types stand side by side in the memoirs as pointedly positive and negative visions of ideal femininity.[46] In contrasting the superiority of French women with the inferiority of German women, memoirs also make an implicit argument about both the vast differences between France and Germany, thereby supporting the *résistancialisme* of the postwar period.

On trial

"The Gestapo of Rue de la Pompe," intoned the court, "was . . . most infamous. . . . The tragic figures can be translated thus: more than 300 arrests, 160 deportations to Germany, of whom 50 died in concentration camps, 40 shot as of Aug. 16, 1944."[47]

"The most terrible drama of the year . . ." –Janet Flanner[48]

This was how *Time* and the *New Yorker* magazines, respectively, described the scene as, in 1952, the French courts began trying the "rue de la Pompe" case. During these proceedings, members of the *Abwehr*-linked Berger cell, headed by the German Friedrich Berger, were put on trial for their wartime crimes.[49] These included the infamous massacre of Resistance members in the Bois de Boulogne outside of Paris in August 1944, as the Berger cell members were retreating in the wake of the Allied advance. This crime in particular horrified the French public, so violent and so close to the end of war. During the war, when Resistance members were captured, they would be brought into the rue de la Pompe cell headquarters for questioning. The members of the cell would then press them for as much information as quickly as possible before sending them along to another, more formal prison, often the one at Fresnes, just south of Paris.[50]

During their postwar trial, the mainstream press heaped attention on rue de la Pompe cell members, particularly Denise Delfau, the lone woman member standing trial.[51] Delfau had worked as a secretary within the cell, primarily typing confessions as others did the physical torturing. This section will largely focus on her portrayal within this newspaper coverage, which was striking for its pointed criticisms of Delfau's femininity, as well as its notations of her disrespect of strong French masculinity. During the postwar period, a woman like Delfau could be considered even more threatening to French society than the women in the camps, precisely because of her French nationality. When a French woman like Delfau betrayed the nation through her collaboration with the Germans, discursive attacks on her took on added urgency because the symbolic stakes were higher. It was crucial to stress her transgressions publicly in order to crystallize the difference between this person and a French woman.

In this section the analysis will center on reporting from three major newspapers: *Combat, Le Monde,* and *Figaro,* each of which embodied a fairly mainstream—yet different—political ethos.[52] The reporters from these papers were *Figaro*'s Roland Bochin, *Combat*'s Jean Pichon and René Hericotte, and *Le Monde*'s Jean-Marc Théolleyre, who wrote many pieces on postwar justice, including extensive work on Klaus Barbie. While Théolleyre did describe a lack of interest on the part of the public in the case at its onset, this is a questionable statement. First, the trial is regardless important, and it is possible to speculate that interest in the proceedings grew by virtue of the fact of its intense coverage on the part of the major French papers.[53] This does not even take into account the large amount of reporting done by international media, such as *Time, The New Yorker,* and *The New York Times.*[54] Also, Théolleyre stated that the lack of attention to the trial was indicative of French people's short historical attention span. Théolleyre was arguably attempting to cajole the French into paying more heed—to his dispatches, no less. In the same article, he claimed that interest in the trial would grow greatly: "It will arouse an exasperating astonishment [on the part of the people] that at the end of seven years there still remain in jail" as untried prisoners.[55]

Despite the cell's known twenty-one person membership, it was Denise Delfau, the only woman present, who, throughout the coverage of the trial, became emblematic as the symbolic instigator of the torture. Delfau, the reports emphasized, had subverted normal patriarchal expectations of power without a care. At one point during the trial, according to *Figaro,* Delfau was called out by a witness, M. Victor Marius, for having gathered a group of collaborating women to snicker right in front of a group of prisoners. The article immediately goes on to quote Marius as testifying, "'I thought more than once that my final hour had come', sighs the witness, 'and with my nails I wrote on the walls of the cave:

We have been tortured by French people.'"[56] It seems that the two vignettes are separated chronologically; indeed they may have come from separate moments in Marius's testimony. However, Bochin placed the two stories one after the other, so that they are at least linked in terms of his writing. Delfau's disrespect for French men clearly struck a nerve, and Bochin's article emphasized this national indignity.

The newspaper coverage of Delfau even portrayed her as the person most responsible for the cell's actions. In *Le Monde*, for example, Jean-Marc Théolleyre reported that one witness, M. Susen-Ber, stated that Denise Delfau had helped others to burn the bottoms of his feet, calling Delfau "horrible, she was the most horrible [of all of the torturers]. She helped them in this nasty job." This sentiment, that Delfau was the least humane of all of the torturers, is telling in light of the fact that earlier in the same article, several witnesses had testified that Berger, the actual head of the cell, had decided to play "the game of William Tell" with a Jewish prisoner, and Susen-Ber himself states that Delfau "helped." Additionally, M. Susen-Ber had testified about the many tortures he underwent at the rue de la Pompe: he faced the baths, he was beaten, and his body was bent so that his hands and feet could be shackled together.[57] Yet Susen-Ber, and Théolleyre in turn, focused on Delfau's supporting role in the burning of his feet. Why would they focus on Delfau's role? Presumably, the very fact that Delfau is a woman was enough to separate her from the rest of the cell members, while coverage depicted her as the absolute worst of all of the cell members.

Other newspapers also stressed Delfau's purported singularly heinous role in the rue de la Pompe cell. In *Combat*, for example, Jean Pichon reported that Delfau took down the confessions of the tortured, "exciting [*excitant*] the men in their exercises of cruelty."[58] Pichon's language invites a sexual interpretation as well; the men are trying to please Delfau sexually through torturing poor prisoners. A few days later, Pichon reported that during the trial a woman had recalled Delfau's presence at her torture session as though she were the queen of the room: "In the midst of these 'beasts', Mme Sauvanet saw a young woman in a white dress appear with as much ease as elegance, [it was] Denise Delfau, smiling and almost delighted to find herself there [amongst the tortures]."[59] *Le Monde*'s Théolleyre went even further in his description of Delfau, representing her as thrilled at the sight of torture. According to him, Mme Sauvanet stated to the courtroom, "You would have thought [Delfau] in full hysteria, ecstatic to find herself in this milieu, dressed in a white dress."[60] Delfau is a mad bride in Théolleyre's piece, subverting the traditional nuptial meanings and symbols of pure femininity and virginity. In these portrayals, Delfau clearly ran the show, and the actual physical torturers were simply trying to please her through doing her bidding and successfully torturing prisoners.

Roland Bochin's coverage in *Figaro* reinforced the notion that Denise Delfau inspired the torturers to commit their crimes, arguing that she pushed them to visit worse and worse punishments upon the bodies of the victims. He wrote: "Denise Delfau . . . watched the scenes of torture complacently in order to type the confessions that the pain extracted sometimes. 'Continue,' she ordered the torturers. 'He hasn't had enough yet. You know well that he hasn't said everything.' And come the evening, she breathed easy: 'Ah! we have had some beautiful sessions today.'"[61] Here it is clear that for Bochin, Delfau was the engine of the torture, if not the actual abuser. In *Le Monde*, Jean-Marc Théolleyre echoed this iteration of Delfau as the inspiration for increased torture, describing a scene where she stood "before a certain exhausted body [and said]: 'I think he has not yet had his [full] number [of blows].'"[62] Like the depictions of the prison guards in French women's postwar memoirs, Delfau had lost the qualities of femininity—nurturing, caring, domesticity, mothering—that were purported to be innate to French women. Additionally, she had taken power over the victims, caring little for the sanctity of their lives while calling for further violence against their bodies.

In fact, much like the German female prison guards, the coverage of Delfau transitioned from a focus on her deficient femininity to a sense of concern regarding her masculine attributes. Where above *Figaro*'s Roland Bochin quoted a witness describing Denise Delfau as saying "Ah! we have had some beautiful sessions today!," in *Le Monde*, Jean-Marc Théolleyre reported that Delfau said, "We have had some beautiful sessions of nudism today."[63] Here, Delfau subverts the normal male gaze of consuming female sexuality, and she makes it a female one.[64] The gaze was about cementing desire, virility, and power, and a woman was not to be the driver of any of those motivations.

Articles stressed how Denise Delfau took pleasure in nudism, consuming the naked bodies in the same way that the male gaze is supposed to work upon the female body. Yet Delfau's gaze, which Théolleyre later described as "notorious,"[65] rather than occurring within the normal guise of heterosexuality, exists in an inverted world: she is consuming nudism, but, unlike a virile French man who would use this gaze to produce babies, she is not sexualizing it in a way that is productive for the nation. She is thus neither entirely male nor particularly female. The more important aspect of Delfau is that, according to the coverage, she has so abandoned her femininity that she has begun to adopt aspects of masculinity that are anathema to French womanhood in the postwar period.

The coverage of the rue de la Pompe trial emphasized that while it might be difficult to conceive of Denise Delfau, seemingly a simple, unthreatening woman, as a cold-blooded torturer, this was indeed reality. Her exposure as such was a crucial component of trial press. René Hericotte of *Combat* said that her image had transitioned from one of the secretary of the cell to "something else" over the course of the trial. He quoted the testimony of one witness at the trial, a Mme Folgoas, who said, "I was burned on the arms and on the breasts with a cigarette. With a cigarette that 'Mademoiselle' plucked from my own case in order to give it to 'Jules' [another cell member]." Hericotte went on to discuss his own ambivalence about Delfau, linking it with her femininity. He writes: "One hesitates still at placing her as low as the others. But this is not the first time that a witness comes to recognize in her something other than a simple secretary."[66] Here, Hericotte singles out Delfau and allows the question that apparently dominates his own thought process to come across to the reader: Can a woman be an evil torturer? He unequivocally answers yes.

Trial reports also emphasized how a once-alluring woman such as Denise Delfau, who at one time could entice men into torturing for her, became far less attractive in her powerless state. The discursive stripping away of Delfau's beauty was important in the aesthetically conscious context of the postwar, when a woman's perfectly feminine appearance in public became a way for her to display her allegiance to France. When portrayals of Denise Delfau showed her as pathetic, meek, and unattractive, they also spoke to her inability to be a French female, contradicting as they did the constitutive values innate to French women. In *Figaro*, Bochin detailed Delfau's quick outburst when she felt she was being unfairly accused of holding a woman's feet so that they could be burned more easily by the male torturers: "Finally, we again saw the pale and puffed up features of Denise Delfau who, accused by M. Suzenberg, came out of her torpor and consented to raise her head which, these days, has remained plunged shamefully in the shadow of the [defendants'] box." Delfau protested the accusation and then quickly shrunk back. According to Bochin, "She disappeared again, as though caught up by a trap, and we only perceived her abundant hair which, from afar, seemed to be a wig, splayed out on the edge of the stall."[67] Bochin reiterated this theme a few days earlier when he described how Delfau was "tearful" and hiding her "puffy" face in her handkerchief."[68] Similarly, in *Combat*, Jean Pichon described how Delfau "tried to dissimulate her flabby traits under her brownish hair."[69] Even the *New Yorker* reporter who covered the case stated that Delfau "looks the worst, with a yellow, pouched face."[70] Her meek and retiring posture highlights Delfau's powerlessness; she can no longer be a threat to French men because she is now under the control of the restored French state. Similarly, her unattractive appearance means that she can no longer use her alluring femininity to tempt French men to torture or otherwise betray the nation. She has lost her physical appeal, and hence she has lost her power.

As the trial progressed, Delfau only seemed to deteriorate physically. On December 13, 1952, toward the end of the proceedings, Théolleyre portrayed Denise Delfau in *Le Monde* as a broken woman: "Denise Delfau is no more than a phantom, where one occasionally sees the heavy cheeks, the tired eyelids."[71] For those covering the trial, justice for Delfau meant the loss of her femininity and even her self. Through France's capture and trial of Delfau, the courts had not only brought a criminal to justice, but they had also taken an insubordinate woman and rendered her impotent. During the war, the newspapers showed, Delfau had delighted in taking control of French men; this could not be tolerated. Thus the postwar coverage effectively took away any pretense that Delfau possessed power. In this way, just as the control of unregulated sexuality could allow for the restoration of national virility, the French could restore their own masculinity in removing female threats to that national masculinity.

Those women who came to testify against the rue de la Pompe cell members were, by contrast, portrayed as visions of true feminine strength in trial coverage. Jean-Marc Théolleyre depicted Mlle Andrée Mérope, for example, as "a black silhouette, a face of wax, a soft voice, infinitely soft and painful in its reserve." Mérope testified succinctly and calmly, Théolleyre reported, and then another woman, Mme André Sauvanet, came to the stand. Sauvanet as well was "calm and soft, but precise," according to Théolleyre.[72] Later in the trial, the presiding judge even labeled Mlle Marie Medard a new Joan of Arc—a symbolically laden moniker in postwar France, as evidenced in the first chapter—by virtue of her testimony, during which she calmly detailed how she faced ice baths, kicks, and burns at cell members' hands.[73] These women were acting as witnesses for France in the case, and as such, they, unlike the once-alluring/masculine and now meek and unattractive Delfau, were both strong and feminine in their courtroom presence.

Perhaps unexpectedly, despite this context of clear gender delineations, male torturers' portrayals in the trial were not strikingly different from those of their female counterparts, because both male and female torturers subverted the prescribed postwar gender roles.[74] Postwar newspaper coverage regularly portrayed male torturers as weak; the state had reasserted itself over them, the men who had so dishonored France. For example, during one court session, according to *Figaro*, Georges Guicciardini, one of the main torturers of the rue de la Pompe cell, was moved to make a small excuse for himself in the face of overwhelming accusations of torture: "Me, in any event, says Georges Guicciardini in his *feeble* voice, I offered cigarettes to these gentlemen [who were being tortured]."[75][emphasis mine] Similarly, Roland Bochin reported, Guicciardini's son, Adrien, seemed to lose his vocal strength, becoming "hollow" when confronted with the crimes he committed.[76] Additionally, during their statements to the court early in the trial, fellow rue de la Pompe cell members Jacques Reymond and Georges Gorisse "concede[d] that they lacked courage and that they ought to have left this 'wasp nest' [*guêpier*], but there were Berger's threats."[77] The coverage of Reymond and Gorisse presented them as cowards, and the Guicciardinis as weak and discredited. The physical inferiority of those who had betrayed France extended to the top of the government.

It was clear that the authority of the French state reigned over these male torturers in the courtroom. In one article for *Le Monde*, Jean-Marc Théolleyre detailed the explanations of some of the cell for their actions. They argued that although they had been involved in arrests and the like, they had not tortured prisoners. In describing this same incident, coverage by reporter Armand Gatti in the paper *Le Parisien libéré*, which had been founded as a Resistance organ, emphasized how other male members of the cell each spoke in a "trembling voice" when called upon to explain their actions.[78] However, a sharp reprimand by the judge, Robert Chadefaux, whom one reporter described as "handsome" and "grey-haired"[79]—a virile, distinguished combination—chastised them for simply belonging to such a group. The rebuke, according to Gatti's description, had much to do with gender: "But, in the end, *you are men*! [Chadefaux] finally exclaimed."[80] [emphasis mine] For the judge, French masculinity was antithetical to the torturers' behavior. According to Théolleyre, the judge's reproof left the men speechless: "So they stayed there, silent, stunned, this one the hands behind the back, that one the arms pinned to the side of his body, that other one with fingers frozen on the side of the box."[81] Whereas before these men had terrified and tortured at will—the *Le Monde* article from the previous day included an abbreviated list of their crimes—now they were physically powerless, contained by the authority of the restored French state.

Male torturers' physical appearances also came into play in trial coverage, which often portrayed the men as the opposite of the robust French male defender. For example, Jean-Marc Théolleyre of *Le Monde* described Ferdinand Poupet as "bony" and "pale."[82] Additionally, later in the trial, *Figaro*'s Roland Bochin noted that Guicciardini was so "bony"[83] and weak—and presumably weighed down by the severity of his crimes—that he could barely raise his head in protest at an accusation he deemed false.[84] Bochin also described Guicciardini's appearance as "disgusting" [*sale*] and "stupid," while other men, such as rue de la Pompe cell member Georges Favriot, were described as "bilious," all apparent physical manifestations of their inner characters.[85] The power and strength of the members of the rue de la Pompe cell were called into question during the trial, standing in contrast to the real men of France, those who had fought for the Resistance. Just as this particular trial communicated messages about proper femininity, it did the same with masculinity.

Certainly the reporters' editors wanted to sell newspapers, and it is possible that they focused on witnesses' testimony about Delfau's actions because they knew it would shock the populace. This alone is revealing about the state of affairs in postwar France. But an analysis of the articles reveals that Delfau did not actually physically torture; rather she was potentially guilty of encouraging physical harm. The very fact that her participation was the most sensational aspect of a trial in which cell members purportedly maimed and harmed at will reveals the severity of gender boundaries in the postwar period. In highlighting Delfau, newspapers made her the main villain of the trial; in attacking her for her appearance, misplaced sexuality, and afemininity, they made her an anti-exemplar for postwar French women.

Violette Morris

Violette Morris, "the hyena of the Gestapo," certainly served as one of the most potent examples of the terrors associated with a woman who renounced femininity in postwar France. It seems that nearly every aspect of Morris's life was—or was portrayed as—a rejection of femininity. A caveat: sources for Morris, especially for her life after her sporting career, are often either sensationalized or rare; they tend to overly condemn her or overly rehabilitate her.[86] She represents such a compelling character, however, that her inclusion is instructive despite its potential drawbacks.

Violette Morris was born in France in 1893 to a prominent military family (her grandfather was one of the original invaders of Algeria in 1830), and she spent a good amount of her youth in a convent school.[87] She married Cyprien Gouraud, a businessman, in 1914 and worked as a motorcycle nurse during the

Figure 5 Violette Morris.

Great War, purportedly developing a deep hatred of weakness and desertion in favor of strength and action. Morris was an incredible athlete, competing—often at the national level—in sports as varied as boxing, swimming, archery, wrestling, soccer, water polo, discus, and hammer, among others. She held numerous world records in various events, she was one of the first French female aviators, and she even won the Bol d'Or, a famous vehicular endurance race, in 1927, when she was the sole female competitor.

Even early on, her fellow competitors were intimidated by her fierceness. Hélène Delangle, another female driver, remembered that before one race, Morris was "marching around her vast Donnet [car] like a policeman on duty, cigarette glued to the corner of her mouth as she barked out orders at a kneeling mechanic. . . . Turning as if she could sense the watchful stare, Morris took the cigarette, dropped it, and slowly ground it out, her eyes on the rosy-cheeked girl in the white beret."[88] Whether this incident was meant to convey a sexual or simply competitive nature is difficult to glean. Either way it is clear that Morris, in physically threatening men and glaring at her competition, as well as her participation in traditionally non-feminine activities, did not conform to the niceties expected of women.[89]

By 1919, Violette Morris was commonly dressing in male clothing, and in 1923, she and Gouraud divorced, purportedly because he "surprised her in a full lesbian orgy at the conjugal domicile."[90] She lived a lifestyle that rejected many of the feminine norms of the day; according to biographer Bonnet, she "smokes, she dresses like a man, she does not hide her sexual orientation, she contests official decisions, she transgresses all limits placed on women, including those of the body itself."[91] As one newspaper put it in 1926, "Is this a man or a woman? She wears male dress with such an ease, and for so long now, that everyone who sees her for the first time says without hesitation: 'Monsieur.'"[92] Over the course of 1927 and 1928, Morris was denied a place on the French Olympic squad and lost her training license from the Fédération féminine sportive de France (FFSF) because the committee, once a vessel for feminism through sport, declared their disapproval of her overly masculine appearance and inappropriate public conduct: she engaged openly in heterosexual and—more importantly for the FFSF—homosexual affairs.[93] Morris went to trial against the FFSF and lost; the presiding judge ultimately decided that her conduct was "deplorable" and that she was endangering French youth through her depraved public example.[94] Attesting to the fears of the time about the impact on the younger generation, one newspaper of the time, *L'Intransigent*, expressed hope that this would be the sole trial of its kind and that "young, sporting women in the future will consent to wear more than puffy pants and not cut off their right side like Amazons."[95]

While her appearance and open bisexuality were controversial in the 1920s, perhaps the most shocking characteristic of Violette Morris was her decisive physical rejection of femininity. She dressed as a man and kept her hair short, which were extreme manifestations of the figure Mary Louise Roberts has termed "*la femme moderne*."[96] Most radically, in 1929, Morris voluntarily decided to undergo a double mastectomy. Writers who have touched upon Morris's life in their works disagree about her reasons for this: Marie-Joseph Bonnet, Raymond Ruffin, Wendy Michallat, and Miranda Seymour all argue that Morris cut off her breasts in order to better grip the wheel during automobile racing. Seymour posits that she found "that her heavy breasts impeded her control of the steering wheel of her Donnet racing car, [and] chose to have them lopped off."[97] Indeed a *Time* magazine article from the era quotes her as saying, "Sport is my life."[98] Christian Gury offers a different interpretation, stating that she underwent the surgery in defiance of the French sporting elite, whose judgment she found intolerable and suffocating.[99] Gury even quotes her as saying, "Since they are 'cutting' me from the world of *sportives* and 'guillotining' me, I myself will 'cut' off the symbol of my femininity."[100] Either way, her protest was a public scandal which received worldwide attention, for Morris announced the operation defiantly to the press.[101] It even figured prominently in her trial, where, according to Wendy Michallat, FFSF lawyers portrayed the double mastectomy "as a further example of Morris's potential to perniciously influence impressionable young women."[102] At the end of the trial, Morris allegedly announced to the press: "I will get a pilot's license. The air is the only place left where a woman can wear pants."[103]

During the 1930s, Violette Morris spent a significant amount of time in Germany, where she could still participate in sport. There, she became involved with the Far Right, even winning a medal for her past sporting achievements and participating—at Hitler's invitation—in the opening of the 1936 Berlin Olympics.[104] According to Raymond Ruffin, Morris was "seduced by the [Nazi] type of society," with its order and ceremonial celebrations of strength and virility, in contrast to what Morris viewed as a weak and passive France.[105] Several of her biographers allege that Morris viewed French men as feeble and was disgusted by what she perceived as her nation's effeminacy; in a 1930 interview, she called the French a "country of small people [who are] not worthy of our ancestors, not worthy to survive."[106] She returned to Paris, and even before the fall of France, she was recruited to join the Gestapo and became a "well-regarded spy," leading many missions in the Rouen area and becoming part of the notorious Bony-Lafont Gestapo ring.[107] Seymour states that she even provided "detailed plans of the Maginot Line defenses" to Germany.[108] And, in a sign of the dangers associated with women and sport, Ruffin highlights how she used her sporting connections to procure information about the French army, only to turn around and give it to Germany.[109] Morris thereby subverted the dominant image of the female spy, often associated with the figure of the seductress, using athletics rather than sexuality to betray her nation. She became friendly with Karl Oberg, the head of the SS in France, through much of the Second World War, and was quickly promoted in the Gestapo ranks.[110] Free France even described her as an "honorary citizen of Germany for services rendered."[111]

During the war, Violette Morris was apparently infamous for her hatred of resistors, who she perceived as traitors, and she quickly gained a reputation for extreme torture tactics; Auguste le Breton, later known as the writer of the Rififi novels, even called her the "hyena of the Gestapo."[112] At first she had been part of a reconnaissance cell, one which would track down Resistance members and turn them in, and she also concerned herself with economic requisitioning for the Germans.[113] She denounced members of the French Resistance and participated in deadly raids, and she was at least partly responsible for the deaths of dozens of resistors.[114] As the war went on, she transitioned to physical violence, becoming, according to one historian, one of two "chief women's interrogators" for the Gestapo."[115]

One young woman remembered her interrogation at the hands of Violette as sexually humiliating and excruciatingly painful. Violette slapped her and forced her to remove her clothing. When the young woman, Odile S., continued to refuse to speak, Violette "throws her to the ground and beats her black and blue on the back, the thighs, the face on which the whip prints some reddish stripes." Odile remembered that she passed out, and when she awoke, she was laying on a sofa, and she looked over at Violette and mistook her for a man.[116] Her reputation was such that she was known in the Resistance as "la terrible Violette Morris"[117] and the most "obsessed"[118] of all the torturers. One Resistance member, Suzanne Leverrier, remembered her questioning by Violette as horrific. She was detained and taken to the rue des Saussaies for questioning, and heard awful screams as she was led upstairs:

> The first thing I saw, it was a woman entirely nude suspended by her wrists to a big hook set in the ceiling. Her head fell forward on her side like that of Christ on the cross, and her hair masked her face. Her body was covered with red and blue marks [and] criss-crossed with trickles of blood.... Violette Morris headed over to the woman and, seizing her by her hair, threw her head back: "You recognize her?" [she asked Suzanne]

Suzanne denied knowing the woman, and thus provoked Morris's anger toward the suspended woman. Suzanne remembered watching the scene: "I was petrified, terrorized, I was shaken by a nervous trembling. . . . La Morris was enraged, she alternated the bursts of blows with burnings with a lighter."[119] Through these and other sessions, Violette was able to break several Resistance cells, thus becoming, as Ruffin calls her, "the incontestable star of the rue des Saussaies" Gestapo cell.[120]

The brutal violence that Morris perpetrated upon Resistance members, male and female, was reflective of her entire adoption of a masculine persona. Unlike Denise Delfau, she did not inspire people to commit acts through her sexuality or her beauty, rather she used her force, akin to that of a man, to torture the heroes and heroines of France.[121] This violence cannot be separated from her sexuality, though. Descriptions of Violette's anger at French men and her insatiable lust for pain echo medico-moral statements about lesbianism that were common in interwar France.[122] In liberated France, these gender boundaries again calcified through fantastical discourses about abnormal women and their behaviors. As Capdevila et al. argue, "During the course of the two world wars, images of ferocity marked the representations of women who diverted from their normal roles."[123] A woman who wanted to be "normal" thus had to be sure to remain sexually pure and appropriate in terms of gender, the opposite of someone like Violette Morris.

Like Denise Delfau and the German prison guards, Morris rejected normative femininity through her espousal of violence and her assertion of superiority over French men. According to accounts of her life, she broke with traditional French femininity in an extreme way, cutting off her breasts in an act of defiance and sympathizing with the Nazis because of their embrace of visceral masculinity. It is difficult to glean how familiar people were with Morris's activities during the postwar period. Her reputation as a successful athlete was certainly widespread, as evidenced by the amount of coverage she received both in domestic and international papers, and the fact that the Resistance put a hit out on her speaks to her renown as a torturer and traitor. As the newspaper *L'Humanité* reported during the Liberation:

> This Violette Morris, she was certainly an informant for the Nazis. A sort of monster hybrid, this creature incessantly wore men's clothes, made an exhibition of herself as a "champion" of shot putting and weightlifting, had even had her breasts cut off to appear more masculine. She put herself in the service of the Gestapo to be able to satisfy her sadistic instincts while torturing patriots.[124]

Similarly, *Le Figaro* described her death at the hands of Resistance fighters, referring to Morris as a "hideous shrew who delivered hundreds of resistors to the Gestapo."[125] These articles were published in 1944, in the midst of what Capdevila et al. refer to as the "battle of images" during the Liberation.[126] Here, Violette Morris was a woman who had discarded her femininity and in the process had become a "monster" and "sadistic." In the postwar period, such discourses functioned to rhetorically alienate Morris—as well as women like the German prison guards—from French society. Her behavior—and that of those like her—was unacceptable in the postwar period and had to be punished.

Gender and punishment

One of the main purposes for making female torturers public fodder in venues like newspapers was to communicate both the severity and symbolism associated with their defeminizing punishment. This is particularly true given the context: much of the publicizing of torturers' activities occurred after the war rather than during it (when, admittedly, the Vichy press would not have done so). Through the public punishment of a woman who had stepped out of traditional feminine boundaries, French society could reassert gender stability. Consider these statistics: 54 percent of all women in prison in 1946 had been arrested for collaboration,[127] and while women were usually no more than 10 percent of the criminal population, they constituted one quarter of the cases before the Liberation courts.[128]

Now French men could regain their virility and supremacy over French women: the bodies of female torturers became a symbolic field upon which to reassert male hegemony, and their punishments reflected that. Representations of these torturers rendered the women ugly and sexually deviant. These representations went even further: the rhetorical defeminization of female torturers stripped them of their power. The consequences associated with having challenged the virility and strength of French men during the war were severe in its aftermath as French men and women sought to reestablish domestic life in peacetime.

In terms of her official punishment, Denise Delfau ultimately received a sentence of twenty years of hard labor for her crimes, less than her male rue de la Pompe counterparts.[129] In this case, though, the public aspect of her punishment, especially the attention paid to her during the trial, is more important than her sentence, which would be served out in private. The newspaper coverage and the disproportionate attention paid to Delfau created a new boundary confining French femininity.

Denise Delfau attempted to use contemporary articulations of prescribed femininity to plead her case once she was put on trial. For example, she argued that she was coerced into torturing by a violent man. In this way, Delfau constructed herself as a victim by virtue of her own physical abuse at the hands of a German man. Jean Pichon of *Combat* reported that Delfau testified that her actions were the result of her own victimization: "I was scared of Bergé [Berger], monsieur le président. He was an alcoholic. He beat me."[130] In the same article Pichon showed himself to be clearly skeptical of Delfau's motives: "Denise

Delfau, for her part, got out the handkerchief. How far it is from the time where, seated on the edge of the tragic baths, she listened for the confessions of patriots like a she-cat [*chatte*]."[131]

Also, Denise Delfau argued that if she encouraged people to talk and confess their Resistance activities, it was only because she could not stand to hear their cries and wanted to alleviate their misery as quickly as possible. During her trial, the judge accused her of being present for the torture sessions and doing nothing to stop them. In response, Delfau argued that "so as not to see these unfortunate people suffer, I advised them to confess." In this way, Delfau constructed her role as that of a friend and an alleviator of suffering, even a confidant during a time of duress. Delfau evoked tapping into the idea of woman as nurse which was prevalent at this time. Just as any French woman's caring side would prompt her to rush to the sick and people in need, no matter the consequences, so Delfau sought to end the pain in front of her. But again the author of the article, Roland Bochin, shows his skepticism about Delfau's claims of nurturing, calling it a "mediocre defense."[132] Though Delfau does use these tropes to try to save herself, the skeptical writing of the newspaper reporters made it clear that readers ought not trust her motives.

Perhaps most alarming for people following the trial was the attestation that there were many such Delfaus out there. A reporter for *Le Parisien libéré* stated that several women had watched and even participated in the torture sessions at the rue de la Pompe cell, but they were "unfortunately not pursued" at the end of the war.[133] Accurate or not, this suggests that French people needed to be wary of potential Delfaus they might encounter, but it does not specify who they might be. This indicates the potential culpability—and hence untrustworthiness—of all French women.

Like Delfau, Violette Morris, the "hyena of the Gestapo," faced a grim fate at the end of the war, and her punishment also symbolically reestablished the masculine authority of France over a woman who had co-opted traditionally masculine power over French men. In her case, Violette Morris was targeted for death by a Resistance cell in Normandy. One evening, as she was out driving with a family, Resistance members staged a diversion and then jumped out of the bushes along the side of the road. They then fired directly into the stopped vehicle, killing everyone inside. Violette apparently survived the initial round of bullets, and according to the Resistance story, she prepared to return fire. However, according to Ruffin, "The chief commando is not a novice and his own reflexes are also prompt: the burst left in a fraction of a second and it fells

[Violette] on the grassy border [of the road]."[134] Although Violette was an elite athlete, her reflexes were not as quick as the Resistance leader, who was able to overpower her. In this way, a French man physically bested Morris, who had wiped away all traces of her femininity and then begun to dominate French bodies. The man becomes the actor in the scene, while Morris is the receiver of justice. Where Morris rejected France because she perceived it as an effeminate country, ultimately France rejected Violette Morris's adoption of masculinity in order to reclaim its own virility.

In postwar France, women faced punishment not just for torturing, but also for being *female* torturers at a time when women's natures were being essentialized into domestic, nurturing creatures. Scholars like political scientist Francine D'Amico have bemoaned certain cultural critics' and media outlets' tendency to make female torturers "gender representative," stating that one woman's poor judgment ought not to affect general conceptions of femininity.[135] Making French female torturers "gender representative" served specific purposes after the Second World War, delineating the lines of national belonging. The mass media, with depictions of women like Denise Delfau and German prison guards, rendered these women outcasts and miscreants. But in constructing them as the opposite of what a proper French woman ought to be, they were also helping to reinforce a set of essentialized notions of femininity as docile and nurturing and to punish those who strayed from that femininity publicly.

Espionage

In 1945, the women's magazine *Marie-France* printed "Along the Clandestine Route," a fictional piece by M-P Salonne about a young female spy named Aïde who was biking on a country road in Brittany, on her way to deliver mail to fellow Resistance members. While out, she thought about a close call she had experienced a while ago. She had been biking down the road with a bunch of freshly picked flowers in the basket of her bike, and she ran into a German soldier, who was also biking. They chatted, and "on the side of the road, they overtook an old country woman, one of those old women in the [Breton] headdress, who have retained all the vehemence of their race." In a reference to the thousands of head shavings across the country, the woman cried out to Aïde that she was "shameful! You will be shaved, you, my girl, you will be shaved!" Aïde laughed to herself—if the old woman only knew the truth of the matter. Then, she and the German soldier ran into a checkpoint. The soldiers who manned the station forced Aïde to show her papers, which were largely falsified reproductions, and they proceeded to rifle through her things. They asked her what was in the packet of papers, and she told them not to disturb her flowers, thereby buying herself a little time. Then she told them the truth about herself, knowing they would never believe her. "Don't you think that I look like a terrorist?" she joked with them. They sent her on her way.[136]

This story reveals more than the bravery of certain French women who participated in the Resistance or how femininity could benefit female resistors. It also exposes a deeper perception of French women in general: just as the elderly Brittany native assumed that Aïde was a German consort rather than a Resistance member, it was impossible to discern the difference between an honorable woman doing her duty for France through espionage and a rogue female spy who betrayed France using her sexuality and flirtations.

By their very job descriptions, female spies traversed all manner of boundaries, including gender ones. As historian Tammy Proctor writes, "The female spy blurred the distinction of private and public . . . by performing 'public' work in 'private' spaces, making her both effective and dangerous."[137] Their gender allegedly rendered them more nurturing and caring, and, ultimately, trustworthy. However, whereas here Aïde happened to be well-intentioned, other sources from the time suggested that even the most honorable of French women, a Resistance member doing her duty for France, could easily deceive and betray French men. Even more insidiously, it was difficult for anyone to distinguish between a female spy and a proper French woman.

Ironically, while female spies after the war could appear as the embodiment of fearsome enemy sexuality, during the war, Resistance women's femininity often served as their greatest asset in their guise as spies and fighters, because it placed them outside of enemy suspicion. Paula Schwartz argues that Resistance leaders recognized this and often put women into dangerous situations, "because it was commonly recognized that of all resisters, they had the best disguise: they were women!"[138] Schwartz goes on to posit that these female spies enjoyed a certain level of "invisibility," which significantly aided the Resistance.[139] In fact, during the war, Schwartz shows, "Sometimes men actually 'borrowed' gender aliases as women for safety and protection."[140] Although not all women enjoyed full membership in certain Resistance groups because of long-standing stereotypes about women's gossipy natures and fears that they would disrupt masculine camaraderie, women were nevertheless central to the Resistance, and their femininity was in turn central to their success.[141] After the war, Resistance women's wartime exploits were assimilated into wider discussions about victimhood and exceptionality, while widespread fears of the harm associated with female espionage turned up in newspapers, court cases, and fictional pieces. It is hence important to ask what changed between the war and the immediate postwar period to cause this adjustment.

One explanation for this shift has to do with postwar French masculinity. If the restoration of virility and masculinity was crucial for the reconstruction of "Frenchness," it was also important for the public image of the Liberation to be French and masculine. Charles de Gaulle understood this need, hence French troops led the way into Paris in August 1944, rather than American or other Allied forces.[142] In his speech at the Liberation of Paris, he claimed:

> This is why the French vanguard has entered Paris with guns blazing. This is why the great French army from Italy has landed in the south and is advancing rapidly up the Rhône valley. This is why our brave and dear forces of the interior will arm themselves with modern weapons. It is for this revenge, this vengeance and justice, that we will keep fighting until the final day, until the day of total and complete victory.

Using the imagery of a strong, vigorous, victorious army, de Gaulle crafted a masculinized narrative of the Liberation of France in which French men reclaimed both their capitol and the masculinity they had lost in the surrender. Similarly, within the Resistance, as the tides were turning in the Allies' favor, women slowly began to be phased out of fighting units. Paula Schwartz argues that this was part of an effort to "normalize" the ranks and to turn "partisan fighters into 'real' soldiers" who would ultimately become part of the French army.[143] It also served to construct an image of victory as orderly and masculine at a time when stability and virility were constant themes. As women became less crucial to the fight for France, their presence in public became more of an embarrassment and even a contamination. Schwartz concludes that "the very 'invisibility' that had been women's stock in trade during the illegal period, now doomed them to obsolescence when underground fighters emerged into the light of day."[144] As the need for a strong image of masculinity grew in the postwar period, those women who had spied for France during the war—in a way that benefited the nation—were silenced. Women who had betrayed France through their espionage, however, remained in the limelight as examples of the dangers of public women.

This section deals with the rhetoric surrounding female spies during the Liberation period when, as Susan Gubar writes, "espionage played a much more prominent role . . . than ever before."[145] First, it analyzes Mathilde-Lily Carré, a double agent for the Allies and the Germans who was alleged to have caused the deaths of many French resistors. Whatever her actions during the war, in postwar newspaper coverage of her trial and biographies of her life, Carré's depictions took a sensual, dangerous cast. Ultimately, after demonstrating the threats of a woman like Carré, contemporary portrayers showed her to be cowed by the French state, thereby reinstating masculine authority over a woman who had challenged the boundaries of gender through her wartime actions. The section then moves to an analysis of a popular spy novel, *V5*, by the French writer Valentin Mandelstamm. In the novel, a spy seduces a strong, masculine hero, to the detriment of his relationship with a wholesome, moral young woman. In the end, though, the hero reasserts his masculinity, punishing the spy and cementing his relationship with the good woman. Female spies showed that any woman in public could be mendacious and hence threatening to the masculinity of both the individual male actor and the state, and she needed to be stopped.

The female spy traverses a contested gender territory: in postwar France, depictions highlighted that she was a public woman using her sexuality, traditionally intended for the private sphere only, to gather public information. Unlike the female torturer, the female spy did not necessarily abnegate her femininity. Rather she weaponized it in order to bring out male weakness. In doing so, she represented a threat to all of France: if the French had universally resisted, as the Resistance myth propagated at this time, then the female spy threatened and betrayed the French nation. The female spy thus embodies what Susan Gubar refers to as a kind of "contamination"[146] in that she pollutes public space with her sexual manipulations. Whereas Gubar uses the concept of "contamination" in reference to women who could potentially spread sexually transmitted diseases to soldiers in wartime, this chapter suggests that the women themselves were perceived as contaminants to the reconstruction of a virile republic.[147] These alternate gendered metaphors of contamination present a useful conceptual model to discuss the female spy. In an atmosphere in which confinement was the prevailing model for French women, female spies represented a fearsome picture of women, in public, who looked like regular women, but who in fact wielded their femininity as a weapon to weaken men and the state.[148]

Mathilde-Lily Carré: The She-Cat

In post–Second World War France, an eroticized, perilous vision of the female spy functioned to counter that of proper French womanhood. Her image was meant to show the dangers of unbounded sexuality and publicly unsanctioned femininity, which could contaminate society. Into this context stepped Mathilde-Lily Carré, aka *La Chatte* (The She-Cat), who came to exemplify the fears and potential havoc caused by a female spy in France after the Second World War. In fact, Carré subtitled her 1960 autobiography, "the most remarkable woman spy since Mata Hari," a moniker also adopted by her (admittedly sensationalistic) biographer, Gordon Young, a Paris correspondent for the *Daily Mail* who called her "a new Mata Hari."[149] There were certainly other female spies at this time, perhaps most notably Marthe Richard, but Carré's betrayal captivated the media—especially the Resistance newspapers—and the public.[150] The story of Carré's wartime doings—and the truth about her guilt or innocence—remains somewhat unclear. What is known is that she was born in 1908 in Le Creusot, in Burgundy, and, following some formal education, she married a teacher and moved with him to Algeria. After that, her personal life becomes somewhat murky. Some accounts say that at the outbreak of war she returned to Paris, and her husband joined the army and was later killed in combat. Gordon Young writes that she had filed for divorce before the start of war upon learning that her husband's family had a history of insanity.[151] He also recounts how, in contrast to the loving French woman who always wanted to please her husband, Carré refused even to read his letters from the front. Instead, she was already plotting to be free of him: "'Don't worry', Mathilde Carré told [her new lover] reassuringly, 'I will soon get rid of him.'"[152]

After meeting a new paramour who was already involved with the Resistance, a Polish air force officer named Roman Czerniawski (also known as Roman Garby-Czerniawski), Carré joined up after the French surrender, and she became a leading member of the *Interallié* Resistance group, based in Paris. Carré was arrested by the Gestapo in 1941 and quickly became a double agent. If she had any "misgivings of conscience" about her betrayal, Young writes, "nobody will ever know."[153] Margaret Collins Weitz describes Carré's disloyalty to France and her Resistance colleagues as absolute:

> And so former Resistance agent Mathilde-Lily Carré accompanied the Germans to all the rendezvous listed in the agenda they found on her when she was captured. [Hugo] Bleicher [the German leader] listened as she called others in the Interallié group—including her own mother—at his direction. At a pâté

and Champagne feast that the jubilant Bleicher held to celebrate his success in rounding up network members (with her assistance), Carré again claimed to feel as if she had been hit with a sledgehammer—one that affects the mind. That night, she became Bleicher's mistress—a fact that weighed heavily against her in the postwar trial.[154]

Thus Carré betrayed France both politically, through the delivery of resistors to the Germans, and sexually, through her affair with a German man.

Following this betrayal, Carré became what Young refers to as the "toast of the *Abwehr*," actively spying for the Germans again and infiltrating yet another Resistance group.[155] This last Resistance group began to suspect that she was a double agent, and they in turn used her to gather information about the German campaigns. In 1942, Carré was arrested in England, and after the war, she returned to France, where, according to Weitz, "several of her former Resistance colleagues supported her; others denounced her."[156] She went on trial in 1949, and was sentenced to death, a sentence which was later reduced to hard labor for life. Eventually, in a move that patterned many war criminals' prison terms, Carré was released from jail in 1954.[157]

The personage of Mathilde Carré certainly captured the imagination of the French press, becoming a focus of media attention, especially during her trial in 1949. At this time Carré's looks became a source of intense speculation on the part of the press. Much like reporters painted Denise Delfau as quite unattractive and the opposite of the beauty associated with French women, Carré's own biographer, Gordon Young, described her as "stocky. . . . Her nose was a little too large and prominent, her jaw a shade too square and determined, and her wide, sensual mouth would part sometimes to reveal teeth which were widely spaced and somewhat fang-like."[158] Young also recounted how a British security guard derided the applicability of her nickname, "La Chatte," saying, "I can't think why they called her The Cat, old boy; she always looked more like a ferret to me."[159] Another postwar account from a British spy dropped in France, Ben Cowburn, described her as "slim and pleasant, but very short-sighted. She apparently considered that glasses would spoil her looks and constantly peered at us from puckered eyelids."[160] In considering his situation at having to work with her, Cowburn again reinforced her subpar looks, writing, "Here I was, in the midst of an intrigue straight out of a cheap edition, complete with a beautiful blonde spy. [Carré] was neither blond nor beautiful, but she would have to do."[161] Similarly, newspapers plastered unflattering images of her, such as the one shown in Figure 6, on their front pages, perhaps to counteract her seductive powers.

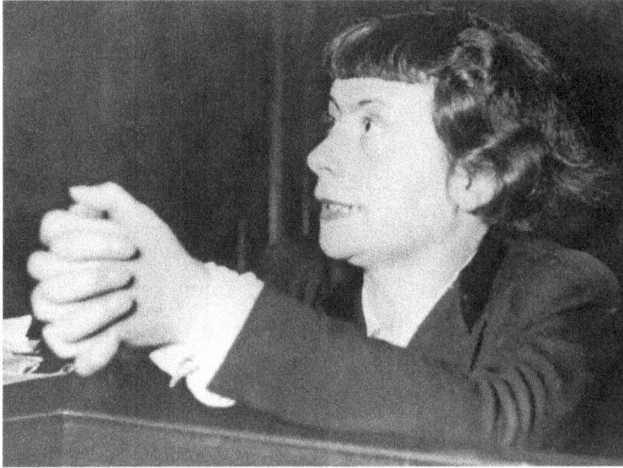

Figure 6 Carré on trial.

In the newspaper *Combat,* the reporter Robert Collin even referred to Carré as a "*femme-fauve,*" or a "woman-beast." He also intimated that she was possessed, wondering "what demon" would cause her to keep all of her dates with her cell members and knowingly lead them to their captures after confessing her own Resistance participation. In keeping with the feline theme, Collin called these setups Mathilde Carré's "mousetraps."[162] In this portrayal, Carré is an evil vixen despite her unfortunate looks, luring her presumed friends to their unfortunate destinies.[163]

If Mathilde Carré was not described as a beautiful woman, she was certainly depicted as a very sexual one. Somewhat similar to female torturers, newspapers and biographers depicted Carré's sexuality as a weapon she wielded on her path of selfishness and betrayal. It had little to do with the heteronormative love associated with a proper French woman's femininity. As noted above, Young referred to her mouth as "sensual" and "fang-like" in the same sentence.[164] In British archives, she was described as "voluptuous" and "sultry," her sexuality a threat to even the most committed Allies.[165] She used her sexuality to get what she wanted, according to one sensationalized biographer, wearing tight suits and walking sensuously through the streets of Paris: "she had something to show and she showed it in her tight-fitting black suit."[166] She was a frighteningly sexual character, described as "the inhumane spy with the green eyes."[167] Indeed one of her victims called her as a "dangerous nymphomaniac."[168] Men were rendered powerless by her sensuality: "Mathilde Carré," one biographer wrote, "could not be described as beautiful, but she possessed that certain *chic* which renders men as soft as wax in a woman's hands."[169]

Carré intended to divorce her husband, having taken up with the head of the *Interallié* group, an illicit affair which was an absolute taboo for a proper postwar French woman. While other French women faced the perils of war by becoming nurses or honorable members of the Resistance, the danger excited Carré sexually, prompting her to state: "There's almost a sensual pleasure in real danger, don't you think? Your whole body seems suddenly to come alive."[170] Young portrays this as a bizarre facet of her sexuality, which he links with her lack of fear at experiencing bombings or even the horrors of medical clinics at the front. Another biographer described her as sexually aroused by the experience of being a spy: "Danger stimulated her."[171] And British spy Ben Cowburn depicted her as abnormal in her feelings, saying she had a "peculiar nature" that likely felt "elation" at being a spy and betraying people on several levels.[172]

In contemporary depictions, Carré seemed to feel no remorse for her actions, furthering her image as a cold seductress and linking her to a certain extent with the female torturers. When reacting to her role in the capture of other members of the *Interallié* cell, she apparently said, "He (or she) should have left [the rendezvous spot]. It's his fault he was taken. You shouldn't reveal yourself [as a Resistance member] to someone when they're accompanied [by someone else]."[173] Cowburn remembered her frustration at being caught herself, not because her betrayals troubled her, but because of her "megalomania."[174] Even when Carré's death sentence was read in court, coverage emphasized how she barely seemed to care. According to reports in *Le Monde*, she "received her sentence without blinking, signing her appeal to the high court, and worrying only about the diet that is going to be given to her from now on."[175] In this article, Carré's vanity is still very much alive, thereby distinguishing her from the ugly female torturers of the previous chapter.

It is interesting to link Carré's concerns about her femininity with her concerns about her appearance and her food intake, both of which were major worries of proper French women. Within normal French femininity, though, a French woman's aesthetic ultimately applied to the happiness of her husband, rather than herself. Here, Carré's concerns were all about her own well-being, the opposite of what was required of a French woman. Unlike Violette Morris, for example, Mathilde Carré was still a woman, with a woman's essential seductive powers, only without the appropriate characteristics (such as private sphere confinement) to temper the dangers associated with her femininity.

In fact her biographer attributed her deviousness to shortcomings within her femininity. Her lack of children, Young wrote, could potentially explain her traitorous actions: "This fact that the young Mathilde Carré was denied her normal desire for children may, perhaps, do something to explain the restless, driving energy with which she was later to pursue quite other objectives and ambitions."[176] Another biographer called this "the whole tragedy of [her] unfulfilled life."[177] It is interesting that during the natalist context of the postwar period, Young used Carré's lack of children to try to shed light on her treason. Similarly, Young calls Carré's "cruelest stroke" the incident in which she separated a fellow female resistor from her infant. He wrote: "As the weeping Madame Hugentobler was dragged out of her home, her former trusted friend 'Micheline' [as Carré was often known in the Resistance] said only one word to her, '*Pardon*'—and turned away."[178] Hugentobler allegedly hanged herself that night in her cell. In this depiction, Carré lacks the maternal nurturing of a proper woman that cultural sources depicted as innate to French women of this time.

Carré did attempt to rehabilitate her own image, much like rue de la Pompe cell member Denise Delfau did during her own trial. According to scholar Christopher Lloyd, Carré was one of many people who, feeling that the creation of their images had been unfair, painted themselves as "wronged and tragic survivor[s]"[179] Indeed, according to an article in *Combat*, Carré presented herself to the court as the victim of Bleicher's machinations, saying that she was "physically shocked" by Bleicher, who was simply using Carré as "bait."[180] Additional coverage in *Le Parisien libéré* reported that Carré testified that Bleicher kept her in a state of "semi-liberty," constantly threatening "to have me shot if I didn't obey his orders."[181]

In his preface to Mathilde Carré's autobiography, *I Was La Chatte*, her lawyer, Albert Naud, explicitly stated that one of his strategies in the trial was to "restore to 'la Chatte' her [womanly] face."[182] During the trial, for example, he called Carré's mother to the stand to testify, and her mother, Madame Belard, "affirmed that her daughter could not have betrayed."[183] According to press coverage, Belard stated that her daughter was "raised with patriotic sentiments, with love for her native soil," and she "gave herself to the Resistance body and soul."[184] Belard here argues for a sexual connection with France, and specifically with the French Resistance, thereby allying Carré with narratives about strong, upstanding, even masculine values and connecting her sexuality to the French nation, rather than making it an unbounded free manifestation of Carré's self-expression. Naud argues that rather than being a "diabolical spy," Carré was simply a fragile woman, naked and trembling, so weak, so feminine, so sadly human."[185] For his part, Lloyd sees these sorts of efforts as "a means of self-justification or as an attempt to avoid passing into historical oblivion."[186] And Carré herself, in a letter to her lawyer, stated that she was now "small, lost, and unhappy."[187] The language Carré and her defenders employed was also indicative of an attempt to place Carré strongly within the bounds of proper femininity, a potent image at the time. This language painted Carré as a defender of her nation rather than a traitor to her gender—and, by extension, to masculinity as well.

Sources from the time reflect skepticism about Carré's inherent goodness, as the reporter from *Combat*'s description of her as a "woman-beast" during the trial implies. For example, the journalist from *Le Parisien libéré* followed his description of courtroom attempts to deny or lessen the impact of Carré's actions by stating, "However, M. René Aubertin [Carré's prewar friend] details the conditions in which 'la Chatte' gave him up, him and another of his Resistance compatriots; his friend, deported to Mauthausen, was clubbed to death."[188]

Much of this doubtful coverage focused on reporters' impressions of Carré's attitude. Indeed Young posits that "throughout the . . . trial The Cat did herself incalculable harm by her pert manner and her apparently unrepentant air."[189] As *Libération* reporter Madeleine Jacob wrote, "Her cynicism had planted on her face a fixed expression of self-satisfied insolence. From under her lowered eyelids her eyes shone hard clear; on her lips there was a vague smile permanently fixed." And another reporter for *Libération* described Carré as more like a snake than a cat.[190] In describing her reaction to the verdict, *Le Parisien libéré*, like *Le Monde*, focused on how Carré's response was abnormal. The paper's reporter noted that she smiled throughout the reading; in fact the paper printed a front-page photo of Carré "still laughing" during the verdict.[191]

For his part, Young asks whether Carré felt any remorse for her disloyalty, and responds that she most likely did not. Certainly, he argues, "if Mathilde Carré was in reality at this time a tortured soul keeping up an outward appearance of bravado she . . . acted her role remarkably well. She . . . at no time seems to have shown any undue emotion as she watched her friends being carried away to imprisonment and, in many cases, torture and death."[192] Her remorse and her attempts at feminine propriety were merely an act.

Carré attempted to digest and analyze her experience many years later in two autobiographies, which seem to betray her awareness of the forces at work in the state's treatment of her as a female spy. For example, Carré pointed out the suspicious nature of her capture and sentence, noting that "only those who had once had German lovers" remained in prison with her after 1949, as "the prison began to empty of female prisoners incarcerated on war-related crimes."[193] (In fact, historian Christine Bard argues that even though women "normally make up only 10% of the criminal population, women formed 25% of the population prosecuted in Liberation tribunals."[194]) Carré thought herself specially castigated for her own sexualized betrayal and her womanhood, arguing more blatantly: "I must never forget that men (particularly the French) do not love an equal . . . and since I feel no inclination to be a slave—unless it be to God—I must outgrow them."[195] While Carré's works are undoubtedly at least partially public relations campaigns, they also seem to reveal a nuanced understanding on Carré's part of the gender forces at work in postwar France.

If the female victim's experience was to be universal—that all French women heroically resisted, and then returned to the private sphere—then someone like Carré, whose betrayal of France was political, sexual, and public, needed to be portrayed as an aberration. Margaret Collins Weitz's work stresses this dichotomy, saying, "The 'saint' who resisted was contrasted [in French views of women] to the 'sinner' who collaborated."[196] Such distinctions performed complex functions within the context of postwar France. The victim image universalized French women's wartime experience and send them home, thereby constructing a new female identity (which would be complemented by images of appropriate French femininity, which would teach women proper comportment within the private sphere). The image of the female spy, on the other hand, marginalized and contained such women who threatened to contaminate the French populace, which had to do with illicit, uncontrolled sexuality and femininity. She also served as an example of the dystopic possibilities associated with unbounded women in public.

Fictional female spies

Fictional accounts of spies flooded the postwar period. According to scholar Eric Neveu, "Espionage [became] a mass literary product" for the first time, enjoying a "golden age" in the wake of the Second World War and the onset of the Cold War.[197] In France, for example, the famous imprint *Série noire* was first begun right in 1945 by Marcel Duhamel.[198] Also, beginning in 1950, publishers produced a series of extremely popular spy novels called *Le Fleuve noir*.[199] These series dominated the French publishing market through the 1950s.[200]

Additionally, famous genre authors of the time included Gabriel Veraldi, Jean Bruce, Jean Bommart, and Dominique Ponchardier, whose books in the *Gorille* spy series numbered in the dozens during the 1950s. Spy films also began to become popular, with examples like *This Man Is Dangerous* and *Le môme vert-de-gris* ("The Grayish-Green Gal"), two in the Lemmy Caution series, achieving notable financial success in the early 1950s.[201]

Despite the fact that a large number of these spy novels and films deal with Americans or import elements of American culture, they still provide a vision of postwar French life.[202] Literary scholar Pierre Laszlo has described the spy novel genre as "a documentary tableau of France in the 1950s."[203] While spy fiction especially took off with the intensification of the Cold War, this project more closely considers earlier manifestations of this type of literature, which continued to react to the Second World War. According to one scholar, the postwar success of spy fiction is attributable to its newfound links with political reality and its insertion into the political consciousness of readers.[204] In short, spy fiction's new plausibility for readers rendered it more successful.

This section will examine one particularly compelling example of this genre, the spy novel *V5* by Valentin Mandelstamm. Mandelstamm was a prolific and well-read French writer during the interwar and postwar periods, both nationally and internationally.[205] His *V5* was prominent enough that even the US-based *French Review* recommended it for light reading to all Francophone readers.[206] In the novel, published in 1945, he articulated a vision of the female spy—and her more proper counterpart—in a paradigmatic way, as a dark and mysterious temptress, a woman who could destroy masculinity and stability through her wily femininity. The novel opens with a young American, Jack Morton, encountering the alluring and enigmatic Irène Lambesco-Thurston in a café in Casablanca. Irène is Romanian, and she had married an American who died a while ago. Mandelstamm paints Irène as a "young woman, in all the flowering of a woman of thirty, with bronzed hair, coiffed a little in the old style in a heavy chignon on her neck, with a little snub nose, with slightly slanted black eyes. Dresses, of a perfect cut, underlined her svelte figure, and haute couture shoes her arched feet."[207] Irène notices Jack and strikes up a conversation with him, and by the end of their time at the café they are acting like old friends.

This description of a foreign seductress—dark, a little bit older, and somewhat voluptuous, with telltale signs of deviousness—stands in direct contrast with the novel's heroine, the young American Dorothy Sharpe, who eventually outwits Irène. Dorothy is "thin, of average height, with a fresh face, the delicate traits of a true blonde, a profile with a pure line and large grey eyes, full—at least in appearance—of candor."[208] Where Irène's description begets suspicion and suggests dissimulation, Dorothy, with "true" blond hair and "candor," is a physical embodiment of transparency. Dorothy is also the daughter of a very rich self-made man, but she lives simply, as these are the values her father instilled in her. Note the contrast between Dorothy and Irène, whose dresses are "of a perfect cut." Mandelstamm's language—specifically "at least in appearance"— briefly leaves the reader in the dark as to who the true heroine is, but it soon becomes clear that Dorothy, driven by love for Jack, will help bring down the temptress Irène.

In the novel, the female spy's appearance and actions both raised alarms about women and espionage specifically, and all women more generally. Irène, who was first introduced in the novel as sitting in a public space, a café/bar, by herself, used her feminine wiles to earn Jack's trust. She then plied him with drink until he revealed that he was an engineer working on a high-tech, secret robot. As the time passes, Jack and Irène strike up a deeper friendship, until Jack finally agrees to procure a visa to the United States for Irène, who has been dying to go back—she left after the death of her husband. Here, Irène's dirty and dissimulating tricks—using alcohol and seductiveness to gain Jack's trust—reveal the instability and treachery of the female spy.

In *V5*, Irène even broke up a stable relationship, the ultimate goal of women in the postwar period: Dorothy and Jack had planned to marry before he had to go away for work and to help with the war. Now Jack has returned to the United States and apparently spurned Dorothy by running off with Irène. Dorothy catches Irène as she is up to some nefarious doings, and she decides to inform Jack that his new love is, in fact, a spy for the Nazis, even cavorting with a known German who is wanted in the United States. Jack, in turn, locks Dorothy in his office, leading to a crisis of conscience on her part: Is Jack really a Nazi sympathizer, and if so, where should her loyalties lie? Even though it was Jack who had imprisoned Dorothy, she still placed the blame for what happened on Irène, wondering, "This woman was so captivating, this was sufficient to turn a head as solid as that of a man like Jack Morton! Was this, thus, the effect of what people call amorous passion?"[209] Dorothy's concern about her predicament is short-lived, for like any good woman, she is only willing to betray her man under one set of circumstances: if he turns against her nation. Dorothy comes to the conclusion that if such treason is the result of "amorous passion," she "would never be able to conceive of a passion like that!"[210] Dorothy acts as a foil to the treachery of Irène, for she is of constant character, and acts in the interests of her country and her relationship, while Irène only uses men for what she needs and then discards them.

The spy Irène continues her dastardly ways until the novel's climax, but ultimately the novel restores both political and gender balance. Irène eventually tries to discard Jack, who has followed her to her meeting with the Nazi spy. He goes to see Irène at the house, and she is there, and at first acting like a hostage as well. She claims she was brought to the house under false pretenses. Jack confesses that he had made a deal to sell his engineering plans to an enemy, pay off his debts, and start a new life in South America. She does not believe him, and refuses to go with him. A little later, he reveals that he knew she was a spy before they met in Morocco, and he used her to get closer to the enemy, as he is a spy for his country. Jack was thus in control the whole time—he knew how she would approach him, he knew what he was saying to her, he had only pretended to be drunk and talkative, all of it. She is angry, *especially that he never really loved her*, and he says, "You are a sorceress, Irène, and I am sure that you have thrown many heads into a spin! But, one day, didn't you even say that I had never said: 'I love you'? That ought to have made you think." Jack was not fooled by Irène's seductiveness, again a quality of a superlative masculine hero at this time.

To the affront that her seduction never worked, Irène responds: "Oh, naturally! I should have perceived that your heart was taken by that little stuck-up Dorothy Sharpe! Oh well, to each his tastes! I would have thought you more eclectic. Grave error on my part!"[211] Irène goes and gets Umbdecker, the aforementioned German spy, and he comes in and has Irène chain Jack to a chair. Umbdecker goes out of the room, and they hear shots. Irène opens the door, and the authorities storm into the room, followed by Dorothy who has learned the truth. In all the chaos, Irène escapes, but Jack and Dorothy only have eyes for one another. Later they learn that Irène committed suicide.

Ultimately Mandelstamm restates the "normal" order in terms of both politics (the rocket Jack developed is safe and not in the hands of the Germans) and gender. Irène, a female spy and as such a single woman in public, disgraces herself further through suicide, and Jack and Dorothy end up together. The man was in control the whole time and the true heroine won him.

Male spies

Portrayals of the *espionne* clashed strongly with images of male spies of the time, who came to resemble suave, calm James Bond types. Fears of contamination do not plague descriptions of male spies; their transparency is assumed, an assumption made in no small measure because the presence of men in public is normal and nonthreatening, unlike that of women. Rousseau-ian conceptualizations of gender stipulated that men were virtuous in public, while women were naturally devious.[212] Legally adapted during the French Revolution, the implications of this philosophy of gender included, according to Joan Scott, that "the political individual was . . . taken to be both universal and male; the female was not an individual, both because she was nonidentical with the human prototype and because she was the other who confirmed the (male) individual's individuality."[213] Almost a century later, men's ability to act autonomously, as Judith Surkis has shown, was foundational to definitions of male citizenship in the Third Republic.[214] Much like Mandelstamm's Jack, men's individual ability to act for the nation was not in doubt at the end of the war, and thus their masculinity did not need to be confined, unlike women and femininity.

Suaveness and calm, hallmarks of the male spy, were crucial for the reconstruction of French masculinity in a time when Charles de Gaulle called for French citizens' "order and ardour" in a speech on the day of Paris's Liberation.[215] If France was a female victim of Nazi aggression, as mobilizers of the Resistance myth intended to show, then her defenders—during the war, after the war, and in postwar accounts of wartime action—were both masculine and single-minded in their defense of the victimized, female nation. In that same speech, de Gaulle insisted that all men in France only wanted to "show ourselves, up to the end, worthy of France." Indeed Mathilde Carré's biographer describes her Resistance circle as full of men who were itching to fight for France, either through combat or espionage. Young points to Marc Marchal as one such example. "By the time the Second World War arrived," Young writes, "Marchal was happily married with four children yet, at 49, he had promptly volunteered again for a tank regiment." France's surrender did not diminish Marchal's commitment to his nation: "When his friends congratulated him on his safe return [from combat] he told them, echoing the words of de Gaulle, 'Not so fast—I joined up for the duration of the war, and for me the war isn't finished—it's only just beginning.'"[216] Marchal was betrayed by Carré and sent to Mathausen concentration camp. He survived the war, but died in 1950. Young remembered Marchal as a true Resistance hero in the vein of French male victims, who encouraged his children to "think of your duty before you think of your rights."[217] Male spies were strong, decisive, and unswervingly loyal in their work for the interest of the nation.

Depictions of male spies stand in marked contrast to images of Mathilde Carré, who cracked immediately under interrogation and became a double agent. She was therefore neither cool nor trustworthy. Contrast this with depictions of one such French agent, Pierre de Vomécourt, whom Young refers to as "dapper, with lively intelligent eyes, a calm manner and a cool, clear brain. He had also a fervent sense of patriotism and great personal courage."[218]

Perhaps most importantly, male spies were seen as always in control of their situations. For example, in *V5*, Jack was playing a spy game that occurred well over Irène's head; he pretended to be interested in her, but was really exploiting her rather than the other way around. Philippe de Vomécourt, Pierre's brother and head of a major spy network, was described in *Figaro* as having "duped" the Germans through his mastery of secret spy techniques. An article in *Le Monde* emphasized that Vomécourt had "parachuted into France in May 1944," again signifying his bravery and patriotism.[219] A headline from another article about Vomécourt, which appeared on the front page of *Le Monde*, stated that he was a *compagnon de la Libération*, furthering his credibility as a French hero and as a masculine fighter for France, categories which had a good amount of crossover.[220] Vomécourt testified in court that he came to suspect Mathilde Carré's motives early on, for she was a little "too curious." As a superlative French hero, he was impervious to her treachery. Once he found out for sure, he testified, he sat her down and "ordered" her to confess, saying, "Your turn to talk, *mignonne*." At this point Carré tearfully broke down—Young states that she lost her trademark "jauntiness"—and agreed to work with Vomécourt to undermine the Germans.[221] "She was a woman without scruples," *Le Parisien libéré* reported Vomécourt as testifying, "but she permitted us to strike a great blow."[222] Vomécourt's contemporary, Ben Cowburn, reported the incident in his memoir as well, highlighting Vomécourt's utter control over the situation: "He could, of course, have killed her on the spot, but decided not to. . . . [She] could be put to our own use with skilful[*sic*] handling."[223] Through his cool assessment of the situation, Vomécourt reestablished French authority over a rogue woman's challenge and even played the situation to France's advantage.

In fact Vomécourt, according to coverage, still had the power to weaken Carré. While other reporters emphasized Carré's relatively jaunty attitude toward the trial, after Vomécourt's testimony, Armand Gatti of *Le Parisien libéré* described her as "doubled over in her box [waiting] for the storm to pass. But it could well be that once this storm passes, there remains for her only the view of the washed-out mornings reserved for traitors."[224] Later, Young reports, Vomécourt ended up a well-to-do businessman in Paris "with an attractive wife."[225] Here his wife and wealth appear as natural rewards for the masculine spy Vomécourt's loyalty to France.

Likewise, another male French spy reported later that he suspected Carré's wavering loyalty well before her betrayal of France. Michel Brault, a lawyer, reported that "The She-Cat worried me almost from the start. For one thing, she would sometimes quite gaily boast of the personal contacts which she was having with people working for the Germans and with the Germans themselves—it was enough to scare you out of your wits!"[226] Whether or not Brault actually did have suspicions about Carré during the war, his postwar damnation of her is more important, for this was the time when it was crucial to reestablish a strong masculine authority, from the highest levels of government down. In these cases, a male spy was in control and a female had been put in her place in an exemplary manner. French masculinity was firmly in charge of the feminine threats to the public sphere in France.[227]

There is a highly telling counterpart to the story of Mathilde Carré: her lover, Roman Czerniawski, was also imprisoned by the Germans as a result of her betrayal. However, the Germans freed Czerniawski, who was known as Brutus in espionage networks, and sent him to England to work as a spy for them. Once there, like Carré, he went to MI-5, became a double agent, and ran missions for the Allies, including spreading false intelligence to the Germans about the D-Day invasions. Yet it was Carré who was put on trial. Perhaps Czerniawski never betrayed anyone, and that is the crucial difference between the two, but it also seems as though the French and Polish had more faith in the intentions of this male spy than in Mathilde Carré.[228] Unlike the female spy, the male spy is not transgressing gender boundaries, he is not automatically presumed to be lying; while his actions might be problematic, his publicity is not.

Portrayals of feminine espionage, like that of Irène in Valentin Mandelstamm's *V5*, showed that the dissimulation of the female spy was threatening to the extent that she could influence international affairs through her uncontrolled sexuality. Additionally, the case of real female spies, such as Mathilde Carré, also promoted the perils of women in public. Carré had no real loyalty to any side, but simply took the most expedient course. Perhaps most pernicious about both Irène and Mathilde Carré, their true natures were unidentifiable; any woman could be a spy. In contrast, male spies were cool under pressure and unwavering in their loyalty to their countries, a crucial criterion for public credence in the postwar period when "order and ardour" were of the utmost importance.

Taken together, images of female spies and torturers presented a dystopian vision of the possibilities of unconfined womanhood in postwar France. Without authentic attachments to love, beauty, and family, the unbound woman threatened the stability of postwar society. In order to combat the threat posed by her, governmental and social institutions punished accused spies and torturers—real or fictional—quite harshly, even when compared to their male counterparts. The public component of these punishments served to instruct all Frenchwomen of the perils of nonconformity and confine the potential range of their behavior.

Women as Voters

Introduction

In 1944, a report issued by the Renseignements Généraux (RG), France's intelligence service, expressed ambivalence about women voting:

> At present, French women constitute more than 60% of the electorate. With this right and this majority, can we say that the French woman, and her country, find themselves at the dawn of a new era? It is indisputable that the vote of women is the great unknown of the next elections. Too much data remains imprecise, the confusion of political positions is currently too great for us in this study to make clear prognoses.[1]

The RG need not have worried. In 2014, for the seventieth anniversary of women's enfranchisement in France, the television channel TV5MONDE interviewed several women who had voted for the first time during that first election in 1944. One of the women, Christine Auvray, remembered that it took years for her to realize that voting could be a tool of power for her—and for all women—in society. For that first election, though, she recalled, "I voted like my husband. I was not the only one. I had no personal opinion at the time. I posed all my questions to my husband. In the beginning, I asked him for advice, for at 23, I knew nothing about [politics]. In our day, nobody told us about it. *And we women did not talk about it so much with each other.*"[2] [emphasis mine]

The French press played an outsized role in shaping the actualities of and narratives around women voting. Historians have particularly studied how major newspapers acted to instruct women about the machinations of the voting act.[3] Newspapers also, historian Sandra Fayolle has argued, could influence women voters politically in an outsized way. If people in most French homes read only one paper, and that paper was purchased by the male head of the house, then his political proclivity, as expressed by his newspaper, became the major influence on the home's female occupants.[4] But this narrative does not take into account the massive presence of the feminine press in homes at the end of the war, as well as their potential influence on women in ways that are both obviously political and more subtly so. Expanding the definition of political speech to include the feminine press allows for a more complete analysis of those early elections.

Historians and political scientists have noted how women's early voting trends tended to mirror the political opinions of their husbands, echoing the experience of Christine Auvray. Women's deference to their husbands, at least politically, seems unsurprising given the conditions and exigencies of the long Liberation. This book has dealt with the reestablishment of masculine authority and the confinement of femininity at the end of the war, despite the enactment of women's enfranchisement following generations of struggle.

Women voting deferentially to the male authorities in their lives having been established, there exists a further, unexplored factor in the history of women's suffrage: the active suppression of female solidarity which, while not measurably linked to the vote,[5] enjoyed a stunning concomitance worthy of analysis. While Auvray describes what could best be called mutual ignorance at the onset of the vote, more actively, postwar women's magazines were full of letters and stories about women who feared the pernicious presence of other women in their lives. These women were portrayed as licentious and potentially harmful to the stability of the home. The advice pointed to a theme of fear among women about other women in general, as well as a sense that her man needed her protection from these types. In *Marie-France* in April 1949, for example, a woman wrote to the magazine with just such a problem. In the letter, "A Shadow Passes," from "Little Forlorn Mother," a young widow was making overtures onto LFM's husband, causing tumult in her personal life. "I am 36 years old," she wrote, "we were living happily, my husband, our two daughters and me. A young widow made advances towards my husband. I came upon her by chance in a car with him." It is impossible to say how this seduction scenario actually played out, even assuming that the letter is actually genuine, but either way it is interesting that LFM assumes that it was the "other woman" who was responsible for seducing the man. The fact that LFM argues that the other woman seduced her husband rather than the other way around, and constructs her letter to say: "I came upon her . . . with him" rather than "I came upon the two of them" emphasizes that the other woman is to blame. The letter goes on to universalize her plight: "It's always the same thing, women throw themselves around the neck of men, [the men] feel flattered and poorly defend themselves."[6] Here this statement creates universalized gender norms and fears of women: women are desperate, they throw themselves at men, and men are too weak to resist.

Women's magazines seemingly fomented a heightened sense of fear about other women. In November 1947, for example, a young woman, "Jacotte, from the Sarthe," wrote to *Ève* asking for advice about her fiancé. While he "seemed very attached to me," Jacotte had just recently found out that he had been with another woman while he was away and that the other woman was pregnant and he had to marry her instead of Jacotte. The catch, according to Jacotte, was that "the child was born more than ten months after their marriage: so he lied to me? I am in despair, as, at least, I thought him sincere." The response from *Ève* suggested that while it was possible that the woman had believed that she was pregnant, it was also possible that both Jacotte and her erstwhile fiancé had been victims of the other woman. The response went on: "She could have told him [that she was pregnant] while knowing that it wasn't true: that happens. So he could have been in good faith."[7] Here the magazine plants the possibility that the woman in question deliberately deceived the man, and in turn Jacotte, by seducing him, claiming to be pregnant, and then entering into a marriage under false pretenses.

This chapter will explore anxieties about women voters, first looking at women's magazines and messages of anti-solidarity, as well as more mainstream press sources, and then exploring the lack of a feminist movement. If confinement was the common element to explaining postwar femininity, then nowhere would its expression be more potent—or important—than at the ballot box.

Magazines and universal female suspicion

In a 1946 fictional piece in *Elle* magazine, "It happened last night," by Claude Letourneur, the author gives a description of the appearance of a dangerous postwar pariah, a woman who chose not to conform to postwar gender norms. In this case, Letourneur described the incomprehensibly alluring Adèle: "Her hair is red, which is fine, but most people like blondes or brunettes. Adèle doesn't care. She even puts rouge on her hair to accentuate it. And she doesn't put a wave or a curl in her hair—she straightens it! You get the picture." In this case, the description of Adèle is that of a nonconformist, a woman who bucks the trends and has her own look and cares little if others like it. Here, the author assumes a sort of camaraderie with the readers about Adèle, assuming both that readers know women "like this" and that they are not this type of woman. Clearly, a nonconforming woman like Adèle was an undesirable and even threatening model for other women.[8]

The theme also appeared that women who eschewed proper feminine behavior possessed a mystical quality that lured men, despite men's better sense and their existing romantic ties. Most importantly, though, those women were indistinguishable from adherents of proper behavior, rendering them all the more threatening. In the preface to Claude Letourneur's "It happened last night," for example, the description of the story is: "He could have chosen the most beautiful woman, or the richest, or the most spiritual, but he was taken with Adèle."[9] Just as a female spy was unmarked and as such could seduce a man and steal his secrets at the most delicate of times, so a more generic seductress could lure a man away from his obligations through some mysterious elixir she possessed. A woman had to be aware of this possibility and stay on her guard, wary of other women's motives. The war continued for the proper French woman, but now the battle focused on warding off female threats to her man.

If a spy by definition could hide her true identity, similarly, a seductress could be so unrecognizable that she could take the most familiar forms, including a woman's best friend. In one advice column, a woman, "Fleur des Champs," recounted how, during her third pregnancy, she asked her best friend, a single woman, to come and help keep her house in order. As the chapter on beauty showed, being an efficacious housekeeper was a way to retain one's man and keep him happy. In this case, though, such efforts backfired, as the friend grew uncomfortably close to the husband, and FdC wrote in because she was unsure of what to do. The response from *Marie-France* was unequivocal: get rid of her. The magazine urged the letter writer to act quickly: "It is necessary to create a very serious pretext, and quickly, in order to regain the harmony of your home. . . . It is always a great danger to move a female friend into one's house."[10] In another example of this, an advice column in *Ève* magazine printed a letter from, a young woman, "Michou, la petite Tourangelle," (Michou, the little woman from Tours), who wrote that her boyfriend wanted to get engaged, despite the interdiction of her parents, who had reservations because of Michou's age. Michou's dilemma is that she desperately wants to tell someone and seek outside advice, and she asked if *Ève* recommended that she trust her best friend, Jacquotte. *Ève* responded: "If you have confidence in Jacquotte, be frank with her: but be sure, beforehand, that she deserves your trust. There are so many disappointments in friendship, as many as in love."[11] Any outside woman, even a woman's best friend, faced severe scrutiny over her trustworthiness and the potential that she could contaminate romantic stability.

A woman's skepticism and resourcefulness in the face of a female menace could be a source of great pride. One story, "Perfidy," by Marcelle Segal, also the editor of *Elle*'s *Courrier du cœur* advice column, depicted Toinon, a French war bride who married an American and moved to New York with him. While there, she met Barbara, Patrick's erstwhile girlfriend, who was obviously still smitten with Patrick. Barbara invited the two of them to a dinner at her parents' house, and while there it became clear that the entire point of the evening was to show Patrick how he had married beneath him. Barbara spent the whole night emphasizing Toinon's humble beginnings and her lack of education. Toinon was upset, and let it show, and later Patrick told her: "Darling, I was ashamed of you today. It is the first time and I want it to be the last. Do you hear?" A few weeks later, a gift arrived from Barbara, and Toinon hid it. Patrick asked about it—apparently Barbara had written to ask how he liked it—and Toinon asked why Barbara was contacting him at all, prompting another lecture from Patrick. The next day, Toinon opened the gift, discovering a broken mess of porcelain. Toinon panicked because she thought Patrick would assume she had broken it in anger, and so she spent two whole days putting it back together. She presented the reconstructed flying bird to Patrick, and he tried to put it in the wooden box in which it arrived, but it would not fit: "He looked at Toinon. In the gray eyes of the petite Burgundian, silent, he saw a kind of gleam, like an air of triumph."[12] No other woman would get the best of her.

Fears of other women were not necessarily limited to those who could become sexual rivals; all women could potentially disrupt the sanctity of home life and relationships. In February 1948, a reader, "Mlle H.P . . . à Troyes," wrote in to *Ève* about her boyfriend's stepmother, who had told her some "displeasing things" about the stepson. The boyfriend found out and stopped seeing Mlle H. P., but "chance reunited us; he is again paying attention to me." She wanted to know what to do, as she still loved him. The magazine responded that she still had a chance at real love with the man, who was probably just fearful that "the idle gossip of his stepmother influenced you and that you ceased to hold him in esteem." The magazine advised Mlle H. P. to go to him and tell him that she did not believe his stepmother and she still loved him.[13] Here a meddling stepmother, rather than a sultry seductress, almost prevented the all-important stability of marriage.

In a much more thorough example of non-seductive threatening women, in June 1948 *Ève* published a story by Vera Volmane called "Should she remake her life?" The story centered on the relationship between two wealthy sisters, Colette and Solange, who live together in their parents' old house. One day, the mail comes, and there is a letter from Georges, Colette's estranged husband. As always, Solange takes control of it, reads it, and then discards it. Apparently, Georges wants Colette to come with him to sign papers to get an advance on his insurance. Solange forbids it, but Colette is willing to do it. Solange tells her to think of all of the pain he caused, wonders how he even dares to write her, and Colette responds that he did not do anything. Solange says that he cheated, and Colette says, yes, but nine of ten husbands cheat. This certainly reflects the sentiments of the chapter on love, where women were to expect infidelity on the part of their men.

Ultimately, Solange persuades her that Georges was unacceptable, as she always does—Solange has a way of arguing that Colette cannot seem to counter. And she tells Colette that she will go with them to the insurance agency that evening. Secretly, Colette thinks of helping Georges with her own money. After Solange leaves for the day, Colette thinks of all the memories she and Georges have together: going to their favorite restaurant, vacations... her favorite memory was of a time when he needed her help and said she was "indispensable" for him. He always liked a bit of distance from her normally, though, with his Sundays spent playing sports and the like with his male friends. It was true, he never prevented her from spending time with her friends, and he and his friends never did anything untoward. Once, Colette fell ill with a nasty flu and went to Bourges for two weeks to recover. Upon her return, she saw that the house had fallen into total disorder, and so she enlisted the maid to help her clean. "In her zeal" to clean, Colette even went through her husband's wardrobe. There, she found a note that proved his infidelity. She laid it out for him and left before he came home, fleeing to Solange's, where there was the familiarity of her youth. She had intended to stay for a few days, maybe as punishment, but Solange convinced her to stay longer, and then to get a divorce, convening a court of public opinion and convincing all of Colette's friends that she should leave him. But divorce? No, for "[Colette] would never consent to a divorce, saying that this procedure couldn't change anything, for religious marriage remained indissoluble." For her part, Solange had to cede this point.

Colette had to admit to herself that she was getting really sick of Solange—she could barely stand her anymore. She thought back on her days of courtship with Georges. Georges was from such a different background, as he told her, working already at fifteen; he would never take any of her money. One night, she did have hints of his infidelity—they went out dancing in Montparnasse and the dancers knew him there; they left quickly and he did not want to talk about it.

Then the doorbell rang, announcing that Georges was there. He was early! She thought about waiting for Solange, but then just went with him. It was like no time had passed. Things were so familiar. They went to the insurance company and signed the papers, then he suggested a drink, and so they went. He made a phone call, and she ordered their usual: two French Vermouths. And she bought his usual daily and separated out the sports pages for him to read, as always. And he read them, making his comments, which were a little rough, but which she had always found so attractive.

While she and George were spending time together, Colette began to feel pity for Solange. They left the café and got into the car; because of all the traffic, Georges asked her to help get him out of his spot. She did, as always. And then he asked where they would dine that night, and she said their usual restaurant, "of course!" And then he said, "in a muffled voice, 'And to think it was so simple!'" And so many emotions ran through Colette, so many things she wanted to say, to tell him about Solange and her "destructive work." But all she could muster was, "Yes."[14] In this instance, it is not the seductress who ultimately proved to be the greatest obstacle to Colette's happiness and the stability of her union; rather it was her imperious, single older sister, whose selfishness nearly wrecked Colette's marriage. Thus any (and every) woman could become a source of romantic instability.

Mistrust among women was not limited to the pages of women's magazines. It even affected the phenomenon of the *femmes tondues* during the Occupation, when the inaugural issue of the newspaper put out by the *Union des femmes françaises* (UFF), born of female Resistance groups, encouraged French women to promote shaving to those around them. They viewed this as a way for proper French women to protect their sons from the pernicious influence of dissimulating women:

> French mothers, defend your sons against the females of the Gestapo. . . . Explain how they should resist these revolting bitches of the Gestapo. First never reveal their true identity and introduce themselves to them under a false name. Then pretend to accept all they are offering, get them into a trap, punish them severely, shave off their hair down to the skin, and finally take their identity card. The photograph will help identify them and punish them later when the time comes. A number of fine young men have been deported and even shot as a result of the actions of prostitutes working for the Gestapo. Say it, repeat it to yourselves, you will then steer them clear of one of the most serious dangers threatening us at the moment.[15]

The angry rhetoric the UFF espoused in this piece indicates that women ought to be extremely wary of the influence and intentions of the women around them. Since denunciations were often faulty and could be the result of old grudges and problems, it could be unclear who was actually in the Gestapo, and thus a mist arose around who was actually a threat.[16] Ironically, in this case the quote promotes dissimulation among men in order to catch these apparently threatening women. As seen previously, dissimulation could be a positive tool in the interest of gender stability, especially if it was clear that the primacy French masculinity remained unthreatened.

It is interesting to consider how the labeling of certain women as seductresses, and, as such, threats to the stability of relationships, might have ultimately created a subversive sense of unity among French women, who could bond against such "bad" women. But the stories do not necessarily allow for that possibility; because the characteristics of such women were not fixed or knowable, the stories above highlight that it was important to trust no one. And even such groups as the UFF, whose ultimate goal was to support women's rights and solidarity, put this aside in favor of the public punishment of female threats to men.[17] In this context, every other woman represented a potential threat, and if French women were still at war to regain their homes, then they needed to take drastic action to counter all such threats.

Confining the vote

"In France politics is a machine, and women detest mechanics."
—Marcelle Segal, advice columnist for *Elle*[18]

"A woman who took interest in politics, for narrow-minded people, this was inevitably a woman whose life was incorrect."
—Odette Roux, PC, Mayor of Sables d'Olonne, 1945–47[19]

Many historians have pointed out that the Liberation of France did not translate into a more expansive liberation for French women, despite the enfranchisement of women in 1944.[20] Female enfranchisement achieved two main postwar political goals: it rewarded women for their Resistance participation and it allowed France to come into line with all of the rest of the Great Powers.[21] On the surface, and perhaps in the long run, it was an important shift in women's political lives. Through their voting, women gained an official public role, and perhaps ultimately the dissonance between their political rights and their actual lives caused some women to agitate against a patriarchal system. However, the addition of the cultural imperative against female solidarity—along with strong pushes for female domesticity such as the caveat that female Resistance participators were expected to return to the home—changed this picture of progress. It allowed for the preservation of the political status quo, which was entirely masculine.

An article in the newspaper *Combat* from September 1944 supports the idea of the vote as both reward for Resistance heroism and a bribe for not challenging postwar gender norms, and it negates the idea of the vote as a liberating force. It detailed the first marriage performed by a female in the seventeenth *arrondissement* of Paris, by a Mme Fillatre, whose husband had died during the war while he was being held hostage. Fillatre argued that she and other women had the right to enjoy citizenship in France because "French women led, for four years, side by side with men, the war against the oppressor. . . . They revealed themselves to be [men's] equals in the hours of danger. They have won the right to be [men's] equals in liberated France."[22] This woman, whom *Combat*, a leftist newspaper, presents as justification for women's participation in French political life, was herself clearly a victim in the vein of the earlier chapter. The article tells her story, about how she was with her husband when he was killed, and how she was spared only because she was pregnant with their third child. This presents her as a widow, a Resistance member, and a mother, and thus a safe public woman. Her public identity of widowhood automatically suggests a masculine complement, her deceased husband. During the marriage, the article continues, Mme Fillatre became "emotional," which the author attributes to her thoughts of her husband's sad fate and her own marriage in happier times: "Maybe she relived her own marriage. She thinks perhaps about her husband, whom she will never see again."[23] In the guise of supporting female enfranchisement, *Combat* renders emblematic a woman who argues that she deserves the vote because of her wartime sacrifice, not her innate right to be a citizen. The vote represented repayment for women for their wartime service as well as a bribe to send them back to the private sphere and put a definitive end to any thoughts of extending their public lives.

Attempts to minimize or marginalize the power of the female vote at official levels began almost immediately upon its being granted, preventing women from assuming a measure of equality and political power. As historian

Sandra Fayolle argues, "This attitude [of diminution] was reflected at all levels of government and reflected a clear political choice: not to emphasize the 'exceptionality' of this first ballot. No official statement makes any reference to it, and when de Gaulle spoke before the elections, he did not mention the subject."[24] When he did actually address women's enfranchisement, Charles de Gaulle sought to render it more palatable, presenting it as "continuing a feminine tradition of duty and thinking of others."[25] The enfranchisement of women was undoubtedly a major development, a rectification of a long-standing injustice, and probably allowed for greater gains for women in the future. It also, as this book has argued, served the French both nationally and internationally. Voting was not, however, meant to be empowering for French women, and cultural sources played a role in the mitigation of the influence of this expansion of rights.

There were numerous cultural attacks on female solidarity which occurred at the very moment when women were being enfranchised. This is interesting given that one of the greatest historical fears surrounding women and the vote was that they would weaken men. As Margaret Collins Weitz shows, political players on the French Right feared that women would be overwhelmingly influenced by the Left or indeed become "militant leftists," while those on the Left were apprehensive of close ties between women and the Church.[26] Each of these fears had to do with concerns about undue influence by others over women's voices (and lost votes), but each also reflected a general anxiety that women's political participation would be monolithic and thus threaten male political dominance. On top of this, there was also the controversy of giving women the vote while so many French men were still prisoners and out of the country. In this context, some members of the provisional government in Algiers feared that "women's vote would 'distort' the political balance."[27] "Is it really appropriate," the politician François Giacobbi asked, "to replace universal male suffrage with universal female suffrage?" In addition to overpowering men demographically, politicians cited fears of voter fraud, lack of education, and an inability to functionally create voter lists as impediments to women voting.[28] Thus tensions over female power and its potential to unseat existing male dominance ran high even during wartime debates about female enfranchisement.

Primary sources from the time reflect these continuing anxieties—on the part of both men and women—about women's newfound role as *électrices* and their potential for causing disarray and corrupting the standing political order. In the Resistance paper *Combat 44*, for example, a young woman penned an article about women's roles in these confusing times. She came down solidly on the side of women staying in the private sphere:

> And all this, education, customs, this has always been our own domain, us women. The thoughts that live in the home, the words and the examples that gently influence husbands, that slowly form the sensibilities of the young—and the silent demand of young girls, whom we know will prefer a bold heart and a noble life to money and security. All of this was our kingdom. Well before the ballot. And it remains so, with the ballot.[29]

Lest there be any doubt about what the newspaper hoped for in terms of women's post-enfranchisement roles, an article the next month—this time presumably by a man—was also about the vote and the headline urged women to "Stay Naïve."[30] In the Leftist Resistance newspaper *Le Centre Républicain*, a writer said that he was less than "enthused" about women voting, and went on to argue that women "owed [men] obedience and fidelity," for men had been quite "tolerant" of women's needs and digressions, even under the unmodified Civil Code. With all of this good will toward French women on the part of French men, the writer posed the question, "What are you [women] still hungry for?" He also emphasized that he was not even sure women actually wanted to vote or would vote given the chance; he cited the example of women in Spain and their support of Franco as evidence of the dangers of the female franchise.[31] The famous satirical newspaper *Le Canard enchaîné* depicted three types of women at the ballot box: nun, homemaker, and prostitute. These three women stood for all women of France and, the paper noted, none voted appropriately.[32]

In the context of these persistent anxieties, media sources such as magazines and mainstream newspapers emphasized that female enfranchisement was not as groundbreaking as it seemed, and it would not threaten the stability and sanctity of masculine French politics. In making these arguments, they effectively confined the power of the vote, just as other sources had confined the boundaries of women's proper postwar behavior. Newspapers addressed the continuing ambivalence surrounding women's influence on French life through the vote. An article for *Le Monde* in May 1945 about women voting in Great Britain soothed readers' anxieties about women voting just as the results of the municipal elections were coming in. First it posed the question, "What have been the consequences of their participation for the political life of the country?" It then answered by saying that British women, who had voted since the end of the Great War, tended to concern themselves much more with "social and moral issues" than with the business of serious policy.[33] Georges Ravon, a columnist for *Figaro*, also attempted to allay male fears about women voting in a front-page piece: "We [men] were assured that the accession of women to political rights would destroy the good harmony of households and would compromise [our] marital authority. Loyalty obliges me to say that political discussions are less acerbic, under my roof, than those born of deficient *ravitaillement* or false announcements at bridge games."[34] *Elle* magazine also held the view of the vote as an international measuring stick, a place for France to prove itself, rather than as a step in the direction of political equality, thereby dismissing the enfranchisement as a major sociopolitical moment. In the very first issue of the magazine, an article used the number of women France had elected as proof of the country's superiority over the *anglo-saxonnes*, where yes, women had the vote for much longer, but they were doing so poorly in terms of representation.[35] On a governmental level, the state did organize orientation meetings about voting rights for women. When politicians spoke at the meetings, however, any remarks addressed to women dealt only with *ravitaillement*. As famous feminist Louise Weiss remembered:

> During the electoral meetings I had the pleasure of attending, either from the audience or from the stage, I noticed that the candidates spoke to the women only about soup, bottle, steak, laundry, gas or metro prices. They did not give them any sense of the general order of things. Sometimes they ventured to talk to them, in slightly higher terms, about their role in the home, their role as educators, but never about the relations between France and England, the United States, Russia, our economic or colonial interests, or details of the future constitution. It was pitiful.[36]

The vote was simply a way for France to retain (or perhaps regain) Great Power status, *not* a revolutionary change. Major newspapers and magazines, along with the state itself, explicitly and implicitly acknowledged male worries about women voting, and more specifically the "female vote," and then dismissed them with claims that women were simply disinterested in high politics, and thus they would not damage male authority.[37]

Additionally, if women feared and mistrusted other women, a sentiment promoted by the women's magazines of the day, any female cohesion and resultant undue influence and contagion would be rendered far more difficult; women voting would make little tangible difference in France. In fact, in France as in other Western countries, such fears were ultimately unfounded, as female solidarity did not materialize in women's actual voting records; there was no "female vote."[38] Nor did women make up a major proportion of elected officials;

they represented 4 percent of deputies and 5 percent of senators, and that number very quickly dropped off.[39] Claire Duchen cites contemporary French political scientists' conclusions that "women tended to vote like men from the same social class" rather than along sexual lines, a fact she regards as proven by the markedly similar voting trends between 1936 and 1946.[40] The female solidarity that men had feared as a threat to their power ultimately did not transpire; the menace of unified female contagion was neutralized.

Voting and women's magazines

Just as there was diversity in women's voting affiliations, so there could exist competing messages in the pages of women's magazines. Perhaps this ambiguity, at least at *Elle*, can be partially attributed to the seemingly opposing viewpoints of the two editors, Hélène Gordon-Lazareff, who thought it was women's duty to be seductive, and Françoise Giroud, who was somewhat more expansive in her views on women's roles.[41] In fact the Swedish art director for *Elle* from the 1950s to the 1960s, Peter Knapp, later said of Lazareff: "She sincerely believed that women were equal, if not superior, to men. . . . That's why she wasn't much of a feminist. She never understood why women wanted to fight for something they already had."[42] The expectation that the magazine would in some way transcend rather than reflect or create a more staid reality in terms of gender norms is misguided.

It is important to acknowledge the possibility of a more positive view of the historical contribution of women's magazines to French women at this time, that they represented at least some sort of voice for women after the war. Françoise Giroud herself believed this, and indeed she encouraged *Elle* readers to vote in elections.[43] As is clear, the magazines also provided useful advice to women facing the material shortages and other difficulties of the postwar era. However, magazines like *Elle* were not liberatory vehicles. As Véronique Vienne writes, "In 1945, French women voted for the first time but the magazine's only comment on election days was to tell readers what to wear to the polls." Vienne agrees to a certain extent with Giroud's own assertion that the magazine could ask deep and controversial questions, and she especially points to Giroud's own work as an example of this, "but," she continues, "the answers were always deeply conservative."[44] The magazines, while occasionally progressive for their day, still emitted messages about disunity alongside their potent embrace of femininity to French women that would ultimately negate magazines' rarer progressive visions.

In the magazines, there were calls for women to have an independent voice within the voting process, but only to a certain extent. For example, in a column by Paul Géraldy, a short-lived advice columnist for *Elle*, he seemed to embrace women's independence of thought, but he preferred women's opinions to be tied to those of their husband. At one point, seeming to hope for women's autonomy in voting, he states, "Younger women romantically vote the same way as their husbands, lovers, boyfriends. More experienced women often vote the opposite. Hopefully more women will join the ranks of the experienced." Yet earlier in the article he writes that he wishes that a wife would "share all of her convictions with her husband. . . . This would be a dream. I'm not saying you shouldn't dream, of course. Reality needs Dream as its correction and its opposition. Female voters should apply all of their strength to sharing the convictions of the man that they love." According to Géraldy, this sharing of convictions does not at all imply a woman's subordination to her man.[45] Instead, he considers this to be her natural role. This article appeared in the same issue of *Elle* as the article from the previous paragraph which celebrated the number of women elected to the Assembly. The confluence of two inharmonious messages further highlights the ambiguities women's magazines seemed to espouse when it came to women's enfranchisement and polling choices. Reading the magazine, it is unclear what a woman ought to do and be as a voter—exactly like her husband or true to her own beliefs. The answer seemed to be resolved in 1947, when *Elle* printed a survey devoted to how men liked their women, entitled, "A Grand Survey from *Elle*: This is How Men Like You." The survey listed a large number of qualities men either liked or disliked in their women, including "Be a gourmand," and "Have another man look at you." One of the most one-sided answers was for the statement: "Vote according to her opinions and not according to yours."[46] This was fairly striking, especially in the postwar context, when attracting and pleasing one's man was a woman's primary duty. In this way, messages about women voting could imbue a mild subversion into women's magazines. The subversion was especially gentle, considering that it was only acceptable because it was explicitly sanctioned by women's husbands.

Ultimately, these types of messages praising women's independence of thought were rarer exceptions to a more confined, traditional portrayal. Just two weeks after printing the survey that showed that men wanted women to vote for themselves, *Elle* printed another article, "Monsieur Mayor Wears a Long Skirt," praising the success of the vote and of female politicians, who "remain women and are interested in their family, their home, their beauty."[47]

The depiction of motherhood as the opposite of politics, or at least completely outside of the political sphere, served to separate women from voting and limit their potential scope. The newspaper *Figaro* added to the confusion about women's voting roles in 1946 when it printed an article about Mother's Day that portrayed motherhood in opposition to politics and campaigns.[48] A similar message appeared in *Elle* in 1951, seven years after women's enfranchisement, in the *Elles à Elles* column, in which readers could write in and respond to articles or even other readers' letters. In this particular column, a reader named Mamie addressed the question of feminism: "Feminism? . . . Emancipated, woman must remain woman and not dress herself as a poorly raised child. We are, after all, the weaker sex, it's sometimes so good to feel so small near someone much stronger than yourself."[49] Just prior to women's first election, *Elle* counseled readers to look to their husbands for clarity at the ballot box, lest they become too overwhelmed and confused by the experience.[50] Finally, a May 1946 issue of the magazine *La Femme*, which was published by the official *Mouvement de Libération nationale* (National Liberation Movement), advised women to retain their femininity throughout the voting process so as not to discomfort their men: "If at the exit of the voting bureau, you fix up your mouth or use your compact, your husband will be reassured."[51] The magazine does not directly address the source of the man's stress, which seems to normalize and universalize these concerns.[52]

Presumably, a French man needed to be reassured that his woman had not lost her femininity in the voting booth, that she was still interested in pleasing him. In this way, the magazines did not necessarily view voting as a revolutionary act for women. Instead they rushed to encourage women to retain the stability of their romantic relationships and not upset the gender order through the public act of voting.[53] They did this while simultaneously promoting a culture of universal female suspicion, helping to preclude a feared female solidarity that would unseat stable, masculine power. Where marriage and romantic stability gave men a stable platform from which to exercise public power, universal female suspicion would help to prevent challenges to political stability.

A lag in women's postwar feminism and activism in France runs parallel to the lack of female solidarity that was evident in women's voting statistics as well as the messages proffered by women's magazines.[54] Women did not vote together, nor would (or will, potentially) they ever, but the general lack of energy for feminist movements suggests a larger lack of concern or solidarity about causes impactful for women. It seems to reveal that the confinement of women's roles was successful. Historian Sylvie Chaperon suggests that the feminist movement did not fade away at this time, but rather refocused, arguing that "diverse new organizations emerged and rubbed shoulders with the older ones." She goes on to note, though, that "these new groups rarely managed to last," and furthermore, any organization among women became increasingly polarized "between those influenced by Communism and those influenced by Catholicism." Chaperon uses the fact that female activists "knew each other" and "saw each other socially" as evidence that feminism was alive.[55] If feminism was indeed alive, it was certainly in a seriously depleted state.

The question of whether or not certain feminist groups remained active, especially politically, in the years immediately after the war becomes one of size and influence.[56] Staying prominent was admittedly a difficult task for feminists in the context of confining gender politics. In terms of size, Christine Bard points to a general silence among feminist groups after the war, many of which were simply shells of first-wave feminist associations: "It is necessary to wait for the middle of the 1950s to see the signs point to a renewal [in feminism], out of the remains of these aging associations."[57] Chaperon herself argues that the postwar years saw a continued decline in participation in the feminist movement from the interwar years, although she argues that this is more positive than the steep decline which other historians have cited. Other than Catholic and Communist feminist groups, Chaperon continues, such organizations were rare.[58] Structural and cultural pressures combined to urge women to return to the home and be constantly pleasant about their positions within the private sphere. These kinds of pressures could certainly contribute to precluding a strong advance in feminism in the immediate postwar years.

Pursuant to influence, it seems that feminist groups were again less important in the postwar years. Sylvie Chaperon herself states that these women "carried little weight in the new political context"[59] including the constitutional arena where, "after 1946, any progress in the field of women's rights slowed down to a snail's pace," despite the efforts of existing feminist groups.[60] Historians of postwar France echo the sense that traditional feminist groups "carried little weight" in the wake of war. Robert Gildea talks about the end of war as a strong return to femininity, and mentions only Simone de Beauvoir's *Second Sex* as a feminist moment in the immediate postwar period. It was not until 1964, according to Gildea, that Beauvoir's work helped to spark a cohesive feminist group, the Mouvement Démocratique Féminin, or MDF.[61] That leaves twenty years since the end of the war, and fifteen years since *Second Sex* was published. Likewise, Claire Duchen also locates the origins of postwar feminism during the 1950s and 1960s, and argues that Beauvoir's ambivalence toward feminism complicates any use of *Second Sex* as a founding text for postwar feminists.[62] The evidence strongly points to the fact that feminism as a whole was largely insignificant in French society following the Second World War.

Even among female writers, few directly expressed an overt feminism. Higonnet et al. point only to Virginia Woolf, Vera Brittain, and Simone de Beauvoir—who, ironically, would not self-identify as a feminist until the 1970s—as examples of feminist authors.[63] Revealingly, it was Simone de Beauvoir, the un-feminist, who was the most prolific of these three in the immediate postwar years. (Virginia Woolf died in 1941, and Vera Brittain's pacifism, born of her Great War experiences, rendered her somewhat of a pariah during the Second World War and the immediate postwar period in Britain.) While Higonnet et al. do suggest that some Western women authors, such as Mollie Panter-Downes, indirectly addressed injustice in her postwar writings, these examples emphasize how female artists after the Second World War did not necessarily lead a charge for a new feminist movement.[64] The end of war saw a domestic revolution in France, but this revolution, like the one that preceded it by nearly two hundred years, perceived women as a threat, and minimized their solidarity and access to power, despite female enfranchisement.

Conclusion

The concurrence of French female enfranchisement, the continuation of fears that women could wrest political control from men through their votes, as well as a strong and pervasive discourse about how women could not trust other women is quite remarkable. Attesting to the power of this narrative of separation, it was not until 1997 that French numbered more than 5 percent of elected officials.[65] As one historian has noted, despite Charles de Gaulle's gift of the vote, "the Gaullian scheme of things was always essentially masculine" in all spheres.[66] All of the anxiety was essentially for naught.

Scholars have long seen voting as the ultimate measure of national belonging, a joining together of natural and political rights into human rights. Once this occurs, people are thought to be full citizens of a country, to enjoy both the state's protection *and* an active voice in determining the makeup of that state.[67] In theory, women's ultimate access to political rights in 1944 completed a circular journey they had begun in the Enlightenment and French Revolution and was a rejection of a certain definition of female agency that had held powerful traction in France since those times.

The press played a major role in shaping narratives of voting, but a focus on more traditional political media ignores a rich source of political language: women's magazines. Placing the feminine press in dialogue with political developments actually reveals a concerted weakening of enfranchisement's potential power. If women did not trust other women, they would not band together and they would not unseat the patriarchy that had been a unifying thread of all French governments. The vote was not the end of anxieties about women's fitness for public life. To simultaneously officially release women from the bounds of patriarchy AND subtly reinforce it: this is the paradox of women's rights in Liberation France.

French women in the immediate postwar period had to take on many responsibilities, both tangible—be well dressed and present a varied and delicious cuisine, for example—and intangible—she always had to be pleasing to her man, no matter what her personal feelings, needs, or desires. The weight of these responsibilities must have been difficult to bear at times, and in a context when complaints were unwelcome, to say the least, many women were probably quite lonely, especially in the context of culturally enforced silence. This chapter points to why it was so strongly encouraged for women to be proper for France— not necessarily just for themselves and for the future of France and the French population, although this was quite important—but also because being a proper French woman was a way to identify oneself as NOT a spy and NOT a lesbian, and NOT a prostitute. In doing so, most importantly, one identified oneself as NOT a threat to France and French masculinity. In this context, the isolation of women politically, socially, and emotionally from each other bears extra significance. Ultimately, though, the silence would be broken.

Conclusion: *Le déluge*

Beginning in the late 1940s, a series of major cultural and political events combined to shift the boundaries of French gender identity created following the Second World War. While none point to national identity as a marker, several commentators have located a new historical moment in the early and middle 1950s in France. In fact, Françoise Giroud later called 1952 "the end of a certain postwar period."[1] She remembered this as a time when the national tides turned, stating:

> I have a feeling that if 1952 wasn't felt by the French as a whole to be a major turning point in history, it was nonetheless an important date. It was in that year that people began to be aware of the burning issues which involved the French: the war in Indochina with all its attendant consequences; Tunisia, which was a veritable tinderbox; the degree to which France was dependent on the United States.[2]

In 1953, Giroud herself left *Elle* for *L'Express*, a news magazine she co-founded with Jean-Jacques Servan-Schreiber, marking a subtle shift in direction for *Elle*, moving it further away from political topics.

In the realm of French politics, commentators began to historicize their wartime experiences and turn to new concerns.[3] Economically, it was in the early 1950s that French consumers felt the fruits of the *trente glorieuses*, or thirty glorious years; rationing had been heavy and common through the 1940s.[4] Print media, which had reached the apex of its readership immediately after the war, saw its circulation numbers drop from 15 million print copies per day in 1946 to 9.6 million in 1952, a trend which has continued almost without fail to this day.[5] The rise of television in the 1950s also contributed to this precipitous decline. The fashion industry and the nation of France mourned the death of Christian Dior in 1957 and fretted anxiously about the role of France in the fashion world—on a practical level, the House of Dior had come to constitute over half of French fashion's export sales.[6] On a more symbolic level, Dior's successor, Yves Saint Laurent, moved the House of Dior away from the aggressively feminine silhouette of the New Look, inventing the Trapeze line, which, despite maintaining an impressive invisible shaping structure, flared out from the shoulders in a triangular shape and sported a much higher hemline, a departure from the hourglass silhouette and more modest length of the New Look. Designated as a "youthful silhouette" by *New York Times* fashion reporter Anne-Marie Schiro, the Trapeze was another sign of attention turning away from postwar standards.[7] Saint Laurent also promoted ready-to-wear collections as the province of the most exclusive design houses.

Geopolitical developments also mark 1954 as a moment of major sea change. Henry Rousso argues that prolonged economic growth, Dien Bien Phu, and the beginning of Algerian escalation, among others, marked a turning point for the French, in which interior politics moved away from the war and toward questions of empire.[8] The imperial questions challenged the war generation's conceptions of gender, particularly of a pure, honorable masculinity. As Robert Gildea writes:

> The scandal that erupted over torture after 1957 exposed the cult of the French liberating and civilizing mission for the sham that it was and precipitated a painful reconsideration of French national identity. The myth of the French Resistance had reinforced the view that the French were always on the side of liberty and justice against oppression and injustice, but now it was demonstrated, little more than a decade after the Occupation, that the French were using the same tactics as the Gestapo.[9]

French atrocities helped to turn the next generation of Algerians against France. Instead Algerian fighters looked inward for government structures and Liberation-related inspiration. Indeed, Martin Evans argues, such accounts turned even some French people against the *patrie*, challenging accepted truths about the nobility of France's international and national goals. He cites the example of François Maspero, a leftist activist who, having founded a publishing house that first published Frantz Fanon's *The Wretched of the Earth* with Sartre's foreword, "[accused] the Republic of a betrayal of the spirit of Resistance. . . . In his opinion the cruelest irony was that the personal and collective liberation embodied in the Resistance was no longer located in France, but in the very Algerian rebels against whom the French army was fighting."[10] If, as historians have suggested, the Resistance myth was intimately linked to the construction of French masculinity and virility, the implications of this reconsideration of gendered French identity were no doubt great.

The confining boundaries of ideal French womanhood also faced challenges on several fronts in the middle of the 1950s. For example, new medical studies demonstrated French women's tendency toward nervous depression, linking this phenomenon to the limitations gender exigencies placed on their lives.[11] Another challenge to the dominant gender norms, albeit a complicated one, came in the form of Dominique Audry's *Story of O*, published in 1954 under the pen name Pauline Réage. The novel was quite well received, winning the Prix des Deux Magots, a major French literary award, in 1955. That same year French authorities also brought obscenity charges against the author, attesting to its shocking nature. It is in part a story about female subjugation in male/female relationships, as well as overall female objectification. The story centers on a female fashion photographer, O, who becomes a willing sexual slave for several masters. In the book's final scene, O dons a bird mask and is paraded on a chain, naked, in front of a large party. Authorship is a thorny issue here. Audry's identity did not become known until 1994, and many people assumed up to that point that it had been written by a man, despite the author's pseudonym. Thus some readers thought they were reading male fantasies about female sexual subjugation. However, the work does depict O in a series of sexually graphic situations that decidedly contradict the contemporary call for a heteronormative, natalist female sexuality.[12]

Perhaps the most important challenge to constructs of postwar womanhood came from Simone de Beauvoir's *Second Sex*, published in 1949, which Gildea refers to as a "lead balloon" in the postwar "atmosphere."[13] Beauvoir weaved her way through a thorough discussion of women's political, economic, and social status using existentialist and leftist theories, biology, and literature. In more than seven hundred pages of evidence and analysis, she disputed women's innate docility and nurturing, both of which had been painted as intrinsic to French femininity. In fact, Beauvoir issued a direct challenge to the notion of essential femaleness with her famous statement: "One is not born, but rather becomes a woman." This statement suggests that femininity and masculinity are not linked with a series of "eternal" or "natural" traits, but rather they evolve in response to ever-shifting cultural, social, and political variables. Beauvoir also defined men as the universal normative subject, and women as opposite: "He is the Subject, he is the Absolute—she is the Other."[14] Through these statements, Beauvoir provocatively asserted the subjugation of women. People read her work in high numbers—the book sold over

22,000 copies in the first week—but Beauvoir also faced harsh criticism for her theories.[15] In her memoirs, Beauvoir wrote of the response:

> I received—some signed and some anonymous—epigrams, epistles, satires, admonitions, and exhortations addressed to me by, for example, "some very active members of the First Sex." Unsatisfied, frigid, priapic, nymphomaniac, lesbian, a hundred times aborted, I was everything, even an unmarried mother. People offered to cure me of my frigidity or to temper my labial appetites; I was promised revelations, in the coarsest terms but in the name of the true, the good and the beautiful, in the name of health and even of poetry.[16]

Her work, however, served to question the gender norms that underpinned French society, specifically French femininity. Upon its appearance, Claire Duchen notes, the French public regarded the *Second Sex* with "outrage and hostility," and in January 1955 the newly reappeared women's magazine *Marie-Claire* even published an article discussing parents' fear of the book and its potential impact on their children.[17] These fears were apparently justified. As Duchen continues, "many women," especially those involved in the Second Wave of feminism, "pointed to the book as the turning-point for their own awareness of women's oppression and their own questioning of their lives."[18]

Each of these phenomena helped to tip the scales away from the confining gender identity posited at the end of the war and closer to the situation as it exists in France today. France is a multicultural society that, at least officially, turns a blind eye to identity-based differences such as race, gender, and sexuality. The French system does so in the hopes that this national blindness will bear out justice and equality. At the moment, the country again faces strong challenges to its official identity, especially from nonwhite, non-Christian, non-male members of society. This project posits that France adopted specific gender norms that confined the scope of women's lives in the postwar period because these norms functioned for the benefit of the nation. It will be interesting to see how long the current system's benefits for the nation will continue to outweigh the increasingly urgent protests of its detractors.

The blindness associated with justice in France must not translate to historical inquiry, though. In their *Vichy: An Ever-Present Past*, historian Henry Rousso and journalist Eric Conan called on the French to end the third phase of the Vichy Syndrome, and asked France to stop beating itself up over its wartime travails. It is important to study the past accurately, they say, but not without an historical framework. Indeed they state that nonscholarly hand-wringing over the past only prevents France from having a productive future. "The duty to remember,"

Rousso and Conan argue, "is nothing but an empty shell if it does not proceed from knowledge. It is nothing but a test question or a pompous moral lesson if it is not connected to a respect for the truth."[19] It is crucial, they argue, not to put an end to historical inquiry about this tumultuous time in French history, but rather to open it up more fully for analyses from diverse vantage points.

By framing the postwar with gendered analysis, this book exposes how the establishment of democracy in France after the war reaffirmed that system of government as masculine, despite the enfranchisement of women. The postwar gender norms were not separate from the rebuilding process, which took place in the realm of the physical, but also the realm of the intangible. Instead, they were central to France's process of moving past the war, and their specific components guided the French—often consciously—away from a reckoning with the events of war and toward an idealized, confined identity.

The process of moving on took place on two main, interrelated planes. First, the Resistance myth, as Henry Rousso has cogently argued, functioned to willfully blind the French people to the complex choices and realities of the lived experience of the Second World War. This book has exposed how the Resistance myth functioned in tandem with gender to create a masculine, virile France at the end of the war. Written and visual narratives about France as a female victim, Charles de Gaulle's rhetorical deployment of self-identifications with Joan of Arc, and even the postwar memoirs of women wartime victims painted France as wholly different from Germany. In depicting France with masculine strength and erasing women's activities from the Resistance record, however, France prepared itself for a postwar resurgence defined by a liberal democratic, masculine state.

Second, the vote acts in many ways as the lynchpin of this entire book; the imagery of postwar women described in these pages seems dissonant with traditional narratives of voting as accession to full citizenship. Cultural narratives, it posits, must be taken as political language in a context in which the vote was used by the postwar government as a corrective rather than an expansion of rights. These cultural narratives, which form the chapters of the book, together present a picture of confinement, despite the possibilities offered by enfranchisement. Postwar cultural sources painted female spies and torturers as anathema to the boundaries of that confinement. Depictions of their misdeeds went beyond simple description; rather these women, like Violette Morris, Denise Delfau, and Mathilde-Lily Carré underwent a simultaneous defeminization and dehumanization in cultural sources. These sources portrayed them as anti-French, but also as ugly, powerless, and empty, particularly once punished by the strong arm of the French state. The establishment of parameters of confinement also took the form of lessons on love, beauty, and motherhood, many of which originated in the pages of popular women's magazines, like *Elle* and *Marie-France*. In their pages, women could learn how to function as a normal woman; ignore such lessons, magazines warned, and prepare for a solitary, unfulfilling, unhappy life. The confinement of women in the postwar period worked to minimize the power of women voting and reinforce the androcentrism that had defined the French Republic for at least seventy-five years.

More broadly, this project seeks to make an argument about women's relationship to power. Official citizenship—the ability to participate in the governance of a nation either by standing for election or selecting representatives—does not necessarily translate into actual power or rights. That calculus is far more complicated. This project has shown how people's relationship to the nation depends on what their societies and cultures contextually need. If, as in the case of postwar France, the culture as a whole—government, mass media, and even the people themselves—bolsters a confining vision of gender, then the issuance of rights is not necessarily sufficient to prevent the larger diminution of roles and possibilities for women *and* men. In postwar France, rhetoric about the people contextually at the margins of gender—torturers, spies, homosexuals, *femmes tondues*, single women, and others—combined with discourses about heteronormative French people to define acceptability.

In 1949, four years after women won the right to vote, Simone de Beauvoir wrote, "What is beyond doubt is that until now women's possibilities have been stifled and lost to humanity, and in her and everyone else's interest it is high time she be left to take her own chances."[20] The vigorous cultural attempts to diminish women's roles and voices at the end of the Second World War, when they might have become a political force, constitute France's reassertion of masculine democracy, despite women's newfound political participation. The process of confinement in France functioned across the cultural landscape in an attempt to negate the potential inherent in women's enfranchisement. A women's magazine fostering anti-solidarity, the pressure on women to return home, the burden exerted to look a specific way in order to be considered "normal," and the demonization of public women who had transgressed social norms all shaped public behavior in ways that limited women's possibilities. Each of these strains worked separately and in unison to distance women from a common experience, to consolidate diverse behaviors into a complex ideal type, and to alienate women from public participation. In addressing these cultural themes as political language, scholars can better understand why women even today seem like nonnative speakers.

Notes

Introduction

1 Guéhenno, *Diary of the Dark Years, 1940-1944*, 272.
2 Beauvoir, *Second Sex*, 152.
3 See, for example, Scott, *Only Paradoxes* and *Parité!*; Landes, *Visualizing the Nation*; Hunt, *Family Romance*; Surkis, *Sexing the Citizen*; and Read, *Republic of Men*.
4 See Smith, *Feminism and the Third Republic*; see also Reynolds, *The 40s and 50s*, 210–12.
5 Scott, *Only Paradoxes to Offer*, 162.
6 Here I am referring to European nations like Denmark, Norway, and the Netherlands. Italy also enfranchised women in 1945, but I do not count Italy among the major Western democracies.
7 Quoted in Scott, *Only Paradoxes*, 161.
8 See Reynolds, *The 40s and 50s*, 210–12; and Smith, *Feminism and the Third Republic*.
9 For more on women as officeholders, see Scott, *Parité!*, 11–12, 19–20. Raylene L Ramsay cites the statistic that "over the five legislative elections during the Fourth Republic, from 1945 to 1958, women averaged only 11 percent of the total candidates." Ramsay, *French Women in Politics: Writing Power*. New York: Berghahn Books, 2003, 42–3. Delphine Gardey's recent work makes a fascinating parallel argument to my own about the exclusion of women from even apolitical posts in the physical French government buildings. This exclusion, she argues, is indicative of a more general will to retain the masculinity of the French government and the French polity. Gardey, *Le Linge du Palais-Bourbon*, 214–15.
10 Scott, *Only Paradoxes*, 171.
11 Nor was there any kind of serious women's movement that arose with women's enfranchisement; the final chapter of the book addresses feminism in more detail.
12 See, for example, Scott, *Only Paradoxes*, *Parité!*, and *The Politics of the Veil*; Hunt, *The Family Romance* and "Male Virtue and Republican Motherhood"; Heuer, *The Family and the Nation*; Nye, *Masculinity and Male Codes of Honor*; Surkis, *Sexing the Citizen*; and Roberts, *Civilization without Sexes*, among others.
13 Surkis, *Sexing the Citizen*, 3–4. See also Roberts, *Civilization without Sexes*; Landes, *Women and the Public Sphere*; Hunt, *Politics, Culture, and Class*; as well as work by Geoff Read and Andrea Mansker, among others.

14 Bouglé-Moalic, *Le vote des Françaises*, 319.

15 Scott, *Only Paradoxes*, 5–9.

16 Offen, "Women, Citizenship, and Suffrage with a French Twist," 152.

17 Scott, *Only Paradoxes*, 169–170.

18 Holly Grout, in her *Force of Beauty*, delineates the differences between
    "womanhood" and "femininity," arguing that womanhood "signifies the embodied
    experiences of being a woman," while femininity "supplies the representational
    language and symbolic repertoire through which womanhood becomes coherent."
    My work shows how these two forces act together to limit the potential power of
    actual women in French political and public life. Grout, *The Force of Beauty*, 4.

19 Ramsay, *French Women in Politics*, 21.

20 The long Liberation witnessed a nascent mass media, which, as Brian Rigby
    and Nicholas Hewitt argue, was "essential" after Vichy to the reconstruction of
    France politically and culturally. During this time, they state, "the mass media
    were perceived as playing a vital role in achieving the purposes of unifying,
    educating, and cultivating the French people." While some sectors of the
    population, like Communists and Catholics, resisted mass media—and mass
    culture more generally—Rigby and Hewitt note that scholarly work has shown
    it to be constitutive of a "new democratic culture." Of course, they state, the
    flipside of such a culture would be a less diverse media diet for the people. Rigby
    and Hewitt, "Introduction," 2. This book focuses on that nascent mass media
    and the way it construed women's roles in the wake of both the war and women's
    enfranchisement.

21 Adler, *Jews and Gender in Liberation France*, i, 5.

22 See Rousso, *Vichy Syndrome*, 18.

23 In 1987, historian Henry Rousso pointed to a Resistance myth, or *résistancialisme*,
    in which postwar French people "forgot" the experience of the Second World War
    and its aftermath, and they latched onto the de Gaulle creation that he had resisted,
    and he was France, so France had resisted. Rousso, *Vichy Syndrome*, 10. Rousso,
    Le Syndrome de Vichy, 109.

24 Foucault, *Discipline and Punish*, 138.

25 See, for example, Pulju, *Women and Mass Consumer Society in Postwar France*, 3;
    see also Jackson, *Living in Arcadia*, 44–46.

26 Bartky, "Foucault, Femininity, and the Modernization of Patriarchal Power," 36.

27 Ibid.

28 Judith Surkis sees the margins of categories like gender as unstable, but not
    "delegitimating [because] they can, in fact, motivate and justify efforts to police the
    boundaries of these admittedly unstable, but nonetheless effective norms." Surkis,
    Sexing the Citizen, 8–9.

29 Scott, *Only Paradoxes to Offer*, 169.

Chapter 1

1 In some ways this particular strand of rhetoric is similar to what Ruth Harris has examined in her work on the Great War, when, she argues, the French came to view their nation as a raped woman. Harris claims that this image was favorable for France because it allowed the French to present themselves as a "violated, but innocent, female nation resisting the assaults of a brutal male assailant [Germany]." However, this image of rape was modified in the context of the Liberation, when France needed to present itself not as an utter victim in need of reinforcements (and later reparations), but rather as a strong, internally stable power as well as a deserving player on the international stage. Harris, "The 'Child of the Barbarian,'" 170.

2 Rousso, *Vichy Syndrome*, 16–18.

3 According to Megan Koreman, "was that in 1940 the great majority of the French supported the collaborationist Vichy government, only slowly turning to the Resistance under the pressure of food shortages and the threat of forced labor. Until the Allied armies landed in Normandy, about an equal number of activists supported Resistance as supported Collaboration." Koreman, *The Expectation of Justice*, 3.

4 Saint-Clair, *Ravensbrück, l'Enfer des femmes*, 195.

5 The idea of self-revival is quite important in dealing with France as a victim; it suggests that not only has France taken control of her own destiny, but also that she has the strength and power to rebuild after the pain and suffering she experienced. This is quite evocative in the context of the development of the Resistance myth and of de Gaulle's constant urging of the French people to rebuild France's greatness, both physically and metaphorically.

6 Agulhon, *Les métamorphoses de Marianne*, 93–94. Agulhon later notes that Vichy passed a law on September 8, 1940, requiring busts of Marianne to be removed from town halls across France and replaced with busts of Joan of Arc and images of Pétain. After the war was over, many mayors were accused of collaboration for having followed this law. Agulhon, "De Gaulle et l'histoire de France," 96–7.

7 Margaret Collins Weitz cites an interview she held with Lucienne Guezennec, a Resistance participator, in which Guezennec describes the experience of Occupation in exactly these terms: "The invasion was like a rape. To this day when I read about a rape trial, I am reminded of the Occupation. This was really violation—violation of my country." Weitz, "Art in the Service of Propaganda," 2. It would be interesting to explore how concepts of the invasion as rape waxed and waned with the political fortunes during the war.

8 The literary critic Marina Warner argues that symbolism actively works to enforce this dichotomy rather than erase it: "Often the recognition of a difference between

the symbolic order, inhabited by ideal, allegorical figures, and the actual order, of judges, statesmen, soldiers, philosophers, inventors, depends on the unlikelihood of women practicing the concepts they represent." Warner, *Monuments and Maidens*, xx.

9 Joan Landes and Lynn Hunt have grounded Marina Warner's assertion of concomitant symbolism and political impotence in the context of French history. Landes, for example, notes that Marianne, or Liberty, lost potency even during the French Revolution: "Over time, the representations of Liberty became more sedate and tranquil, reiterating on the symbolic plane the defeat of women's independent, radical political initiatives within the Revolution." Additionally, Hunt points to Marianne's nonthreatening femininity as one of the motivations for her choice as the new symbol of France at the time. Contrary to women like Marie Antoinette or Mme de Roland, who represented challenges to the desired masculine authority of the revolutionaries, "the French Republic could find in the feminine allegory a figure suitably distant from the real-life-heroes-turned-villains of the revolutionary process." In fact it is also Marianne's "abstraction and impersonality," which, Hunt argues, is the very reason Marianne survives as a symbol even today, as opposed to Hercules, among others. After the Revolution, ensuing governments could use Marianne's obliqueness to pursue and justify their specific agendas. See Landes, *Women and the Public Sphere*, 160, and Hunt, *Politics*, 93. For more on representations of Marianne and female symbolic representations in Germany and Britain, and their relationship to their political contexts, see also Mosse, *Nationalism and Sexuality*, 90–99.

10 Galland, "Cette fois tu ne te relèveras pas!" *Les Nouvelles du Matin*, #84, May 8, 1945, 2.

11 Fresneau, Simone, "La France est une âme," *Marie-France*, Issue #8, January 8, 1945, 2.

12 Those who did, such as the *femmes tondues*, received a public, symbolic punishment that clearly marked them as abnormal and not true French women.

13 Weitz, "Art in the Service of Propaganda: the Poster War in World War II," 43.

14 Gates, Jr., Henry Louis and Karen C.C. Dalton. *Josephine Baker and La Revue Nègre: Paul Colin's Lithographs of Le Tumulte Noir in Paris, 1927*. New York: Harry N. Abrams, 1997, 8.

15 For more on Colin and his body of work, see Rennert, *100 Posters of Paul Colin*.

16 Gates, 10.

17 Colin, *La croûte*, 182.

18 Weill, Alain and Jack Rennart. *Paul Colin, Affichiste*. Paris: Éditions Denoël, 1989.

19 Ibid., 17.

20 See Weill, 116, and Rennert, *100 Posters of Paul Colin*, 10.

21 Vichy propagandists, according to Miranda Pollard, preferred the image of the "French Mother" to the "politically charged, feminine symbol of the Republic." Pollard, *Reign of Virtue*, 49.

22 Agulhon, *Les métamorphoses de Marianne*, 108; for a full account of the scene in which de Gaulle refused to proclaim the Republic, see Aron, *France Reborn*, 297. See also Rousso, *Vichy Syndrome*, 17.

23 I should note that this is most likely a direct reference to the state of France physically at the end of the war. For example, in terms of railroads at the moment of Liberation, there were "2.300 ouvrages destroyed. 3.000 kms of unusable railtrack. Out of 131 Major Storehouses. 71 have been annihilated. Out of 31 Repair Workshops. 19 were destroyed. Out of 40 Major Gares de Triage. 24 have been disrupted. Out of 322 Major Stations. 115 have been destroyed." From AN, F/41/453, "Photos de SNCF Destruction, Reconstruction. Photographs prises en vue d'un film." Additionally, in his *Postwar*, Tony Judt notes that "in 1944–45 alone, France lost 500,000 dwellings." Judt, *Postwar*, 17. In fact, Judt states that at the end of the war, 20 percent of French housing was destroyed. Judt, *Postwar*, 82.

24 Marianne had not at all been in favor with the Vichy propagandists, and this is a large factor in why her image is so potent at the moment of Liberation. While there was a battle between Vichy and the Resistance over the ownership of the symbolism of Joan of Arc, Marianne was so linked with the idea of republicanism that her imagery was discarded by the more conservative, religious Vichy regime. In fact, according to Eric Jennings, during Vichy, the "collaborationist newspaper *Gringoire*" referred to Marianne as "the old shrew with the Phrygian bonnet." Thus when Colin employed Marianne to represent the nation, he was making a strong statement against Vichy policies. In this way, the image of Marianne, just like the discourse of gendered victimhood generally, could be politicized to suit the needs of a particular culture and cultural author at a particular moment. From *Gringoire*. April 10, 1941, 3. As quoted in Jennings, "Reinventing Jeanne," 715.

25 Rennert, *100 Posters of Paul Colin*, 4.

26 Ibid.

27 Rey, "Vingt ans de Paris."

28 The French translation, published later, is entitled *Souffrances de Mon Pays*.

29 Vercors, *Souffrances de mon pays*, 13–15.

30 Although I have not found evidence that directly states this, some of the other artists and writers featured in this chapter do seem to have been inspired by Colin's *affiche*.

31 Rennert, *100 Posters of Paul Colin*, 10.

32 Hourdin, Georges. "L'espérance de Pâques," *Marie-France*, Issue #19, March 30, 1945, 2.

33 "Voici Marie-France," *Marie-France*, November 6,1944, 2.

34 Ferniot, *Je recommencerais bien*, 1.

35 See Aron, *De Gaulle Triumphant*, 238; see also Aglion, *Roosevelt and de Gaulle*, 152. Interestingly enough, in his war memoirs, de Gaulle expresses ambivalence at this direct comparison between himself and Joan of Arc; when Wendell Willkie, Roosevelt's Republican challenger, portrayed de Gaulle as Joan in the American press after a private visit, de Gaulle attributes it to the fact that one of his men had used the term "'General de Gaulle's mission'. . . . In this manner, Roosevelt's rival was also his imitator." From de Gaulle, *War Memoirs*, 33. Charles de Gaulle often called upon the figure of Joan of Arc as inspiration for his life, but it is in the postwar period where he metaphorically becomes her, which makes these references extra laden with symbolism and gender. See Pedley, *As Mighty as the Sword*, 180–81.

36 de Gaulle, *The Speeches of General de Gaulle*, 9.

37 Hazareesingh, *In the Shadow of the General*, 21.

38 Meltzer, *For Fear of the Fire*, 6. Meltzer uses an analysis of artistic renderings of the figure of Joan to show how widely they differ and how they correspond to specific gender "needs" of their artists' times. This is also reminiscent of Lynn Hunt's work on the French state's adoption of Marianne as the official symbol during the French Revolution. She argues that it is the abstract nature of Marianne (that she can mean anything and nothing) that allows for her longevity. Hunt, *Politics, Class, and Culture*, 93.

39 Rousso, *Le Syndrome de Vichy*, 109.

40 Warner, *Joan of Arc*, 274.

41 See Gildea, *The Past in French History*, 154–65.

42 Brasillach was particularly fascinated with Joan of Arc and devoted several writings to her, most famously his interpretation of the Trial of Joan of Arc. In this work, originally published in 1931 and reprinted in 1941, Brasillach emphasizes Joan's mystical quality, calling her the "Christ of France" and saying, "people have emphasized her contradictory qualities too much, that her good sense could never marry itself with her exaltations, no more than her clarity with her mysticism." In his work on Joan of Arc, Brasillach clearly uses her character as a sort of vessel to make a point about the possibilities and desirability of fascism, thus supporting Françoise Meltzer's assertion that discourses about Joan of Arc have long acted as symbol-driven languages that reveal the motivations behind particular historical moments. Brasillach, *Le Procès de Jeanne d'Arc*, 6.

43 In fact, the Vichy regime generally did not hesitate to call upon the Jehannic legacy in order to drum up popular support; in Joan of Arc, Vichy leaders found a religious counterpart to Marianne, the secular symbol of the republic. They even used Joan's image to teach children about the heroes of France: Eric Jennings points to a visible

"demarginalization of Joan" in schoolbooks that were produced under Vichy. (Jennings, "Reinventing Jeanne," 715.) Additionally, the government sponsored massive rallies on the day of her festival in early May, and it used her image and the holiday to inspire unity and rail against the English, highlighting that France's historic enemy had caused Joan's death and were now again France's adversaries. According to Robert Gildea, the purpose of such Jehannic symbolism was to inspire "'restoration', 'redemption', and 'resurrection'." Vichy hoped to link itself with a timeless vision of 'traditional' France. Gildea, *The Past in French History*, 163; Margaret Collins Weitz also discusses the connection between Joan of Arc and Vichy/German propaganda. Weitz, "Art in the Service of Propaganda," 60, 63.

44 Gildea, *The Past in French History*, 164.
45 Rauch, "La virginité de sainte Odile et la liberté de Marianne," 265.
46 de Gaulle, *Appels et Discours*, 10.
47 Ibid., *Discours et messages*, 85.
48 Robert Gildea states Pétain was compared with Joan of Arc (*The Past in French History*, 162). It is an interesting idea that these two men were fighting over the soul of France, each with his specific vision, which was somehow contained in the symbolic body of Joan of Arc.
49 See Rosbottom, *When Paris Went Dark*, 370.
50 Like Joan, Cazaux was originally from Lorraine and had been a priest in Domrémy, Joan of Arc's birthplace. When ordained in 1941, he had fought in both world wars and was France's youngest bishop, hence his words held extra symbolism.
51 Cazaux, "La Sainte de la Patrie, 'Les dicts de Jehanne'," 1.
52 Ibid., 3.
53 Ibid.
54 Ibid., 5.
55 Ibid., 3.
56 Ibid., 6.
57 Ibid.
58 Thomas, *Jeanne d'Arc*, 38.
59 Blanchet, *Solitude de Jeanne d'Arc*, 8.
60 Bronner, *La Bergerette de Lorraine*, 2.
61 Rousso, *Le Syndrome de Vichy*, 95–96; quote dates from May 19, 1958.
62 Meltzer, *For Fear of the Fire*, 221n. 10.
63 I would also argue that in using the figure of Joan of Arc, de Gaulle was also reminding the French of their history of grandeur, an important reminder at a time when he was desperate to reestablish France as a great power. I go into the importance of this later in the chapter, in the discussion of images of France as a victim.
64 De Gaulle's actions at this point must be considered to be calculated, meaning that this is likely not an accidental comparison. De Gaulle has been well documented as

quite conscious about the crafting and maintenance of his own image. For example, Maurice Agulhon has detailed de Gaulle's seemingly personal relationship to French history: "This history, he knew it well, and he claimed to be inspired by it and, most essential, to continue it." Agulhon, "De Gaulle et l'histoire de France," 3. It was in this spirit that, as Robert Aron described, de Gaulle conceptualized the Allied landings in France as the culmination of his own sense of personal historic fate: "As the day approached on which [de Gaulle] was to regain the contact he had been denied for four years with the soil of his native land, his personality achieved fulfillment, and his destiny its apogee in history as he conceived it." Aron, *France Reborn*, 43. If de Gaulle thought of himself as the keeper of the legacy of great French heroes, his actions during the Liberation of France were meant to "continue" French history. His references to Joan of Arc must be considered as part of de Gaulle's conscious self-actualization with respect to his sense of greatness and destiny.

65   This discussion of Charles de Gaulle as Joan of Arc complicates the idea posited by historians, notably Eric Jennings in his article "'Reinventing Jeanne,'" that Joan of Arc and Marianne were simple adversaries. As the usage of both images by the opposition to Vichy suggests, both Joan of Arc and Marianne were powerful symbolic forces that de Gaulle and the Resistance wished to harness for their own purposes. Their confluence at the Liberation as symbols for the Republic was a seemingly fleeting moment, however, considering Jean-Marie Le Pen and the French right's repossession of Joan for their own symbolic political purposes. In fact, at the Liberation, both seem to be martyrs who blur secular/religious boundaries and are pedagogical influences on France. Later, Marianne resumes her place as more purely secular, and Joan of Arc resumes her place as more religious. See Jennings, "Reinventing Jeanne," 711–34. On p. 711 Jennings notes, "From the late nineteenth century onward, the competing symbols of Marianne and Joan of Arc began to be claimed by conflicting elements of a rapidly polarizing French society. They were presented as bitter rivals."

66   Warner, *Joan of Arc*, 275.

67   For more examples of martyr imagery as it pertains to towns and cities, see also "Tulle, Ville martyre," in *Combat*, #7, Sunday, November 5, 1944, 7; in *Le Monde*, see "Le Havre, Ville Rasée, a la volonté de vivre," September 19, 1945, 4; in the *French Review*, see Ignatius W. Brock, "Caen, Rennes, Dijon, Grenoble," Vol. 19, No. 2 (1945 December), 103–08.

Chapter 2

1   From *Le Figaro*, part of a series of articles relating to this particular trial that appeared in November and December 1952. AN, 72AJ/385 L'après-guerre,

Folder 7. The reference to Joan of Arc here is evocative of the feminine side of the representation of Joan from the first chapter.

2 "Mauvaise journée pour l'accusée Favriol," *Combat,* mardi 2 décembre 1952.

3 See Bard, *Les femmes dans la société française au 20e siècle*; Weitz, *Sisters in the Resistance*; Duchen, *Women's Rights and Women's Lives*; Rossiter, *Women in the Resistance*; and Diamond, *Women and the Second World War in France.* Olivier Wieviorka has recently asserted that women comprised a smaller part of the Resistance than these scholars posited, and that those who had were exceptional in some way, be it personality or other structural advantages. Still, he views their participation as quite high, given the many barriers to women's public action in society in general. Wieviorka, *The French Resistance*, 403–08.

4 Duchen, *Women's Rights and Women's Lives*, 12.

5 Bard, *Les femmes dans la société française au 20e siècle*, 140.

6 Ibid., 146. Their survival rate was quite low compared to women of other nationalities in the camp, a fact historian Sarah Helm attributes to their relatively late arrival there and related lack of administrative support: "[There were] no French Blockovas to watch out for them, no one in the kitchen to slip them extra food," among other factors. Helm, *Ravensbrück*, 366–67.

7 Mornand, *La vie et la mort de Daisy Georges-Martin, Martyre de la Résistance*, 68.

8 Busson, *Dans les Griffes nazies ; Angers, Fresnes, Ravensbrück, Mauthausen*, 8.

9 Bard, *Les femmes dans la société française au 20e siècle*, 140.

10 Téry, *Du soleil plein le coeur, la merveilleuse histoire de Danielle Casanova*, 10.

11 Saint-Clair, *Ravensbrück, l'Enfer des femmes*, 193–94.

12 It is well known that women have received limited recognition for their roles in the Resistance. For example, as Margaret Collins Weitz notes in her *Sisters in the Resistance*, "Of the more than one thousand medals awarded—including five to municipalities and eighteen to fighting units—only *six* were awarded to women." Weitz, "Art in the Service of Propaganda," 10. Additionally, Édith Thomas remarked in 1947 that of the many resistors acknowledged in Paris with renamed streets, only two women—Berthie Albrecht and Danielle Casanova, who both died during the war—were so honored. Thomas, *Jeanne d'Arc*, 12. This lack of recognition might also be attributed to a denial of women's experiences by forces that wished to re-stabilize French identity through keeping women in the private sphere.

13 Cormier, *Une Bordelaise martyre de la Résistance*, Part II.

14 Delbo, *Auschwitz and After*, 12. Motherhood has long played a role in French women's relationship to the state. In the eighteenth century, republican mothers acted as incubators of republican values for the state, inculcating their children. See Landes, *Women and the Public Sphere in the Age of the French Revolution.* Into the Third Republic, historians have shown, the republican mother acted as an acculturating force for her family. Doron, *Jewish Youth and Identity in Postwar*

France, 98. A mother's "selflessness" and "self-abnegation" became political commodities in the Third Republic as well. Read, *The Republic of Men*, 214–15. In the long Liberation, motherhood and self-abnegation again combined to present a vision of proper femininity. This was, however, a public vision, meant to promote specific behavioral norms to a population reeling from war.

15 Hoisne, *Chambre 535, ou mes cinq prisons pendant l'Occupation*, 82.

16 I interpret the leaving of the child behind to join the *maquis* not as a-maternal for two reasons: Menut finds herself in extraordinary circumstances, and because she is following her husband into the Resistance. She serves her country—as a caregiver—as well as her husband.

17 "Galérie des Martyrs," *Ceux du Maquis*, dimanche 17 décembre 1944, 7.

18 Interestingly, Capdevila et al. cite the Red Cross's insertion of a special provision for pregnant prisoners of war in their 1949 conventions, which "extended" the "particular consideration" for pregnant women from civil society into combat arenas. Capdevila et al., *Hommes et femmes dans la France en guerre*, 287.

19 Farmer, "Postwar Justice in France: Bordeaux, 1953," 200. Quoted from *Le Figaro*, 2 February 1953.

20 *Le Monde*, February 3, 1953 in Farmer, 200.

21 *Figaro*, February 2, 1953 in Farmer, 200.

22 This is very reminiscent of the way mothers in Latin America used their status as mothers as capital to demand investigations into cases of disappeared persons in the face of military dictatorships in the 1970s and 1980s. For more on this topic, see for example Jennifer Schirmer's article, "The Seeking of Truth and the Gendering of Consciousness: The Comadres of El Salvador and the Conavigua Widows of Guatemala," in Radcliffe and Westwood, eds., as well as Bouvard. Unfortunately, as Sarah Farmer and Megan Koreman suggest in their work, justice is not always possible in the context of Liberation France, but the idea of justice is certainly powerful. For examples of discrepancies between notions of justice in postwar France and the conflicting realities of what the government and the people would and could deliver as such, see Koreman as well as Farmer, "Postwar Justice."

23 It is especially interesting that this motherhood and pregnancy is highlighted in the context of an extremely pronatalist atmosphere in postwar France. In fact, the rhetoric of victimhood is employed at this time by government officials and cultural critics to urge families to procreate in the name of the *patrie*. I will address this issue of pro-natalism further in the following chapter.

24 Mornand, *La vie et la mort de Daisy Georges-Martin, Martyre de la Résistance*, 63.

25 Ibid., 85.

26 Wilborts, *Pour la France*, 11.

27 Delbo, *Auschwitz and After*, 20.

28 Tillion, *Ravensbrück*, 34.

29 Please see Chapter 3 for an introduction to and contextualization of women's magazines.

30 "Une héroïne française: Madame de Montfort," *Marie-France*, Issue #17, March 16, 1945, 2.

31 Helm, *Ravensbrück*, 393.

32 "Ce n'est pas par la coquetterie qu'elles portent le cordon rouge," *Elle*, Issue #12, February 6, 1946, 3.

33 Rosane, *Terre de cendres*, 174.

34 Bouteille-Garagnon, *Infernal rebus*, 42.

35 Tillion, *Ravensbrück*, 13.

36 Ibid., 25.

37 Rosane, *Terre de cendres*, 84, 120.

38 Bouteille-Garagnon, *Infernal rebus*, 16.

39 Saurel, *Les femmes héroïques de la Résistance*, 29.

40 Helm, *Ravensbrück*, 365.

41 Hoisne, *Chambre 535, ou mes cinq prisons pendant l'Occupation*, 44.

42 This trauma resonates even more deeply considering the forced shaving of tens of thousands of French women, known as the *femmes tondues*, at the end of war. See Virgili, *Shorn Women*.

43 Téry, *Du soleil plein le coeur, la merveilleuse histoire de Danielle Casanova*, 242–43.

44 Bouteille-Garagnon, *Infernal rebus*, 34.

45 Tillion, *Ravensbrück*, 34; Rosane also asserts that the French block had "almost no" lice as a point of pride, 78.

46 Saint-Clair, *Ravensbrück, l'Enfer des femmes*, 68.

47 Delbo, *Auschwitz and After*, 162.

48 Tillion, *Ravensbrück*, 9.

49 Hoisne, *Chambre 535, ou mes cinq prisons pendant l'Occupation*, 50–51.

50 Bouvard, *Revolutionizing Motherhood*, 179.

51 Wilborts, *Pour la France*, 38.

52 Rosane, *Terre de cendres*, 126–27.

53 While in these cases national pride and aesthetic appearance are inextricably linked, Margaret Collins Weitz argues that female detainees put on makeup to maintain their dignity. This is certainly an important aspect of trying to survive in the camps and sustain a sense of normalcy, but the issue here has more to do with how makeup functioned to allow women to maintain a patriotic dignity and how women used their beauty regimens as a way to distinguish between themselves and other nationalities, to make themselves more French. Additionally, the retention of beauty in its own time and place, the detention camps of France, Germany, and Eastern Europe, is not the focus here. The main concern is rather the meaning of the retelling of these stories during the Liberation, when femininity

was so important and was undergoing a process of definition. Weitz, *Sisters in the Resistance*, 289.

54   Pateman, "Equality, Difference, Subordination," 23–24.

55   Farmer, *Martyred Village*, 88.

56   Brillant, Marie, "Le retour des cloches," *Marie-France*, Issue #19, March 30, 1945, 10.

57   Fabrice Virgili has argued that sounds played a large role in the *femme tondue* incidents, allowing spectators to feel as though they were taking part in the process of head shaving, with all of its implications of punishment and redemption. Specifically, Virgili argues that the French national anthem, the *Marseillaise*, represented a way for the French people to express control over themselves and their environment after the Occupation. (Virgili, *Shorn Women*, 222–26, esp. 225–26) One theme I noted in my research was that one way women acted as caregivers was through expressing their support for France and the French in noise and song. This is noteworthy considering the gender-based tensions surrounding testimony and silence at the time. This sentimentality and symbolism with regard to the national anthem is echoed even during the war, in famous resistor Danielle Casanova's final letter before she left the French prison at Romainville en route to Germany. In this letter, Casanova described how the *Marseillaise* had a sustaining effect on the prisoners there: "The comportment of all is magnificent and our beautiful *Marseillaise* has resounded more than once. What fate do they reserve for us? We will see . . ." (Saurel, *Les femmes héroïques de la Résistance*, 30) Simone Saint-Clair remembered leaving the Sarrebrück prison and shouting out the *Marseillaise* in defiance of the guards. Later, a group of people singing the anthem welcomed Saint-Clair and other women back into France at Annemasse: "this *Marseillaise* so dear to our hearts." (Saint-Clair, *Ravensbrück, l'Enfer des femmes*, 192) The *Marseillaise* also served to inspire the women in the various prisons in France and Germany; at Angers, Suzanne Wilborts remembered feeling invigorated at the patriotism of the French prisoners, who would sing the national anthem all along the route to their executions. (Wilborts, *Pour la France*, 38) The condemned in the Santé prison, who had to pass by the women's barracks on their way to the firing squad, would ask the women to sing for them. When Danielle Casanova was housed at Santé, prisoners would call to her on the way, and she would tell them that they were heroes for France. Then, according to memoirist Simone Téry, "all the women would sing a fervent *Marseillaise* to salute those who were going to die for France. And they went happily and proudly to their destination."(Téry, *Du soleil plein le coeur, la merveilleuse histoire de Danielle Casanova*, 209) The song was thus a vessel for Frenchness and France, a way to express one's identity in defiance or solidarity. The *Marseillaise* provided a comfort for prisoners and condemned people, and it was best administered by the women victims who could reassure

them and thus serve to represent France. In this way, such women again acted in the capacity of secular saints, singing, chanting, and blessing the condemned.

58 Busson, *Héros du sport, héros de France*, 147–50 (quote 147).

59 "Échos des grands bois: Leur dernière lettre," *Ceux du Maquis*, dimanche 3 décembre 1944, 6: « Ne pleurez point, cela ne servirait à rien. Tâchez d'être dans le futur que moi je vais l'être dans la mort. . . . J'espère qu'une fois la guerre finie, vous retrouverez le bonheur pour lequel je donne ma vie. »

60 Claire Duchen briefly touches upon this characterization when she notes that women's Resistance roles were "perceived as less important in the Resistance than the more 'heroic' role of men" because their roles often placed them in less direct danger. Duchen, *Women's Rights and Women's Lives in France, 1944-1968*, 12.

61 "Discours du Général de Gaulle, le 6 juin 1944," BNF Richelieu, Image M130422.

62 Koreman, *The Expectation of Justice*, 190.

63 Weill, Alain and Jack Rennart. *Paul Colin, Affichiste*. Paris: Éditions Denoël, 1989, 100.

64 While this is perhaps one of the earlier and most famous of these Resistance *affiches*, Christine Bard states that there existed a number of other ones which glorified the masculinity of the Resistance and of resistors in general. This, in turn, helped erase women's Resistance participation from the official record. Bard, *Les femmes dans la société française au 20e siècle*, 152–53.

65 "Mlle MANDEL ne déposera pas," *Le Monde*, 19 août 1945, 2.

66 Belinda Davis's *Home Fires Burning* touches upon how widowhood, among others, became an acceptable social role for women in First World War Germany. She examines it in and of itself, however, and does not look deeply at the consequences of the idea that these women perhaps had less of a public role in and of themselves, and more of one in terms of the men they represented.

67 Rosane, *Terre de cendres*, 3.

68 Busson, *Héros du sport, héros de France*, 149.

69 "Elles ont repris le flambeau," *Elle*, Issue #2, November 28, 1945, 3.

70 Scott, *Only Paradoxes to Offer*, 169; William Ghéraiche also addresses how these women served in their husbands' stead, that their surname was their most important quality. Ghéraiche, Les femmes politiques de 1944 à 1947, 34.

71 "Elle aurait tout donné," *Elle*, Issue #9, January 16, 1946, 16.

72 This image of the kiss exists, of course, in contrast to the common postwar image of the triumphant embrace, as seen in photographer Robert Doisneau's work, for example, which symbolized the end of war and the return to normalcy.

73 "Le Baiser," *Elle*, Issue #11, January 30, 1946, 3.

74 Cormier, Part II; For yet another example of work which highlights the power of the French woman's kiss, see also Berthe Bernage's short story, "Si Marguerite lit ces lignes," in *Marie-France*, Issue #5, December 15, 1944, 11.

75 Those women who exercised their sexuality outside of the bounds of this virility were subject to highly intense and public shame, as evidenced by the *femmes tondues*. Other threats to French virility, particulary gay men and lesbians, also faced stigma at the end of war. As Robert Nye points out in his article, "Michel Foucault's Sexuality and the History of Homosexuality in France," there were some places where gay men could meet at this time, such as "drag bars and Turkish bathhouses," however, "they were heavily staked out by the police," presumably in order to discourage men from entering. Nye, *Masculinity and Male Codes of Honor in Modern France*, 232. Additionally, as A.R.H. Copley shows, it was "de Gaulle's post-Liberation administration which was to sanction the Pétain decree against pederasty," further strengthening the state's fight against "immoral" sexual acts. (From Copley, *Sexual Moralities in France, 1780-1980*, 216) I will discuss this in more detail in the following chapter.

76 Salonne, *Fends la Bise ! Scènes du maquis Breton*, 215.

77 See, for example, the work of Margaret Rossiter and Margaret Collins Weitz.

78 Pollard, *Reign of Virtue*, 50. It is not new to France in the Second World War, however; in the Third Republic, many feminists made their case by using women's moral superiority as a justification for the vote. See Mansker, *Sex, Honor and Citizenship in Early Third Republic France*, 193–233. Even earlier, in the time of the French Revolution, "women were expected to behave differently from the way men did. . . . Private morality was seen as intimately tied to public virtue and state interest." Landes, *Women and the Public Sphere in the Age of the French Revolution*, 5.

79 Interestingly, male prisoners were represented in a similar way as females in general. For example, an *affiche* appeared in several issues of *Le Monde* in the spring and summer of 1945 showing depicting an emaciated man standing in front of barbed wire, bare-chested, and looking out at the reader. The text says: "they *are weakened* but they will bring back our strength. they *are depleted* but they will bring back our abundance. They are 250,000 returning workers, fathers, producers, clients. Their return to France is, for France, a return to life." [original emphasis] *Le Monde*, May 29, 1945, p. 2. This similarity in representation is not an anomaly. Imprisoned men were victimized in the same way as the women, they are helpless bodies that represent France, but they are also public figures who will restore French strength.

Chapter 3

1 Pulju, *Women and Consumer Society in Postwar France*, 3.

2 Love itself is a historically contingent concept, subject to the cultural tensions of its time. Historians have traced the advent of new, modern attitudes about love to the

Enlightenment, when familial bonds transitioned from more economic modes of self-preservation to a sense of emotional attachment. Within this new context, a married couple could also have more profound expectations of love for one another. This sense deepened over the course of the eighteenth century, when, Peter Stearns and Mark Knapp argue, "love became a valid element in the formation of marriages, and absence of love a compelling reason for a young person to reject a match." Stearns and Knapp, "Men and Romantic Love: Pinpointing a Twentieth-Century Change," 770. Historians of the Victorian era, most notably Karen Lystra, have presented arguments that counter the traditional image of the cold, separate marriage. They portray Victorian marriages and romances as fraught with emotion and passion. See Lystra, *Searching the Heart*, 771–74; Steven Seidman has argued that while this revision is important, it is crucial not to "[reinvent] the Victorians as moderns who successfully integrated desire and affect." Seidman, *Romantic Longings*, 1.

3   Collins, *Modern Love*, 4; See also Langhamer's "Adultery in post-war England," in which she argues that "companionate marriage" arose at this time in England. Langhamer, "Adultery in Post-war England," 90.

4   Collins, *Modern Love*, 167. Collins does point to certain problems in its implementation, especially with regard to class and race. Collins specifically states that the division of labor within middle-class homes, as women began to join the workforce, was a source of tension. In working-class homes, he argues, patriarchy remained more generally dominant. However, within those middle-class marriages, he does argue that "mutuality was a stated goal of marriage." See 169–73. In France, as I will show, this was decidedly not the case.

5   Cancian and Gordon, "Changing Emotion Norms in Marriage," 308; Laura M. Carpenter also details how *Seventeen* appeared to broaden sexual norms over time, but in reality, it reinforced existing conceptualizations of sexuality and gender. Similarly, Scholars like Kristin Ross and Benedict Anderson have pointed to such magazines as actively constructing a "nationally imagined community," a sense that one's compatriots shared similar problems and a similar ethos about the direction of their lives and goals. Ross, *Fast Cars, Clean Bodies*, 144–45; See also Zdatny, *Fashion, Work, and Politics in Modern France*, 234. Additionally, in her work on the American and British feminine press, Marjorie Ferguson has argued that women's magazines tend to imply that "a female sex which is at best unconfident, and at worst incompetent, 'needs' or 'wants' to be instructed, rehearsed or brought up to date on the arts and skills of femininity." Ferguson, *Forever Feminine*, 2.

6   Feminine press, or *presse feminine*, is a common term in French, defined as "media made for women and read by women." Definition from Eck and Blandin, "*La vie des femmes*," 9.

7   Miller, *La presse écrite en France au XXe siècle*, 80, 143. *Marie-France*, according to one historian of the feminine press, consciously tried to court former readers of

Marie-Claire by adopting Marie, and then adding France to it so it was "adorned with a little bit of *tricolore*, because of contemporary events." Sullerot, *La presse féminine*, 67.

8   Sullerot, *La presse féminine*, 68.

9   Archives Nationales, F/41/354, Folder 1; Kristin Ross defines magazines as "more shareable" than other forms of media. Ross, *Fast Cars, Clean Bodies*, 143.

10 Grumbach, *History of International Fashion*, 195.

11 "Si Elle Lit Elle Lit Elle," *Time*, May 22, 1964.

12 Weiner, "Two Modernities," 400. For quote see Bonvoisin and Maignien, *La presse féminine*, 22.

13 The analysis in the book also includes several selections from *Ève*, a periodical that had existed before the war, had stopped publishing during the war, and started up immediately after the war. I included it because it was the amalgamation of twenty regional supplements, and thus provides a broad regional look at notions of femininity in France at the time. Bonvoisin and Maignien, *La presse féminine*, 19.

14 Zdatny, *Fashion, Work, and Politics in Modern France*, 234.

15 In terms of defining gender, this chapter takes as its cue Joan Scott's "Gender: A Useful Category of Historical Analysis," in which she defines femininity and masculinity in terms of the power they wield, both relationally and singularly. Scott, *Gender and the Politics of History*, 28–52.

16 Rioux, *The Fourth Republic*, 81.

17 Farmer, *Martyred Village*, 81.

18 Jackson, "Sex, Politics and Morality in France, 1954-1982," 77–102.

19 Capdevila, "The Quest for Masculinity in a Defeated France, 1940-1945," 424.

20 Each of these countries also saw a rise in prominence of women's magazines, which took up a call for a more pronounced femininity. For example, in the United States, historian Stephanie Coontz notes: "Marriage experts of the day worried . . . that while the men were off at war, women had gotten too used to being in charge of the house and the checkbook. 'He's head man again,' the American magazine *House Beautiful* reminded its female readers. 'Your part . . . is to fit his home to him, understanding why he wants it this way, forgetting your own preferences.'" (Coontz, *Marriage, a History*, 223). For more information on the experience of Great Britain in the immediate postwar years, see Gledhill and Swanson; for more on the United States, see May; see also Coontz, *Marriage, a History*, 216–28.

21 In describing the collective shock of wartime events, Miranda Pollard states, "Nothing . . . had prepared the French for the devastating speed of the German advance into France and the total collapse of their armies." Pollard, *Reign of Virtue*, 29.

22 Ibid., 32.

23 This is not an entirely new concept; as Judith Surkis has shown, during the Third Republic, "heterosexual masculinity and femininity [were] characteristics of the

national political and social order." Surkis, *Sexing the Citizen*, 183. See also Read and Mansker.

24 Ad for Jil, "N'imitez pas les hommes . . .," *Elle*, Issue #103, November 4, 1947, 15.

25 Quoted in Ross, *Fast Cars, Clean Bodies*, 1.

26 Weiner, "Two Modernities," 404.

27 Sullerot, *La presse féminine*, 67.

28 Rioux, *The Fourth Republic*, 442.

29 "Quel froid!" *Marie-France*, Issue #12, February 2, 1945, 2; see also "Je n'ai qu'une robe," *Marie-France*, Issue #87, 14.

30 "Dans ma chemise de nuit, je n'ai pas froid," *Elle*, Issue #9, January 16, 1946, 10–11.

31 Rioux, *The Fourth Republic*, 24–25.

32 In fact, women staged multiple protests about food shortages and the difficulties of *ravitaillement* in the postwar period. For more on this, see, Annexes, Folder 8, *Synthèse pour la période du 15 avril au 15 mai 1945*, 72AJ/384, Archives Nationales; this report details these protests in the context of worries for the French nation in the immediate aftermath of the Liberation. See also Pulju, "Consumers for the Nation," 68–90.

33 Alsop, *To Marietta from Paris, 1945-1960*, 70.

34 "N'évitez pas les œufs en poudre!" *Elle*, Issue #1, November 21, 1945, 16–17; "Verdict sur l'élégance," *Elle*, Issue #1, November 21, 1945, 11.

35 For an analysis of women's magazines' duality of purpose in the American context, see the Conclusion of Scanlon, 229–34. Scanlon notes that while American women's magazines of the early twentieth century "had to please women readers," they also "set limits both on women's demands for change and on cultural expectations of men."(231).

36 "Sirène en leçons," *Marie-France*, Issue #88, July 24, 1946, 6–7.

37 Périer and Bauby, *Les Années* Elle*, 1945-2000*, 13.

38 Vienne, "The Woman Who Was *ELLE*," 169.

39 Giroud, *I Give You My Word*, 107.

40 "Voici Marie-France," *Marie-France*, Issue #1, November 6, 1944, 2.

41 Ibid.

42 Vienne, "The Woman Who Was *ELLE*," 168.

43 Giroud, *I Give You My Word*, 106.

44 Dujardin, Rosemary, "Il préférait Cendrillon," *Elle*, December 26, 1945, 14, 22. This kind of advice is juxtaposed with the often-present section at the beginning of these magazines which features prominent people's weddings and engagements. *Elle* magazine, for example, did a large profile on Elisabeth de Gaulle, the daughter of Charles de Gaulle, and her engagement/marriage to a Russian nobleman who had fought for France in the war. See "Les mariages officiels et les autres," *Elle*, Issue #9, January 16, 1946, 3.

45   As I point out in the chapter on gendered victimization, the exclusion of women from the historical record of the Resistance also served to render the Resistance and other similar wartime narratives masculine.

46   Fishman, *We Will Wait*, 149.

47   Ross, *Fast Cars, Clean Bodies*, 126.

48   While it may seem odd to have a man writing about women's love issues and the effects of the war, the presence of a masculine authority was quite common in the magazines, particularly in the earlier issues. It also echoes the idea of an ever-present masculine state.

49   Lang, André. "La guerre a-t-elle tué l'amour?" *Elle*, May 28, 1946, 8–9.

50   Francine, "Le Courrier de *Marie-France*," *Marie-France*, Issue #330, March 26, 1951, 7.

51   "Elle et Vous," *Elle*, Issue #56, December 10, 1946, insert.

52   "Elle et Vous," *Elle*, Issue #60, January 7, 1947, insert.

53   Cantineau, Simone, "Mon cœur a cru choisir," *Marie-France*, Issue #3, November 24, 1944, 9, 11.

54   Lynn Hunt argues that dissimulation was considered a major threat to the Republic during the French Revolution, as "it was the chief ingredient in every conspiracy; it lay at the heart of the counterrevolution." She goes on to argue that dissimulation was a "characteristic feminine quality," and a way for women to corrupt otherwise worthy men. Hunt, *Family Romance*, 97–98. See also Scott, *Only Paradoxes to Offer*, 43.

55   Stewart, Maclane, "Vous Ici!" *Elle*, Issue #1, November 21, 1945, 18. I should note that this story was adapted from an English story, "Well of All People!"; details such as names and places were added to make it French, however, and the message resonates in both cultures at this time.

56   Segal, Marcelle, "Êtes-vous si seule que vous l'imaginez?" *Elle*, Issue #125, April 13, 1948, 6–7.

57   "Cinq ans ont passé depuis que vous êtes mariés," *Elle*, Issue #52, November 12, 1946, 20–21.

58   Lang, "La guerre a-t-elle tué l'amour?" *Elle*, Issue #36, July 23, 1946, 18–19.

59   Lang, André, "La guerre a-t-elle tué l'amour?" *Elle*, Issue #30, June 11, 1946, 18–19.

60   De Mongeot, A. Rastoul. "Nouveau départ," *Marie-France*, Issue #10, January 19, 1945, 9.

61   There were approximately 35,000 divorces in 1953. Pulju, *Women and Mass Consumer Society*, 109.

62   Fishman, *We Will Wait*, 131.

63   "Courrier des cœurs," letter from "Une maman isolée," *Ève*, Issue #16, July 26, 1946, 19.

64   "Courrier des cœurs," letter from "Celle qui attend," *Ève*, Issue #3, October 1, 1945, 2.

65 Lang, André, "La guerre a-t-elle tué l'amour?" *Elle*, Issue #29, June 4, 1946, 14–15, 22.

66 Coontz, *Marriage, a History*, 235.

67 Copley, *Sexual Moralities in France, 1780-1980*, 204; Riot-Sarcey, *Histoire du féminisme*, 90.

68 Vinen, *A history in fragments*, 368.

69 Pringle, *Telles qu'Elle*, 24.

70 Duchen, *Women's Rights and Women's Lives*, 28.

71 Pulju, *Women and Mass Consumer Society in Postwar France*, 109.

72 "200000 divorces en instance à Paris," *Elle*, Issue #4, December 12, 1945, 18, 22.

73 "Plus fort que l'Amérique," *Marie-France*, Issue #390, May 19, 1952, 24–25.

74 Mercier, Alain, "Il ne connaît que moi," *Elle*, Issue #29, June 4, 1946, 3.

75 Jackson, *Living in Arcadia*, 43.

76 Fears of depopulation have plagued France not only in the twentieth century. In fact, as Joshua Cole argues, "French thinkers were among the first to create an awareness of population as an object of study in the eighteenth century."(5) During the nineteenth century, concerns about depopulation, Cole argues, "emerged as a central problem for government."(6) Theories about how to handle population problems emerged over the course of the century, and they crystallized around a concrete, conservative vision of the family. Cole, *The Power of Large Numbers*, 5–6. Such familiar policies and discourses, linked as they were with republican governance, no doubt helped to muffle any protest against their reapplication by de Gaulle and the Fourth Republic following Vichy and the Second World War. As Francine Muel-Dreyfus points out, "the surplus of widows and unmarried women had reached three hundred thousand after the war of 1914, and in 1935, the draft contingent had declined by half because boys born between 1914 and 1918 were so few in number." Muel-Dreyfus, *Vichy and the Eternal Feminine*, 63; Mary Louise Roberts complicates this assessment in her work on the period following the Great War. During the decade immediately after the war ended, the birthrate actually rose. Thus Roberts suggests that government reactions in the 1920s represented unfounded fears. In fact, she argues, it was only in the 1930s that births began to decrease. Roberts, *Civilization without Sexes*, 123.

77 In fact, the birth rate rose in 1938–9, which the Vichy regime attributed to stronger anti-abortion measures, rather than what Muel-Dreyfus calls "an effect of the re-establishment of demographic equilibrium." Muel-Dreyfus, *Vichy and the Eternal Feminine*, 63.

78 Jackson, *Living in Arcadia*, 43.

79 F/41/5, Folder 2, Circulaires du Bureau du Personnel, Archives Nationales.

80 Bard, *Les femmes dans la société française au 20e siècle*, 186, 193.

81 Gildea, *France since 1945*, 80.

82 Judt, *Postwar*, 331.

83 Rioux, *Fourth Republic*, 352.

84 For more information on how women themselves attempted to negotiate state demands for children with their new role as full citizens, see Pulju, *Women in Mass Consumer Society*, 68–90.

85 Quoted in Rioux, *Au bonheur la France*, 351.

86 "Le problème des problèmes: la natalité," *Questions actuelles*, Document #64, September 25, 1945, 1–3. While *QA* is a rightist publication, calls for increased natality spanned the political spectrum, from the Far Right all the way to the PCF. See Rioux, *Fourth Republic*, 352.

87 Bordeaux, Henry, "La famille française en danger," *Questions actuelles*, 3ème année, #121, June 1946, 5–6.

88 "Future mamans savez-vous que . . ." *Marie-France*, Issue #151, October 7, 1947, 6–7; "*Ève* vous guide et vous conseille," letter from Mme. L.M. à Reims, *Ève*, Issue #105, April 16, 1948, 6.

89 "Des quadruplés sont nés à la Celle-Saint-Cloud," *Le Figaro*, #1241, September 7, 1948, 1, 4.

90 *Elle* began as a small insert in *France-Soir*, but it quickly emerged as a force in and of itself.

91 "ELLE est marraine," *Elle*, Issue #148, September 21, 1948, 3.

92 Duchen, *Women's Rights and Women's Lives in France*, 19.

93 Mouthiez, Claude, "Son dernier caprice," *Marie-France*, Issue #9, January 12, 1945, 9.

94 For another definition of republican motherhood, see Rendall, *Origins of Modern Feminism*, 33–66.

95 Childers, *Fathers, Families, and the State in France, 1914-1945*, 191.

96 Pollard, *Reign of Virtue*, 45–49. Natalist policies were also intense under the Third Republic, suggesting even stronger continuity between France's liberal democracies and the autocratic Vichy regime. See Roberts, *Civilization without Sexes*, 98–102.

97 Pollard, *Reign of Virtue*, 49.

98 Pollard, *Reign of Virtue*, 201; there is a book yet to be written about the disquieting continuities between Vichy and the postwar government when women and gender are the analytical lens. For more, see also Muel-Dreyfus, *Vichy and the Eternal Feminine*.

99 "Une date à noter: le 27 mai," *Marie-France*, Issue #9, January 12, 1945, 2.

100 See Pollard, Introduction; Sarah Fishman also addresses the tension associated with the continuity of strong family policies after the fall of the Vichy regime. She notes: "After the war . . . the Radical Republican Party emphasized that a radical government has passed the Family Code in 1939. 'Family policy is a republican tradition.'" Fishman, *We Will Wait*, 171.

101 Andrau, Marianne, "Appelez les témoins," *Marie-France*, Issue #266, January 2, 1950, 21.

102 "Quelques recettes pour ne pas rester 'vielle fille'," *Marie-France*, Issue #172, March 9, 1948, 67.

103 Quoted in *Alger Républicain*, "Après son voyage en AEF, le general de Gaulle est rentré hier soir à Alger," February 3, 1944, 1.

104 *Elle* magazine, Issue #3, December 5, 1945, 4.

105 "Le problème des problèmes: la natalité," *Questions actuelles*, Document #64, September 25, 1945, 1–3 (quote from page 1).

106 Rioux, *The Fourth Republic*, 85.

107 Coontz, *Marriage, a History*, 229.

108 Tirza Latimer argues that homosexuality went underground at this time, writing that the interwar community of lesbians and gay men "grew ghostly silent during the Occupation and reconstruction period." Latimer, *Women Together/Women Apart*, 137.

109 Jackson, "Sex, Politics and Morality in France, 1954-1982," 85.

110 Indeed Julian Jackson shows how even the editor of the early male homosexual publication, *Futur*, actually marginalized lesbianism, calling it "weak" in relation to male homosexuality. Jackson, *Living in Arcadia*, 51.

111 Porquerol, Elisabeth, "La Signification du Saphisme à travers les âges," *Le Crapouillot*, Troisième année #10, 33–34.

112 Reboux, *Sens interdits. Sodome. Gomorrhe.*, 231–34 [quote from p. 234].

113 Reboux, *Sens interdits. Sodome. Gomorrhe.*, 67–68.

114 This history is just beginning to receive more needed attention from scholars. Scholars Julian Jackson and Mark Meyers are currently at work on projects that relate to homosexuality in the immediate postwar period. I should also note that these kinds of stereotypes, such as the preying older lesbian, appear during other times of cultural anxiety about gender and sexuality in France, such as the interwar period. For more on cultural and intellectual tropes of homosexuality in the interwar period, see Dean, *The Frail Social Body*, 130–216. Postwar visibility for lesbians only came with the arrival of the Second Wave of feminism, according to Christine Bard. The first associated lesbian magazine, *Lesbia*, appeared in 1982. Bard, *Les femmes dans la société française au 20e siècle*, 174.

Chapter 4

1 "Une grande enquête d'*Elle*: voilà comment les hommes vous aiment," *Elle*, Issue #105, November 19, 1947, 4–5.

2 de Beauvoir, *The Second Sex*, 528.

3 "Vous pourriez être aussi belle qu'ELLE," *Elle* magazine, Issue #12, February 6, 1946, 12–13.

4 Bourdieu, *The Field of Cultural Production*, 37.

5 Arzaroli, *Le maquillage clair-obscur*, 83.

6 See, for example, Holly Grout's *Force of Beauty*, in which she argues that Third Republic beauty culture actively courted women and sometimes encouraged women to broaden their public voices, even if their access to political rights remained strained. Grout, *The Force of Beauty*, 9. See also Roberts, "Samson and Delilah Revisited."

7 Duchen, *Women's Rights and Women's Lives*, 23; See also Veillon, whose work complicates this assertion.

8 Even the pampering that was purported to be so essential to a woman's health and happiness traces back to this idea of a woman in the image of what one's man wants her to be. In terms of the woman herself and her own needs, women's magazines did embrace a small amount of self-nurturing. However, this was probably anathema to most French women who were not part of the burgeoning middle class. Firm statistics on members of the working classes are difficult to come by in this period, for, as Claire Duchen notes, the accepted definition of "working population . . . changed between 1946 and 1954." (Duchen, *Women's Rights and Women's Lives*, 129.) However, Jean-Pierre Rioux reports that the major union, the *Confédération Générale du Travail* (CGT), counted more than five million members alone, eclipsing Popular Front membership, in 1945. (Rioux, *The Fourth Republic*, 76.) This comprised around 12 percent of the population at this time. Additionally, Robert Gildea shows that "at the beginning of the Second World War 45 percent of the population lived in rural communities, defined as having fewer than 2,000 inhabitants." There was a boom in agriculture in the years immediately following the war due to improved technology, although this would lead to severe corrections in the later 1950s and beyond. (Gildea, *France since 1945*, 102–03.) The middle class did comprise a significant portion of the French population, however. Robert Gildea places the percentage of members of the new *cadre*, or "salaried middle class" at 12 percent in 1954, and the percentage of "business people, shopkeepers, and artisans"—historically France's middle class—at 13 percent. (Gildea, *France since 1945*, 109). The question here, though, centers on the creation of a mainstream identity, one which was directed at a very wide swath of French women (see this book's chapter three for questions of magazine readership, for example).

9 See, for example, Jean-Jacques Rousseau's discussion of artifice in his *Émile*. Rousseau, Book V.

10 Veillon, *Fashion under the Occupation*, 141.

11 Blandin and Eck, "*La vie des femmes*," 14; see also Roberts, "Making the Modern Girl French," and Grout, *The Force of Beauty*.

12 Veillon, *Fashion under the Occupation*, 130.

13 "Regardons votre cou," *Elle* magazine, Issue #7, January 2, 1946, 20–21.

14 It is perhaps no accident that 1946 saw the launch of the Terraillon personal scale in France. From Herscher, *Qualité de vie*, 47.

15 "A la recherche de la beauté plastique," *Marie-France*, Issue #111, January 1, 1947, 19.

16 "Méritez-vous qu'on vous critique sur la plage?" *Elle*, Issue #39, August 13, 1946, 21.

17 "Cet hiver, vous devez être pâle," *Elle*, Issue #46, September 3, 1946, 3; For more articles like this, see Chevalier, "La beauté a 27 lois," in *Elle*, Issue #113, January 20, 1948, 12–13; see also Alice Chavane, "14 questions autour d'une gorge ronde," *Elle*, Issue #226, March 27, 1950, 24–25, among others.

18 "Cutex, le vernis à ongles américain!" *Marie-France*, Issue #276, March 13, 1950, 40 (back cover); see also "Cutex," *Elle*, Issue #279, April 2, 1951, 52.

19 "Mon amie américain envie mes ongles!" *Marie-France*, Issue #200, September 21, 1948, 2.

20 This tension mirrors French geopolitical concerns, specifically that the United States was destroying something uniquely French. See Rioux, *Fourth Republic*, 133–34, and Kuisel, *Seducing the French*. It would be interesting to use beauty and gender as a yardstick of anti-Americanism in the 1940s and 1950s. The tension also reflects the American model of advertising, what Victoria de Grazia calls "life-style feminism." It featured young, slender, attractive middle-class women selling to presumably the same make of consumer. Here, the model is somewhat inverted, with a French company using American methods to both attract French women and repel American goods. de Grazia, *Irresistible Empire*, 428–30.

21 de Richard, André, "Je quitte ma femme . . .," *Elle*, Issue #14, February 20, 1946, 16, 22.

22 Kathy Peiss notes this postwar trend of diminished/distorted female sexual agency as manifested in "movies and romance magazines" in the United States: "A woman acted upon her desire for a man by making herself beautiful, in order to catch his attention and awaken *his* desire." Peiss, *Hope in a Jar*, 249.

23 Arzaroli, *Le maquillage clair-obscur*, 60.

24 "Sachez vous maquiller," *Marie-France*, Issue #18, March 23, 1945, 4.

25 Veillon, *Fashion under the Occupation*, 128–29.

26 "Je n'ai qu'une robe," *Marie-France*, Issue #87, July 17, 1946, 14.

27 Lang, André, "La guerre a-t-elle tué l'amour?" *Elle*, Issue #30, June 11, 1946, 18–19.

28 "Pour lui seul plus belle encore," *Elle*, Issue #52, November 12, 1946, 19.

29 Danon, Monique, "Ce soir, il ne veut pas sortir," *Elle*, Issue #52, November 12, 1946, 8–9.

30 Giroud, Françoise, "Comment ne pas se dévaluer?" *Elle*, Issue #357, November 29, 1952, 40.

31 Sandra Reineke attributes *Elle*'s popularity in part to the frankness of the magazine's discussions of sexuality; I am not so sure it is quite as direct. It seems to me that *Elle* presented an escape from the difficulties of women's lives, and then within that, there were some liberatory tendencies, but the messages were larger conformist and not always evidently disclosed. Reineke, *Beauvoir and Her Sisters*, 44.

32 See also Alice Chavane's "Pour plaire à son mari, elle met toutes les chances de son côté," which provides a pictorial of nine images detailing exactly how a woman should prepare for a day of pleasing her man. *Elle*, Issue #268, January 15, 1951, 24–25.

33 Keyer, Georges, "Elle n'était pas jalouse," *Elle*, Issue #52, November 12, 1946, 18, 22.

34 "Pour lui plaire," *Ève*, Issue #2, September 15, 1945, 11.

35 de Beauvoir, *The Second Sex*, 529.

36 For more on this in nineteenth-century Paris, see Lisa Tiersten's *Marianne in the Market*; for more on this in a different context, see in the context of, see Erika Rappaport's *Shopping for Pleasure*, (nineteenth-century London), and Elaine Abelson's *When Ladies Go A-Thieving* (nineteenth-century US).

37 *Elle*, Issue #2, November 28, 1945, 10–11.

38 Lipovetsky argues this at many points in his work; for example, he states, "The distinguishing feature of haute couture is not that it imposed homogenous standards as that it diversified styles in order to emphasize individual personalities, to consecrate the value of originality in dress, even to the point of extravagance." Lipovetsky, *The Empire of Fashion*, 78. The New Look accomplishes exactly the opposite of this: it is couture which speaks to uniformity and conformity. Carolyn Dean's review of Lipovetsky acutely critiques him for this point in arguing that Lipovetsky does not devote any attention to how fashion "sustains gender inequities" rather than challenges the status quo and creates an individual. Dean, "Review: The Empire of Fashion," 477. Malcolm Barnard agrees with Lipovetsky in his *Fashion as Communication*, when he states that "fashion and clothing may be used to challenge or to contest . . . class, sex and gender relations."(102–03) He does argue earlier that "fashion and clothing may be used as fences and bridges . . . they delineate one group from another at the same time as they identify common values in a group."(40) Barnard does not, however, directly address this question of how fashion may be homogenizing the self—the individual—rather than liberating it.

39 Arnold, *Fashion, Desire and Anxiety*, xiv.

40 "On demande mannequins, taille 42, grande," *Elle*, Issue #12, February 6, 1946, 3.

41 Cawthorne, *The New Look*, 86.

42 Ibid., 93.

43 Soley-Beltran, "Modelling Femininity," 312.

44 Leblond, Denise and Nicolas Tikhomirov, "14 heures de Fabienne: Le film qu'elle tourne sans le savoir," *Marie-France*, Issue #310, November 6, 1950, 10–11.

45 Steele, *Fifty Years of Fashion*, 44.

46 Ibid., 47.

47 "On demande mannequins taille 42, grandes," *Elle*, Issue #16, March 5, 1946, 3; Apparently this was true, as the modeling "crisis" situation still existed a few years later, despite the magazines' entreaties. In 1947 it even made front-page news in *Le Figaro*, where a staff writer evaluated the beauty and potential service of the young women. Dartois, Yves, "Pour remédier à la crise des mannequins, 100 jolies candidates ont affronté un sévère jury féminin," *Le Figaro*, October 26–27, 1947, 1; in an odd anecdote, Christian Dior once recalled his own problems finding models: "In despair at not being able to find the type of girl I wanted, I decided to put an advertisement in the paper. As luck would have it, I chose the exact moment when a new law was forcing certain Paris 'houses' to close down, and many of their former occupants found themselves without regular employment." They came down to the house, and unfortunately none of them suited Dior, who still made sure to interview every last one of them. From Dior, *Christian Dior and I*, 35–36.

48 Paul E. Deutschman, "How to Buy a Dior Original," *Holiday*, January 1955, 44–47; quoted in Steele, *Paris Fashion*, 273.

49 "L'heure d'être belle approche," *Elle*, Issue #157, November 30, 1948, 16–17.

50 For skiing, see "Plaisir de neige," which notes that a woman absolutely must have a special ski outfit for the slopes; *Marie-France*, Issue #103, November 6, 1946, 15–16. For gardening, a woman needs "practical" but still "elegant" clothes; see "Jardinage," *Marie-France*, Issue #86, July 10, 1946, 10–11. For the beach, see "Soyez à la plage," *Marie-France*, Issue #236, June 6, 1949, 12–13.

51 "Future mamans . . . soyez à la mode," *Elle*, Issue #241, July 7, 1950, 2.

52 Keenan, *Dior in Vogue*, 30.

53 de Réthy and Perreau, *Christian Dior*, 8.

54 Keenan, *Dior in Vogue*, 30.

55 de Marly, *Christian Dior*, 21.

56 Ibid., 73.

57 The link between fashion and French identity was first set in the reign of Louis XIV, in the seventeenth century, and maintaining French prominence in the industry became a priority for the nation's leaders almost uniformly since that time. For more, see Steele, *Paris Fashion*.

58 de Pietri and Leventon, *New Look to Now*, 23; Veillon, *Fashion under the Occupation*, 93; some couture houses did remain open during the war, see Bertherat et al., *100 Ans de Mode*, 58; see also Veillon, *Fashion under the Occupation*, 85–106.

59 The Théâtre de la Mode was an astounding success, with attendance reaching more than one hundred thousand. The dolls in the Théâtre de la Mode had real leather and textiles; they even sported real hair and real fur coats. For more information on the Théâtre de la Mode, see Campbell, "High Fashion and the Reconstruction of postwar France, 1945-1960," as well as Veillon, *Fashion under the Occupation*, 144; Louise de Vilmorin's article, "Au Théâtre de la Mode, petits personnages parés de grandeur," from the *Album de la Mode du Figaro*, #5, 1945, 50–51; and Edmonde Charles-Roux's edited collection, *Le Théâtre de la Mode*.

60 Giroud, *Portraits sans retouches*, 82.

61 For more context, see Steele, *Paris Fashion*, 270–74.

62 Ibid.; see also Veillon, *Fashion under the Occupation*, 141–45.

63 Alsop, *To Marietta from Paris, 1945-1960*, 93.

64 "Christian Dior," *Le Crapouillot*, Deuxième année, #8, 64.

65 Keenan, *Dior in Vogue*, 43; see also de Marly, *Christian Dior*, 79, and Palmer, *Dior*, 22.

66 Reynolds, *The 40s and 50s*, 19.

67 Dior, *Christian Dior and I*, 16.

68 Dior, *Talking about Fashion*, 36.

69 de Marly, *Christian Dior*, 19.

70 Quoted in Parkins, *Poiret, Dior and Schiaparelli*, 132.

71 Parkins, *Poiret, Dior and Schiaparelli*, 136.

72 Dior, *Christian Dior and I*, 57.

73 Ibid., 46.

74 Roberts, *Civilization without Sexes*, 68; Roberts argues that the Chanel fashions necessitated a new kind of body policing, one which forced women to be extremely thin and conscious about certain areas of their bodies. So, while freeing in the sense that women did not have to wear complicated corsets, it still created a beauty industrial complex.

75 Keenan, *Dior in Vogue*, 31.

76 Forlano, "Voici les **'bombes'** de Dior," *Elle*, Issue #198, September 15, 1949, 11.

77 Roberts, *Civilization without Sexes*, 68.

78 de Pietri, Stephen and Melissa Leventon. *New Look to Now: French Haute Couture,1947-1987*. New York: Rizzoli International Publications, Inc., 1989, 29.

79 "Ces cochons de français," *Le Canard enchaîné*, September 27, 1944, 3; see also Wallach, *Chanel*, 128–32; Interestingly, many other popular culture figures, such as Arletty, Édith Piaf, and Maurice Chevalier, who had entertained Germans, either sexually or professionally, were let go with little punishment or even dishonor. See Gildea, *France since 1945*, 70. Coco Chanel, on the other hand, whose fashions had represented a threat to gender norms, was temporarily run out of the country.

80 Judt, *Postwar*, 89.

81 Rioux, *The Fourth Republic*, 181; statistic about cost of dresses from Cawthorne, *The New Look*, 114.

82 Beevor and Cooper, *Paris after the Liberation, 1945*-1949, 285.

83 de Pietri, *New Look to Now*, 24.

84 Givhan, *The Battle of Versailles*, 33.

85 Partington, "Popular Fashion and Working-Class Affluence," 145–61, quote from 159.

86 Steele, *Paris Fashion*, 274.

87 Alsop, *To Marietta from Paris, 1945*-1960, 93; Dior later asked Alsop to wear the clothes among her social set in order to popularize them further.

88 Bertherat, *100 Ans de Mode*, 67; I should additionally note that this chapter focuses more on the messages that designers and clothes proffered to the public in and of themselves, rather than on their reception.

89 Givhan, *The Battle of Versailles*, 33; Adding to the diminution of Dior protests, Fashion scholar Ilya Parkins labels criticism of Dior a "minority view . . . his garments became the epitome of fashion." Parkins, *Poiret, Dior and Schiaparelli*, 111; Similarly, sociologists Kurt Lang and Gladys Engel Lang refer to incidents of critique as "isolated, if well-publicized." Lang and Lang, "The Power of Fashion," 130.

90 Beevor and Cooper, *Paris after the Liberation, 1945*-1949, 286.

91 "Comment faire apparaître une robe comme dix!" *Elle*, Issue #8, January 9, 1946, 10–11.

92 "Je n'ai qu'une robe," *Marie-France*, Issue #87, July 17, 1946, 14.

93 "Tant d'invitations et une seule robe!" *Elle*, Issue #57, December 17, 1946, 32–33.

94 "Bonjour à la mode nouvelle," *Elle*, Issue #70, March 18, 1947, 4–5.

95 "Conclusion: Vous serez à la mode si . . .," *Elle*, Issue #70, March 18, 1947, 18–19.

96 "ELLE vous présente la MODE 49," *Elle*, Issue #172, March 15, 1949, 9.

97 While economic and material conditions undoubtedly improved between the end of the war and 1949, people still faced serious deprivations. According to Rioux, "In January 1946, 49 per cent [of the population] still gave the satisfaction of basic daily needs as their principal concern . . . proportions which were to remain unchanged until 1949." So the gulf between the two articles—one of making do, one of purchasing new attire, remains vast when compared with basic realities. Rioux, *Fourth Republic*, 27.

98 Chavane, Alice, "14 questions autour d'une gorge ronde," *Elle*, Issue #226, March 27, 1950, 24–25.

99 "Star-Sein," *Marie-France*, Issue #200, September 21, 1948, 27.

100 The concept of a woman's responsibility to decorate her home is not a new one in France, nor is the notion that these decorations carried consequences for the

nation. Lisa Tiersten has shown that in late-nineteenth-century France, during
an era of increasing commercialization and modernization, cultural critics
expressed fears that French society as a whole was losing its grasp of taste in favor
of cheaper, mass-produced products. She argues that bourgeois women were
cast as the bearers of taste for the nation, "creating interiors that were at once
morally pure and artistically designed." Tiersten, *Marianne in the Market*, 158.
This kind of consuming did not, Tiersten argues, challenge male authority. She
shopped to please her husband and care for her family. Ibid., 191–95. Overall,
the bourgeois woman of the time was, Tiersten posits, "shopping for the good of
home and nation." Ibid., 235. This stands in contrast with Deborah Cohen's study
of British homes during the Victorian and Edwardian periods, when, she argues,
men were often the final arbiters of taste in their homes. This was specifically the
case in the Victorian period when "houses . . . served to convey a man's wealth
and standing [in the late nineteenth century]. Where and how a man lived might
do more to advertise his position than could his occupation or profession." It was
only later in the nineteenth century when home decoration became conflated
with effeteness. Cohen, *Household Gods*, 97–100; quote from 97. Women's role as
consumers was no longer subject to questions of legitimacy, but now the national
and international anxieties about France's greatness as a nation permeated the
home.

101   See Pollard, *Reign of Virtue*, 1, 80–84.
102   Roche, Alice, "Quatre femmes sur cinq ne savent pas organiser leur travail," *Elle*, Issue #20, April 2, 1946, 19.
103   "Vous êtes? . . . Vous n'êtes pas? . . ." *Marie-France*, Issue #116, February 5, 1947, 4–5.
104   Sylvie, "Parmi le thym et la rosée," *Ève*, Issue #12, June 28, 1946, 3.
105   "Les bons soins . . . font les bons maris," *Elle*, Issue #52, November 12, 1946, 16–17; see also "Ménagères avec le sourire," *L'Alouette d'Auvergne*, March 1946, (no page).
106   Auslander, *Taste and Power*, 380–85, Introduction.
107   Siegfried, André, "Qualité," *Album de la mode du Figaro*, Issue #5, 1945, 39–40.
108   Segal, Marcelle, "Courrier du cœur," letter from C.R.L., *Elle*, Issue #209, November 28, 1949, 3.
109   Roland-Marcel, Marian, "À vos pieds, Madame!" *Le Monde*, February 3–4, 1946, 4.
110   Fishman, *We Will Wait*, 168.
111   Gildea, *France since 1945*, 148.
112   Masson, Elisabeth, "Rester vraiment des femmes . . .," *Marie-France*, Issue #14, February 16, 1945, 2.
113   de Beauvoir, *The Second Sex*, xxx.

114 "Ann Todd," *Elle*, Issue #2, April 20, 1946, 2; for a similar example, see Dubreuilil, Simone, "Madeleine Carrol pour se consacrer aux enfants a abandonné le cinéma," *France-Soir*, #216, March 4–5, 1945, 1.

115 The Todd piece was not unique. Susan Weiner points to a series of similar articles in *Elle*, all of which profiled a professional woman in her home, performing domestic tasks. Weiner, "Two Modernities," 400.

116 "Le beau métier d'infirmière," *Marie-France*, Issue #103, November 6, 1946, 14.

117 Interestingly, many of the "bad women" types in the following chapter, such as Denise Delfau, were independent, single women who had "unnatural" jobs.

118 Claire Duchen writes that "basic products were still rationed until 1949, coffee until 1950." Duchen, *Women's Rights and Women's Lives*, 18.

Chapter 5

1 Capdevila, "L'identité masculine et les fatigues de la guerre (1914–1945)," 104–05.

2 Virgili, *Shorn Women*.

3 Gentry and Sjoberg, *Beyond Mothers, Monsters, Whores*, 3.

4 Ibid., 108.

5 Ferguson, *Accounting for Taste*, 131–35.

6 Bouteille-Garagnon, *Infernal rebus*, 205.

7 Mornand, *La vie et la mort de Daisy Georges-Martin, Martyre de la Résistance*, 80; Mornand goes on to describe another similar scene with the daily soup rations on 83.

8 Tillion, *Ravensbrück*, 34.

9 Rosane, *Terre de cendres*, 50.

10 Maurel, *An Ordinary Camp*, 54.

11 Tillion, *Ravensbrück*, 25.

12 Saint-Clair, *Ravensbrück, l'Enfer des femmes*, 77.

13 Rosane, *Terre de cendres*, 70.

14 Bouteille-Garagnon, *Infernal rebus*, 28.

15 Ibid., 30–33, quotes from 33.

16 Rosane, *Terre de cendres*, 94.

17 Helm, *Ravensbrück*, 375.

18 Hoisne, *Chambre 535, ou mes cinq prisons pendant l'Occupation*, 92.

19 Rosane, *Terre de cendres*, 38.

20 Quoted in Beevor and Cooper, *Paris after the Liberation, 1945-1949*, 275–76.

21 Tillion, *Ravensbrück*, 68.

22 Tillion, *Ravensbrück*, 69.

23 Busson, *Dans les Griffes nazies; Angers, Fresnes, Ravensbrück, Mauthausen*, 60–61.

24 Rosane, *Terre de cendres*, 43.

25 Delbo, *Auschwitz and After*, 22–23.

26 Rosane, *Terre de cendres*, 34.

27 Delbo, *Auschwitz and After*, 175.

28 See Delbo, *Auschwitz and After*, 36; Richet, et al., *Trois Bagnes*, 111; see also Le Breton, *Les pégriots*. From Ruffin, *Violette Morris*, 7; See also Rosane, *Terre de cendres*, 82, 85.

29 Busson, *Dans les Griffes nazies; Angers, Fresnes, Ravensbrück, Mauthausen*, 54.

30 Rosane, *Terre de cendres*, 34.

31 Bouteille-Garagnon, *Infernal rebus*, 104–05.

32 Rosane, *Terre de cendres*, 95.

33 Ibid., 158.

34 Tillion, *Ravensbrück*, 70.

35 Delbo, *Auschwitz and After*, 80.

36 Saint-Clair, *Ravensbrück, l'Enfer des femmes*, 57–58.

37 Maurel, *An Ordinary Camp*, 56.

38 Wilborts, *Pour la France*, 101; The female prison guard with a dog is an image which seems to abound at this time, which is interesting. I would hypothesize that there are two reasons for this: first, prison guards simply used dogs to control the detainees, and second, there is a sexual aspect to the notion of the woman who has this dog who attacks for her. See also coverage of the Belsen trials in various French newspapers, during which Irma Grese, who became the archetypical female prison guard, was tried. In the small French newspaper *Les Nouvelles du Matin*, the well-known journalist Pierre Scize describes another of the female guards, Folken Hath, as "la femme au chien." [Scize, Pierre, "Kramer, Grese et Cie accusé par leurs victimes," *Les Nouvelles du Matin*, September 22, 1945, 1–2].

39 Richet et al., *Trois Bagnes*, 112–13.

40 Tillion, *Ravensbrück*, 76.

41 Rosane, *Terre de cendres*, 151.

42 Ibid., 50.

43 Ibid., 81.

44 This is highly reminiscent of attempts to categorize lesbianism medically during the Third Republic. In her *Frail Social Body*, Carolyn Dean has shown how lesbianism was divided into two categories at this time: "congenital . . . and acquired lesbianism." (197) A certain contingent of congenital lesbians thrived on pain and torture, even to their own persons. According to Dean, this served to construct them as inherently "perverted" and in stark contrast to normal French sexuality. (197–8) They stand in opposition to the other group of congenital lesbians, whose undomesticated, uncontrolled sexuality in fact represents the essence of femininity.

45 Tillion, *Ravensbrück*, 59.

46 I have not come across work on female prison guards within the German context in my research, but I think this would be fascinating given the different circumstances. Where the French were trying to portray themselves as heroic resistors and hence victors in the war, the Germans had clearly lost and their postwar experience was radically different. Given that, how were these 'non-women' represented in postwar Germany? Trials and German-language memoirs would both yield an interesting contrast with the French constructions and constitute an important subject of study within their own right. I also think that this subject continues into the Cold War, where the idea of the masculine woman seems to become associated with Communism itself, almost becoming a by-product of such a system in the West. Consider, for example, portrayals of female athletes from Soviet bloc countries during the Olympic Games in the 1970s and 1980s. Here again, such women act as stand-ins for their own nations and political systems, but they also can serve as negative pedagogical examples for women in the West. Such a woman is so closely tied to a negative political regime, so much so that she almost becomes a by-product of such a regime, then women in the West must be the opposite of that, both in terms of representations and actualizations.

48 Flanner, Janet, "Letter from Paris," *The New Yorker*, December 27, 1952, 52.

47 "Gestapo of rue de la Pompe," *Time*, December 1, 1952, 27.

49 The *Abwehr* was a German intelligence gathering group, which performed similar functions as the Gestapo but was not the same; it was subsumed under the SS in summer 1944.

50 There were two Germans on trial with this group, and there were others who were still either at large or had died. Friedrich Berger, for example, had been the leader of the rue de la Pompe cell, yet he never faced judgment for his crimes in France or elsewhere. He was captured in Milan in 1948, then escaped and lived in hiding in Germany until his death from illness in Munich in 1960. In all, there were twenty-one members of the rue de la Pompe cell, and fourteen were put on trial in this case. Bochin, "Quatorze tortionnaires du « S.D. » de la rue de la Pompe écoutent le rappel de leurs crimes," *Figaro*, November 20, 1952, 2.

51 The members of the rue de la Pompe cell on trial for their crimes included two women, Denise Delfau and Madeleine Marchand. Marchand was unable to sit through the court hearings because of an illness.

52 *Combat* was leftist, *Le Monde* more centrist, and *Figaro* conservative.

53 Théolleyre, Jean-Marc, "Ça n'intéresse personne," *Le Monde*, November 20, 1952, 1.

54 For a sampling of international coverage, see, "Gestapo of the rue de la Pompe," *Time*, December 1, 1952, 27; "Eight Years' Wait," *Time*, January 5, 1953, 29;

Flanner, Janet, "Letter from Paris," *The New Yorker*, December 27, 1952, 51; "Eight Frenchmen Doomed," *The New York Times*, December 23, 1952, 7.

55 I should note that some of the articles in *Combat* are not attributed to anyone. Pichon and Hericotte seem to have been the most common reporters for the newspaper, however, and I have used them most frequently in my own analysis.

56 Bochin, Roland, "Pour couvrir les cris de leurs victimes les tortionnaires faisaient fonctionner les avertisseurs de leurs camions," *Figaro*, December 13–14, 1952, 2.

57 Théolleyre, Jean-Marc, "Les rescapés de l'Organisation juive de combat ont raconté l'agonie de leur réseau," *Le Monde*, December 9, 1952, 8.

58 Pichon, Jean, "Les 14 tortionnaires de la rue de la Pompe face à leurs forfaits: 300 arrestations, 160 déportations, 42 fusillés," *Combat*, November 20, 1952, 1,8 [quote from p. 8].

59 Pichon, Jean, "Le témoignage des victimes rend inutiles les dénégations des accusés," *Combat*, December 1, 1952, 8.

60 Théolleyre, Jean-Marc, "Les témoignages les plus calmes se révèlent les plus accablants," *Le Monde*, December 2, 1952, 8.

61 Roland Bochin, "Quatorze des tortionnaires du « S.D. » de la rue de la Pompe écoutent le rappel de leurs crimes," *Figaro*, November 20, 1952, 2.

62 Théolleyre, Jean-Marc, "Les quatorze accusés présents ont entendu pendant plus de trois heures le récit de trois cents tortures," *Le Monde*, November 21, 1952, 4.

63 Théolleyre, Jean-Marc, "Les quatorze accusés présents ont entendu pendant plus de trois heures le récit de trois cents tortures," *Le Monde*, November 21, 1952, 4; Armand Gatti of *Le Parisien libéré* also remembered the scene with the inclusion of nudism; see Gatti, "L'interrogatoire se heurte au mur de silence," *Le Parisien libéré*, November 25, 1952, 8.

64 Writing about an early-twentieth-century American context, Lauren Rabinovitz has argued that even when a female returned male gazes in her guise of "flirt," in literature, "she looks . . . only to be held as the object of a male sexualized gaze." Thus in this context even when a woman gazed upon a man in public, she was only doing so in order to objectify herself; she did not hold the power in that relationship. Also, even when artists depicted women in public as actively looking at men, Rabinovitz argues, there was always an unknown man gazing at them. She states: "Women may look at both white and nonwhite men, but they do so only while they simultaneously are held as the unaware objects of other men's gazes." Rabinovitz, 26, 66.

65 Théolleyre, Jean-Marc, "Les résistants polonais semblent avoir subi les pires tortures," *Le Monde*, December 6, 1952, 11.

66 Hericotte, René, "Pour ne pas avoir été à la Cascade le 16 août 1944, les accusés cherchent aujourd'hui un alibi," *Combat*, December 10, 1952, 8.

67   Bochin, Roland, "Les survivants de l'Organisation juive de combat témoignent de la froide cruauté de Berger et de ses complices," *Figaro*, December 8, 1952, 2.

68   Bochin, Roland, "Les coupables expriment des regrets de pure forme," *Figaro*, November 21, 1952, 2.

69   Pichon, Jean, "Les 14 tortionnaires de la rue de la Pompe face à leurs forfaits : 300 arrestations, 160 déportations, 42 fusillés," *Combat*, November 20, 1952, 1.

70   Flanner, Janet, "Letter from Paris," *New Yorker*, December 27, 1952, 52.

71   Théolleyre, Jean-Marc, "Les résistants de Sainte-Menehould évoquent les traitements qu'ils ont subis lors du passage de Berger dans leur région," *Le Monde*, December 13, 1952, 11.

72   Théolleyre, Jean-Marc, "Les témoignages les plus calmes se révèlent les plus accablants," *Le Monde*, December 2, 1952, 8.

73   Théolleyre, Jean-Marc, "Les rescapés poursuivent le récit de leurs supplices," *Le Monde*, December 3, 1952, 11; see also Roland Bochin, "De nouveaux et accablants témoignages sur les tortures infligées aux résistances," *Figaro*, December 2, 1952, 2 and René Hericotte, "Mauvaise journée pour l'accusé Favriol," *Combat*, December 2, 1952, 8.

74   This stands in opposition to the differences between male and female victims. In that case, female victims' bodies took on a heavily symbolic burden in a discursive way which eventually emphasized that women should stay in private. Male victims, on the other hand, were honorable men whose deaths were publicly praised. Where female torturers had taken over a masculine role in terms of power, in the Liberation context, when every man had to have participated in the Resistance in order to restore French virility, a male torturer for the Gestapo had in fact subverted his own masculine role, and his portrayal reflected that. I should note that these are observations about legal proceedings for the most part, rather than attempts at vigilante justice. The authority of the state plays a strong role in discussions about legitimacy, in my opinion, as well as about official public attitudes about gender, as read through these trials. I should also argue that the rue de la Pompe trial fell well out of the scope of Megan Koreman's work, in which she convincingly describes the people's anger at the leniency of French courts between 1944 and 1946. The government, she argues, was fully complicit in attempting to smooth over the Occupation and supported more lenient punishments in the interest of stability. (See Koreman, *The Expectation of Justice*, 92–147) On another note, it would certainly be interesting to compare these discourses with how reactions to French torturers played out in terms of gender a few years later, in the Algerian context.

75   Bochin, Roland, "Le président Chadefaux ouvre le dossier des atrocités commises dans la région de Sainte-Menehould," *Figaro*, December 12, 1952, 2.

76 Bochin, Roland, "Contre Georges et Adrien Guicciardini se succèdent d'accablantes dépositions," *Figaro*, November 28, 1952, 2.

77 Bochin, Roland, "Les coupables expriment des regrets de pure forme," *Figaro*, November 21, 1952, 2.

78 Gatti, Armand, "Ni les larmes de Denise Delfau ni l'invraisemblable croix de guerre de Poupet n'ont atteenu l'horreur des crimes de la bande," *Le Parisien libéré*, November 21, 1952, 7.

79 Flanner, Janet, "Letter from Paris," *New Yorker*, December 27, 1952, 52.

80 Gatti, Armand, "Ni les larmes de Denise Delfau ni l'invraisemblable croix de guerre de Poupet n'ont atteenu l'horreur des crimes de la bande," *Le Parisien libéré*, November 21, 1952, 7.

81 Théolleyre, Jean-Marc, "Les accusés reconnaissent avoir participé à des arrestations mais nient avoir martyrisé des résistants," *Le Monde*, November 22, 1952, 6.

82 Théolleyre, Jean-Marc, "Les quatorze accusés présents ont entendu pendant plus de trois heures le récit de trois cents tortures," *Le Monde*, November 21, 1952, 4.

83 Bochin, Roland, "Un accusé, Raoul Fouché, ayant troublé l'audience par ses vociférations, est expulsé momentanément de la salle," *Figaro*, November 25, 1952, 2.

84 Bochin, Roland, "Contre Georges et Adrien Guicciardini se succèdent d'accablantes dépositions," *Figaro*, November 28, 1952, 2.

85 Bochin, Roland, "Les coupables expriment des regrets de pure forme," *Figaro*, November 21, 1952, 2.

86 For a more nuanced discussion of this, see Bonnet, *Violette Morris*.

87 Bonnet, *Violette Morris*, 18.

88 Seymour, *Bugatti Queen*, 86.

89 In her article, "Droit au but," Wendy Michellat describes several other "scandalous incidents" involving Morris's comportment on the fields of play. Michellat, 15.

90 "Le port du costume masculin par une femme va faire l'objet d'une curieuse controverse devant le tribunal civil," *Le Journal*, February 24, 1930, 1. See also Bonnet, *Violette Morris*, 12; Gury, *L'honneur ratatiné d'une athlete lesbienne en 1930*, 13.

91 Bonnet, *Violette Morris*, 44–45.

92 Musnik, Henry, "Nos Interviews-Express: En neuf ans, Violette Morris n'a subi qu'une seule défaite," *L'Intransigeant*, October 21, 1926, 5.

93 "La curieuse destinée de Violette Morris," *Paris-Soir*, December 28, 1937, A. See also Michallat, 17; Bonnet argues that, on the pretext of not wanting to lose funding or public support, the FFSF had turned much more toward a promotion of traditional female values through sport by the late 1920s and early 1930s. Bonnet, *Violette Morris*, 58-9.

94 "Mme Violette Morris perd son procès contre la Fédération féminine sportive," *Le Journal*, March 27, 1927, 1. See also Bard, Christine, "Les Femmes travesties, un mauvais genre, Le 'DB58' aux Archives de la Préfecture de la Police" (no page numbers).

95 Mazeline, Guy, "Une sportive peut-elle porter la culotte?" *L'Intransigent*, February 27, 1930, 5N.

96 See Roberts, *Civilization without Sexes*, 63–88.

97 Seymour, *Bugatti Queen*, 26.

98 "Pour le sport," *Time*, Monday, March 18, 1929, 46.

99 Ruffin, *Violette Morris*, 109; Seymour, *Bugatti Queen*, 26; Gury, 31-2. I should note that these are all popular biographers and writers, Ruffin and Gury in France, Seymour in England.

100 Gury, *L'honneur ratatiné d'une athlete lesbienne en 1930*, 31–32.

101 Morris later lost a lawsuit stating that it was unlawful for the FFSF to expel her. For some international press, see, for example, "Resent Morality Order: French Women Athletes Call Committee's Apparel Decree Absurd," *New York Times*, July 4, 1926, E2; see also "Woman Sues in Defense of Right to Wear Pants," *Washington Post*, December 22, 1928, 4; see also "Women's Right to Trousers," *International Herald Tribune*, December 23, 1928, 8; see also "The Right to Wear Pants," *International Herald Tribune*, February 25, 1930, 2; see also "Male Attire is Cause for Barring Woman Athlete, Paris Court Holds," *Washington Post*, March 27, 1930, 15.

102 Michallat, "Droit au but: Violette Morris and Women's Football in 'les années folles,'" 16.

103 "Who Won," *Time*, Monday, April 7, 1930, 66.

104 Auvray, "Violette Morris (1893-1944)," 430.

105 Ruffin, *Violette Morris*, 134–35, quote from 134; see also Bonnet, *Violette Morris*, 84–85.

106 Ruffin, *Violette Morris*, 121.

107 Bard, *Une histoire politique du pantalon*, 275. See also Auvray, "Violette Morris (1893-1944)," 431.

108 Seymour, *Bugatti Queen*, 236.

109 Ruffin, *Violette Morris*, 139.

110 Oberg later went on trial in 1954 in what Henry Rousso calls "one of the last great postwar trials" which "revealed the scope and collaboration and repression under Vichy." (Ironically, Jean-Marc Théolleyre also covered this trial for *Le Monde*.) Rousso, *Vichy Syndrome*, 61, 2. Morris was linked to the Gestapo group at the rue des Saussaies by a German interpreter at the end of the war. See Bonnet, *Violette Morris*, 147.

111   Dossier Morris Violette, December 1943–January 1944, "Mise en garde sur la femme Gouraud-Morris Violette," Quoted in Auvray, 431.

112   Le Breton, *Les pégriots*. From Ruffin, *Violette Morris*, 7.

113   Bonnet, *Violette Morris*, 115–20.

114   Weitz, *Sisters in the Resistance*, 279; Weitz refers to her as Violette Moriss.

115   Perrault, *Paris under the Occupation*, 38.

116   Ruffin, *Violette Morris*, 196–98; quote from 196–97.

117   Ibid., 237.

118   Bonnet, *Violette Morris*, 183–84; this comes from the testimony of Kléber Combier, an ally of Morris, whom Bonnet discounts because he disclosed this during a confession. She also argues that Combier's chronology of Morris's crimes is problematic.

119   Ruffin, *Violette Morris*, 238.

120   Ibid., 215.

121   She was apparently known to Friedrich Berger, head of the rue de la Pompe cell, who named her in some of his postwar sworn statements. Bonnet, *Violette Morris*, 135, 148–49.

122   I have used evidence about Violette torturing women here; this is not to suggest that she did not do the same to men—see quote below. Also, according to Carolyn Dean, during the interwar period discourses about *tribades*, women whose lesbianism was innate, posited that they were tyrannical, "but this masculine imperiousness is inseparable from the unrestrained emotion characteristic of female insatiability. 'Dr.' L.R. Dupuy claimed lesbians liked to flagellate men because they harbored tremendous rage against them." In the Third Republic such language served to harden boundaries between "normal" and "perverted" women. At the same time, because it was argued that it was difficult to tell if a particular woman's sexuality was "normal", "all women were subject to more intense regulation." Dean, *Frail Social Body*, 198, 199.

123   Capdevila et al., *Hommes et femmes dans la France en guerre*, 233.

124   *L'Humanité*, September 20, 1944, from Capdevila et al., *Hommes et femmes dans la France en guerre*, 234.

125   "L'affaire Bony-Lafont La Terreur fait une entrée discrete," *Le Figaro*, September 20, 1944. See also Bouni, Henry, "La mystérieuse disparition de Violette Morris," *Le Journal*, May 17, 1944, 1–2.

126   Capdevila et al., *Hommes et femmes dans la France en guerre*, 234.

127   Bonnet, *Violette Morris*, 10.

128   Bard, *Les femmes dans la société française au 20e siècle*, 151.

129   Most were sentenced to death, while three received life sentences for hard labor. See "Eight Years' Wait," *Time*, Monday, January 5, 1953, 29. In fact according to the *New York Times*, which covered the case, the sentences were longer that what the prosecution had originally wanted. "Eight Frenchmen Doomed, Sentenced

to Death for Torture before Liberation of Paris," *New York Times*, December 23, 1952, 7. It is unclear what ultimately happened to most of the defendants in the trial; on the sixtieth anniversary of the Allied landings in Normandy, Radio France put out a pamphlet about the landings and the aftermath of war, describing the rue de la Pompe cell members' fate as replete with "shadow zones." We do know that several of their sentences were commuted, and only three ultimately faced execution. See Bonnet, *Tortionnaires, truands, et collabos*, 168.

130 I should note that Delfau was accused by all three newspapers of being Berger's mistress. Their sexual relationship does not appear to have been a great focus of the trial, though. Still, her acceptance of Berger as a lover represents an extra threat to the virility of French men, and as such it could heighten the consequences of her symbolic representation.

131 Pichon, Jean, "Les gestapistes de la rue de la Pompe reconnaissent leurs dénonciations mais nient les tortures," *Combat*, November 21, 1952, 1, 8.

132 Bochin, Roland, "Les coupables expriment des regrets de pure forme," *Figaro*, November 21, 1952, 2.

133 "Le 'benjamin' des tortures Jean-Paul Schleinger a déclaré: 'Je les considère tous coupables'," *Le Parisien libéré*, December 9, 1952, 7.

134 Ruffin, *Violette Morris*, 248.

135 F. D'Amico, 'One of the Guys', in *Women as Aggressors and Torturers*, ed. Tara McKelvey (Emeryville, CA: Avalon Publishing, 2007), 49.

136 Salonne, M-P, "Sur la route clandestine," *Marie-France*, Issue #14, February 16, 1945, 6. In another similar incident, Fabrice Virgili cites a story from Lee Miller, the famous model and *Vogue* photographer, in which she describes being lauded by the French people because she happened to be at the fore of a procession of four *femmes tondues* who were being paraded through the streets of a town. The people assumed she had been associated with their capture, when in reality she was there in her capacity as a photographer. From Virgili, *Shorn Women*, 83.

137 Proctor, *Female Intelligence*, 124.

138 Schwartz, "*Partisanes* and Gender Politics in Vichy France," 131. See also Wieviorka, *The French Resistance*, 407–8.

139 Schwartz, "*Partisanes* and Gender Politics in Vichy France," 132.

140 Ibid., 134.

141 This was largely a rural-urban division, with rural Resistance groups less trustful of women than their city-based counterparts. Schwartz, "*Partisanes* and Gender Politics in Vichy France," 139–42.

142 According to Robert Aron, de Gaulle ensured that the first troops in Paris would be French. Aron, *France Reborn*, 210–11. For a longer account of the machinations involved between all Allied troops, see Beevor and Cooper, *Paris after the Liberation, 1945-1949*, 30–40.

143   Schwartz, "*Partisanes* and Gender Politics in Vichy France," 146.

144   Ibid., 147.

145   Gubar, "This is My Rifle, This Is My Gun," 230.

146   Ibid., 240.

147   I am not sure whether or not contemporary discourses about female espionage proliferated to the same extent as those of prostitution and lesbianism. However, as the quote about prominence from Susan Gubar suggests, I do think they were present and potent in the postwar era, for espionage itself was much more prominent at this time. Gubar, "This is My Rifle, This Is My Gun," 230.

148   Public women during the French Revolution, like Olympe de Gouges and Madame Roland, as well as prostitution in the nineteenth century are exemplary of this discursive category. In their own specific ways, these groups of women were connected through versions of what Carolyn Dean calls "a metaphor of contamination." (Dean, *Frail Social Body*, 96.) For more on women as contaminants and the masculinization of government during the French Revolution, see Hunt, *Family Romance*, 93, 97–98. For more on prostitution and social contamination, see Walkowitz, *City of Dreadful Delight*, 23; Walkowitz, *Prostitution and Victorian Society*, 22–24, 70; Walkowitz, "Jack the Ripper," 552; and Harsin, *Policing Prostitution*, Chapter 3.

149   Carré, *J'ai été la Chatte*. Also noted in Wheelwright, 149 and Young, 28.

150   Young argues that there was not much interest in the trial on the part of the French. However, an article for *Time* magazine describes Parisians' thirst for news of the verdict, and the coverage itself was prominent in papers. Young, 10, 181; "La Chatte," *Time*, Monday, January 17, 1949, 24. Indeed in *Le Parisien libéré*, the coverage at the beginning of the trial consisted of a small news box. Over the course of the trial coverage expanded, and by the time of the verdict, Carré's picture was on the front page. For a (very) small sampling of articles and evidence relating to Marthe Richard and other women spies, see the following: "L'avocate Juliette Goublet devant la Cour de Justice," *Figaro*, Issue #189, March 27, 1945, 2; "En relations avec la Gestapo, Dita Parlo, espionne au cinema, est arrêtée," *Les Nouvelles du matin*, Issue #272, November 30, 1945, 1; "Poursuivie pour trafic d'influence, Mme Marthe Richard comparaît en Correctionelle," *Figaro*, Issue #1047, January 24, 1948, 2; "Le tribunal militaire de Paris juge une femme accusée d'avoir dénoncé à la Gestapo le duc d'Ayen," *Figaro*, Issue #2546, November 15–16, 1952, 2; Mathilde Carré also allegedly had an accomplice, Renée Bormi (aka Violette), who is mentioned in many of the sources I cite relating to Carré. See, for example, *Figaro*, January 4, 6–9, 1949, 2, for articles.

151   Young, *The Cat with Two Faces*, 17–18.

152   Ibid., 27.

153   Ibid., 68.

154 Weitz, *Sisters in the Resistance*, 283.

155 Young, *The Cat with Two Faces*, 81.

156 Weitz, *Sisters in the Resistance*, 284.

157 Ibid., 284–85; Sarah Farmer cites statistics that point to the typicality of the commutation of Carré's sentence: "Of the 40,000 people who had been arrested for collaboration at the Liberation, only 13,800 were still in jail in December 1948. In October 1949, 8,000 remained. In 1951, on the eve of the first amnesty, only half that number were still in custody." There were two amnesty laws passed, in 1951 and 1953, which eliminated national degradation charges. "The first amnesty law had reduced the number of collaborators jailed from 4,000 to 1,570. When the second had taken full effect in 1956, only sixty-two of those jailed in 1945 remained in custody." (Farmer, *Martyred Village*, 137–38); Christopher Lloyd states that she actually spent twelve years in prison. Again, the truth is murky, further underscoring the nebulousness both of espionage and postwar recriminations at this time. Lloyd, *Collaboration and Resistance in Occupied France*, 133–36.

158 Young, *The Cat with Two Faces*, 17.

159 Ibid., n. 26.

160 Cowburn, *No Cloak, No Dagger*, 67.

161 Ibid., 73.

162 Collin, Robert, "'La Chatte' avait livré à son amant 35 membres du réseau 'Interallié,'" *Combat*, Issue #1400, January 5, 1949, 1.

163 According to *Time* magazine, of the thirty-five people arrested that day due to Carré's betrayal, most were sent to Buchenwald, and only fourteen ever returned to France. "La Chatte," *Time*, Monday, January 17, 1949, 24.

164 Young, *The Cat with Two Faces*, 17.

165 "A Salient Lesson from the Cat and the Lord," *The Independent*, November 28, 2002, 20.

166 Soltikow, *The Cat*, 13; Soltikow, a German journalist, primarily used interviews with Hugo Bleicher, the German spy who was Carré's alleged former lover, as evidence for his story, which he published in Germany in 1956. Clearly this source would have specific motivations which must be kept in mind when utilizing it. Soltikow himself was allegedly a former Gestapo officer who switched sides; one historian has described him as "an opportunist and provocateur." Kirsch, *The Short, Strange Life of Herschel Grynszpan*, 257.

167 Lloyd, "In the Service of the Enemy," 242.

168 Young, *The Cat with Two Faces*, 214.

169 Soltikow, *The Cat*, 75.

170 Young, *The Cat with Two Faces*, 19.

171 Soltikow, *The Cat*, 16.

172   Cowburn, *No Cloak, No Dagger*, 72.

173   Collin, Robert, "'La Chatte' avait livré à son amant 35 membres du réseau
       'Interallié," *Combat*, Issue #1400, January 5, 1949, 1.

174   Cowburn, *No Cloak, No Dagger*, 72.

175   "Mathilde Carré comdamné à mort," *Le Monde*, Issue #1230, January 9–10, 1949, 6.

176   Young, *The Cat with Two Faces*, 18.

177   Soltikow, *The Cat*, 74.

178   Young, *The Cat with Two Faces*, 79–80.

179   Lloyd, *Collaboration and Resistance*, 135; in another piece, Lloyd cites René Hardy,
       who is believed to have betrayed famed Resistor Jean Moulin, as similar to Carré
       in their "abrogation of responsibility." Lloyd, "In the Service of the Enemy," 242.

180   Collin, Robert, "'La Chatte' avait livré à son amant 35 membres du réseau
       'Interallié," *Combat*, Issue #1400, January 5, 1949, 1.

181   "Le procès de 'La Chatte' devant la cour de justice," *Le Parisien libéré*, January 5,
       1949, 5.

182   Carré, *J'ai été la Chatte*, 9.

183   No Headline, *Figaro*, #1345, January 6, 1949, 2.

184   "La mère de l'accusée tente d'apitoyer les juges," *Le Parisien libéré*, January 6, 1949, 2.

185   Carré, *J'ai été la Chatte*, 9.

186   Lloyd, *Collaboration and Resistance in Occupied France*, 135.

187   Soltikow, *The Cat*, 212.

188   "La mère de l'accusée tente d'apitoyer les juges," *Le Parisien libéré*, January 6, 1949, 2.

189   Young, *The Cat with Two Faces*, 180.

190   Quoted in Young, *The Cat with Two Faces*, 180.

191   "Espionne, traître et agent double 'La Chatte' est condamnée à mort," *Le Parisien
       libéré*, 1, 4.

192   Young, *The Cat with Two Faces*, 82.

193   Wheelwright, *The Fatal Lover*, 149.

194   Bard, *Les femmes dans la société française au 20e siècle*, 151.

195   Quoted in Wheelwright, *The Fatal Lover*, 150.

196   Weitz, *Sisters in the Resistance*, 285.

197   Neveu, "Trente ans de litterature d'espionnage en France (1950-1980)," 52; for
       example, this was around the time when authors such as Graham Greene and Ian
       Fleming enjoyed literary excess for their spy fiction.

198   The *Série noire* was hugely popular, with two new titles per month appearing by
       1948, just three years after its launch. See Gorrarra, *The Roman Noir in Post-war
       French Culture*, 14.

199   Series were the most popular form of postwar spy fiction, in which several novels
       centered on the exploits of a single hero. It would be interesting to consider the
       implications of this for the construction of French masculinity. See Coward,
       A History of French Literature, 509–11.

200 Blaza, "Detective/Mystery/Spy Fiction," 4445.

201 Spy novels' success benefited from generally large growth—six percent per year— of the French publishing industry in the Fourth Republic. See Rioux, *Au bonheur la France*, 444. Similarly, the French film industry, while not yet in its "New Wave" heyday, still counted an average of 380 million visits per year in the early 1950s. Rioux, *Au bonheur la France*, 440.

202 The impact of Americanization on French culture is quite sizable, in many ways mirroring the creation of a European mass consumer society with the United States as a financial and cultural base. These phenomena largely begin in the early 1950s, just as the analysis for this book is concluding. See de Grazia, *Irresistible Empire*, 345–50. France, however, resisted Americanization for longer and more strenuously than most of its European neighbors. Rioux, *Au bonheur la France*, 444.

203 Laszlo, "Nothing Added, Nothing Subtracted," 116.

204 Corbel, Danielle, unpublished dissertation, "Roman d'espionnage et science politique," quoted in Hoveyda, *Histoire du roman policier*, 207.

205 Mandelstamm was a French government liaison to Hollywood, passing his time there and in France in the interwar years. During the war, he lived in the United States, which perhaps explains the provenance of his characters. However, he wrote the book in French for a French audience. Vasey, *The World According to Hollywood, 1918-1939*, 81.

206 Langellier, Alice, "V5," *The French Review*, Vol. 19, No. 5 (March 1946), 323.

207 Mandelstamm, *V5*, 7.

208 Ibid., 40.

209 Ibid., 172.

210 Ibid.

211 Ibid., 197.

212 Rousseau, *Émile, ou de l'éducation*, Book V.

213 Scott, *Only Paradoxes to Offer*, 8.

214 Surkis, *Sexing the Citizen*, 2.

215 Aron, *France Reborn*, 297.

216 Young, *The Cat with Two Faces*, 36.

217 Ibid., 78.

218 Ibid., 111.

219 "'La Chatte' et sa complice connaîtront leur sort ce soir," *Le Monde*, Issue #1229, January 8, 1949, 5.

220 LaBorde, Jean, "'A toi de parler, mignonne,' ordonna Pierre de Vomécourt (compagnon de la Libération)," *France-Soir*, 1, 3.

221 LaBorde, Jean, "'A toi de parler, mignonne,' ordonna Pierre de Vomécourt (compagnon de la Libération)," *France-Soir*, 1, 3. Young, *The Cat with Two Faces*, 127. Interestingly, Vomécourt believed that Carré had had a change of heart

after this confrontation, but despite enduring suspicion about Carré, newspapers do not reflect a sense that Vomécourt had also been duped by the duplicitous, charming "Chatte." Perhaps the intimation that one of France's own James Bond types was vulnerable to the charms of a woman such as Carré was untenable in the postwar context, when women needed to be returned to the private sphere, but also masculinity had to stand firm. See "La Chatte et sa complice connaîtront leur sort ce soir," *Le Monde*, Issue #1229, January 8, 1949, 5.

222 Gatti, A., "'La Chatte' saura ce soir si elle mérite le poteau," *Le Parisien libéré*, January 7, 1949, 2.

223 Cowburn, *No Cloak, No Dagger*, 72.

224 Ibid.

225 Young, *The Cat with Two Faces*, 166.

226 Ibid., 32.

227 Images of male spies during the Cold War era in the United States also reflect these British and French depictions. Kathryn S. Olmstead writes that male spies were seen as "action-heroes . . . smart, tough, and strong." Olmstead, "Blond Queens, Red Spiders, and Neurotic Old Maids," 79.

228 See the memoir by Garby-Czerniawski, *The Big Network*, especially the final chapter.

Chapter 6

1 "Les femmes et les problèmes politiques à la veille des élections," 24 avril 1945, Rapport de la Direction générale de la Sûreté Nationale, de la Direction des RG, AN F 7 15588. Quoted in Fayolle, "Réagir aux premiers votes des femmes," 224.

2 Ide, Sémiramis, "21 avril 1944: les Françaises ont (enfin) le droit de voter," TV5MONDE, April 21, 1944.

3 Denoyelle, "Canard Déchaîné et Poules Enchaînées," 18.

4 Fayolle, "Réagir aux premiers votes des femmes," 235.

5 Noël Burch and Geneviève Sellier argue that the disparity between official rhetoric about women voting and anxieties about the potential for liberation that might arise is highly visible in Liberation-era film. See Burch and Sellier, *The Battle of the Sexes in French Cinema, 1930-1956*, 240–41.

6 "Notre courrier," *Marie-France*, Issue #226, April 1, 1949, 37.

7 "Le courrier des cœurs," *Ève*, November 7, 1947, 7.

8 Letourneur, Claude, "C'est arrivé hier soir," *Elle*, Issue #33, July 2, 1946, 17.

9 Ibid.; The issue of wearing pants, a wartime staple for many, also arose in the postwar era as a marker of feminine difference. The filmmaker Marceline Loridan-Ivens recalled being one of the very first women to wear pants in

post-Liberation Paris. She would generally wear them in the more avant-garde quarters of the city, like Saint-Germain-des-Près, she said, and even then she would be in a tiny minority: "It was considered bad form for women . . . we were no more than forty who dared to wear pants." In Bard, *Une histoire politique du pantalon*, 301–02.

10 "Le courrier de *Marie-France*," *Marie-France*, Issue #293, July 10, 1950, 3.

11 "Le courrier des cœurs," *Ève*, Issue #65, July 4, 1947, 7.

12 Segal, Marcelle, "Perfidie," *Elle*, Issue #13, February 13, 1946, 8, 23.

13 "Le courrier des cœurs," *Ève*, Issue #96, February 13, 1948, 2.

14 Volmane, Vera, "Doit-elle refaire sa vie?" *Ève*, Issue #114, June 18, 1948, 14–17.

15 Virgili, *Shorn Women*, 72; quote from *Femmes Françaises*, Issue #1, January 1944. The UFF later morphed into the ironically titled *Femmes solidaires*, a feminist organization.

16 For more on the general haziness that surrounded denunciations at the very end of the war and during the postwar period, see Koreman, *The Expectation of Justice*, 93–95; Koreman calls denunciation "an ambiguous crime that shows how quickly the moral and political sands shifted at the liberation."(93)

17 Interestingly, during the first election in which women could vote, the UFF was, according to Hanna Diamond, largely the sole group that actively sponsored efforts to encourage women to vote at a high rate and also educated women as to how to vote. Diamond, *Women and the Second World War in France*, 185–86.

18 Quote from Ross, *Fast Cars, Clean Bodies*, 82; originally quoted from Grégoire, Ménie, "La presse feminine," *Esprit* (July–August 1959), 26.

19 From "Les premières électrices françaises: Odette Roux," televised interview on women voting in France in 1944, *Fondapol*, April 3, 2014.

20 Sarah Fishman expressly states "women's social status remained essentially unchanged after the war." Fishman, 168. Similarly, Claire Duchen has described the postwar years as ones of "gradual disappointment," when women's great "hopes" for equality eroded. Duchen, *Women's Rights and Women's Lives*, 2.

21 Several historians, including Sarah Fishman, attribute female enfranchisement at least partly to women's participation in the Resistance, which, according to Fishman, "was widely interpreted as the 'rite of passage to full citizenship after the war." Fishman, *We Will Wait*, 169; for others who argue for this, see Françoise Decaumont, "La Préparation des ordonnances à Alger: Le Vote des femmes," in *Le Rétablissement de la légalité républicaine*, and Alice Kaplan's *The Collaborator*, which briefly touches upon the vote, 125–26. Kaplan contrasts French women's enfranchisement for their Resistance participation with American and British women's enfranchisement as a result of long suffrage campaigns. I am not sure that this is entirely accurate; scholars have argued that these women also received the vote as a kind of reward for their participation in the First World War. In fact

the famous American suffragist Carrie Chapman Catt even explicitly "asked for passage of the woman suffrage amendment as a 'war measure.'" From Woloch, *Women and the American Experience*, 359. Hanna Diamond has contested this interpretation of the reasons for women's enfranchisement in her *Women and the Second World War in France*, calling it a "minor concern" for delegates debating female suffrage.(183) For work on France conforming with the other major powers, see Scott, *Only Paradoxes*, 163–64. Interestingly, articles in many women's magazines from the time also express fears and anxieties about keeping up with the world powers like the United States. In the Looks chapter I cited articles that discussed French women's beauty in an international context. Magazines also cited France's higher marriage rates as evidence of French international superiority. Claire Duchen echoes this assertion: "Granting women the right to vote was probably no more than a measure aiming to correct this anomaly [France's female disenfranchisement]—as well as to provide electoral support for General de Gaulle, in whose gift the vote seemed to be." Duchen, *Women's Rights and Women's Lives*, 34. Additionally, Michèle Riot-Sarcey argues that the vote meant little within France, and that the legislation simply corrected "a singularly French backwardness, putting a stop to an anomaly." Riot-Sarcey, *Histoire du féminisme*, 92.

22 "Mme Fillatre adjointe au maire et dont le mari fut fusillé comme otage a célébré hier un mariage à la mairie du XVIIe," *Combat*, September 24, 1944, 2.

23 Ibid.

24 Fayolle, "Réagir aux premiers votes des femmes," 230.

25 Duchen, *Women's Rights and Women's Lives*, 35; Quoted in Reineke, *Beauvoir and Her Sisters*, 23.

26 Weitz, *Sisters in the Resistance*, 303.

27 Ibid.; see also Fishman, *We Will Wait*, 170; here, Fishman argues that rather than being controversial that prisoners' wives votes, these women's enfranchisement was actually seen in a positive light, as they could temporarily stand in for their husbands.

28 Bard, *Les femmes dans la société française au 20e siècle*, 153.

29 "Notre royaume," *Combat 44*, Issue #40, June 24, 1945, 3.

30 "Rester naïve," *Combat 44*, Issue #45, July 29, 1945, 3.

31 R. T., "Citoyennes! . . .," *Le Centre Républicain*, Issue #94, December 12, 1944, 1; this is similar to what Curt Reiss writes in *Elle* magazine, which I quoted in the chapter on female torturers, about the women of Germany deserving their postwar misery because they were responsible for bringing Hitler to power. See Reiss, "De Gertrude Weinert à Eva Grun: sept berlinoises me racontent leur vie," *Elle*, Issue #9, January 16, 1946, 14–15, 23. Despite these concerns, the major French political parties did little to educate and encourage French women to vote. Diamond, *Women and the Second World War in France*, 85.

32 Denoyelle, "Canard Déchaîné et Poules Enchaînées," 3–4.

33 "Le Rôle bienfaisant du vote des femmes anglaises," *Le Monde*, May 14, 1945, 3.

34 Ravon, Georges, "Comment elles voteront," *Figaro*, Issue #42, October 7, 1944, 1.

35 "France record au monde des députés," *Elle*, Issue #1, November 21, 1945, 3.

36 Quoted in Denoyelle, "Canard Déchaîné et Poules Enchaînées," 95.

37 This is quite interesting given that many of these same magazines and newspapers were concomitantly printing messages within their pages about the dangers associated with women trusting other women. These sources thus justified female voting through mollifying their (male) readers' concerns about female power while simultaneously creating schismatic articles and stories for their female readers to digest.

38 In the United States, for example, Robyn Muncy has shown that despite pre-election fears on the part of politicians, "Disunity at the polls reflected economic and social diversity among female voters." Because of this, Muncy notes, "Male politicians no longer worried about women as voters or opposing candidates [and thus] they felt free on the public record to deride professional women, to demean them as policymakers, and certainly to vote down their prized projects." Muncy, *Creating a Female Dominion in American Reform, 1890-1935*, 126, 132.

39 Diamond, "'Libération! Quelle Libération?' L'expérience des femmes toulousiennes," 41.

40 Duchen, *Women's Rights and Women's Lives*, 37.

41 Giroud once wrote: "For [Hélène], women have only one superior vocation: to seduce. She was a missionary of seduction." In Périer and Bauby, *Les Années* Elle, *1945-2000*, 13.

42 Quoted in Vienne, "The Woman Who Was *Elle*," 179.

43 Duchen, *Women's Rights and Women's Lives*, 36.

44 Vienne, "The Woman Who Was *Elle*," 169.

45 Géraldy, Paul, "Ce que j'en dis," *Elle*, Issue #1, November 21, 1945, 19.

46 "Une grande enquête d'*Elle*': Voilà comment les hommes vous aiment . . ." *Elle*, Issue #105, November 19, 1947, 4–5.

47 "Monsieur le Maire porte la jupe longue," *Elle*, Issue #107, December 2, 1947, 4–5; I do want to note that in *Marie-France*, an article appeared praising Charles de Gaulle for awarding women the vote and recognizing in them "the same capacities for exercising the right of suffrage as the blacks in Senegal," thereby echoing some of the racism seen in other women's suffrage movements while still lauding their newfound political rights. See Vogt, Blanche, "La Grande Entente des femmes," *Marie-France*, Issue #73, March 16, 1945, 3; for more on the racism of American suffrage movements, see Louise Newman's *White Women's Rights: The Racial Origins of Feminism in the United States* and Suzanne M. Marilley's *Woman Suffrage and the Origins of Liberal Feminism in the United States*.

48 "Les mères de France sont aujourd'hui à l'honneur," *Figaro*, Issue #553, May 26–27, 1946.

49 "Elles à Elles," *Elle*, Issue #267, January 8, 1951, 3.

50 Bard, *Les femmes dans la société française au 20e siècle*, 154.

51 Ibid., 155.

52 Rebecca Pulju argues that women's voting in France was directly linked with consumerism and *ravitaillement*, revealing the "common tendency to associated women with the home and family despite their political enfranchisement." Pulju, *Women and Mass Consumer Society in Postwar France*, 38.

53 I should expressly state that there is no direct evidence linking women's disparate voting patterns to cultural influences like *Elle* and *Marie-France*. The confluence of the enfranchisement of women and the proliferation of women's magazines that promote, subversively or otherwise, the splintering of female solidarity through a message of mistrust and disruption of stability, is at the very least quite telling about the state of French society at the time, and specifically French gender relations. My purpose here is to explore this confluence and attempt to analyze the deeper meanings behind it, not to make a statistical connection between the two.

54 The major exception, which in itself is quite complicated, is Simone de Beauvoir's *Second Sex*, published in 1949. I will examine this work in more detail in the Conclusion.

55 Chaperon, "Feminism is dead. Long live feminism!" in Duchen et al., *When the War Was Over*, 147.

56 Feminist movements were relatively muted across the West after the war; however, again, French women had just won the vote, and the country was reestablishing democracy after flirting with fascism during the war, making the moment more ripe for potential movements.

57 Bard, *Les femmes dans la société française au 20e siècle*, 163; Certain feminine associations—especially Catholic ones—remained active in the postwar years, according to Bard. There was also, according to Rebecca Pulju, a large amount of female organization around the problems associated with material deprivation at this time. In her work about consumption in the postwar years, Pulju situates this activism under the umbrella of political involvement. I am not sure, however, that I would include this in a category about participation in feminist movements in the postwar period at present. I would argue that women's public sphere demonstrations and actions continue to be in keeping with a more conservative message about femininity. It would be interesting to see if these organizations and activists became part of the second wave of feminism in France. See Pulju, *Women and Mass Consumer Society*, 39–58.

58 Chaperon, *Les années Beauvoir*, 55, 72.

59 Chaperon, "Feminism is dead. Long live feminism!", 147.

60 Ibid., 157.
61 Gildea, *France since 1945*, 145–46.
62 Duchen, *Women's Rights and Women's Lives*, 186–87.
63 Higonnet et al., *Behind the Lines*, 16.
64 Ibid.
65 Bard, *Les femmes dans la société française au 20e siècle*, 159.
66 Hazareesingh, *In the Shadow of the General*, 180.
67 This is largely an eighteenth-century distinction, invented during the French Revolution as a way to deny rights to minority groups, particularly women. See Hunt, *Inventing Human Rights*, 67.

Conclusion

1 Giroud, *I Give You My Word*, 113.
2 Ibid., 117.
3 Adler, *Jews and Gender in Liberation France*, 5.
4 Rioux, *The Fourth Republic*, 360, 372.
5 Ibid., 441.
6 Okawa, "Licensing Practices at the Maison Dior," 93.
7 Schiro, Anne-Marie, "Yves Saint Laurent, Fashion Icon, Dies at 71," *New York Times*, June 1, 2008. *Vogue* later designated the Trapeze dress "epoch-shifting." Mower, Sarah, "Svetlana Lloyd Walked Dior's 1958 Show," June 2, 2016. See also Hill, *As Seen in Vogue*, 88.
8 Rousso, *Vichy Syndrome*, 60.
9 Gildea, *France since 1945*, 24.
10 Evans, "Algeria and the Liberation," in Kedward and Wood, *The Liberation of France*, 264–65.
11 Duchen, *Women's Rights and Women's Lives*, 87.
12 For further discussion, see Dorothy Kaufmann's discussion of Audry in her "The Story of Two Women," 883–905.
13 Gildea, *France since 1945*, 145.
14 de Beauvoir, *Second Sex*, xxii.
15 Bair, "Introduction to the Vintage Edition," *Second Sex*, vii.
16 Beauvoir, *Force of Circumstance*, as quoted in Deirdre Bair's "Introduction to the Vintage Edition," *Second Sex*, vii. Despite Beauvoir's groundbreaking work, which Bonnie Smith calls "perhaps the best and most thorough book about women ever written," her personal feminism wavered, to say the least. She famously refused to call herself feminist until the 1970s, and she would not "participate in so-called feminist groups, which she found too bourgeois, too conformist." Smith, *Changing*

Lives, 519. Duchen, *Women's Rights and Women's Lives*, 187. Additionally, scholars have since challenged some of the basic premises upon which the book rested.

17 Duchen, *Women's Rights and Women's Lives*, 187.

18 Ibid., 188; see also Reineke, *Beauvoir and Her Sisters*, 24–25.

19 Rousso and Conan, *Vichy*, 197.

20 Beauvoir, *The Second Sex*, 751.

Bibliography

Primary sources

Archives & Libraries:

Archives Nationales de France
Bibliothèque nationale de France
    Site Mitterand
    Site Richelieu
Bibliothèque historique de la ville de Paris
Bibliothèque Centre Pompidou
Library of Congress

Published sources:

Magazines & Journals:

Album de la mode du Figaro
Le Crapouillot
Elle
Ève
French Review
Marie-France
The New Yorker
Questions actuelles
Time
Vogue

Newspapers:

Alger Républicain
L'Alouette d'Auvergne
Le Canard enchaîné

Le Centre Républicain

Ceux du Maquis

Combat

Le Figaro

France-Soir

L'Humanité

International Herald Tribune

L'Intransigeant

Le Journal

Le Monde

The New York Times

Les Nouvelles du Matin

Le Parisien libéré

Paris-Soir

Washington Post

Books and pamphlets

Aglion, Raoul. *Roosevelt and de Gaulle: Allies in Conflict: A Personal Memoir*. New York: Free Press, 1988.

Alsop, Susan Mary. *To Marietta from Paris, 1945-1960*. Garden City, NY: Doubleday, 1975.

Besançon, Abbé G. and Curé de Bussières-les-Belmont. *Trois jeunes filles de Bussières-les-Belmont mortes pour la France victimes de la barbarie allemande*. Langres, France: Imprimerie Campenoise, 1945.

Blanchet, Mgr. *Solitude de Jeanne d'Arc. Panégyrique pronounce en l'Église de Saint-Ouen de Rouen le 1er Juin 1947*. Rouen, France: Imp. Lainé et de la Vicomté, 1947.

Bouteille-Garagnon, Marie Jeanne. *Infernal rebus*. Moulins: Éditions Crépin-Leblond, 1946.

Bouvard, Suzanne. "Mort de Rose-Marie Lafitte." In *Simone et ses compagnons*, edited by C. Séailles, 178–90. Paris: Éditions de Minuit, 1947.

Brasillach, Robert. *Le Procès de Jeanne d'Arc*. Paris: Gallimard, 1941.

Bronner, René. *La Bergerette de Lorraine, pièce épisodique de la vie de Jeanne d'Arc en 2 tableaux*. Gundershoffen (Bas-Rhin), France: Édition de Théâtre et de Musique L. Jaggi-Reiss, 1948.

Busson, Bernard. *Héros du sport, héros de France*. Paris: Éd. d'art Athos, 1947.

Busson, Suzanne. *Dans les Griffes nazies; Angers, Fresnes, Ravensbrück, Mauthausen*. Bayeux: OREP, 2014.

Carré, Mathilde-Lily. *J'ai été la Chatte*. Paris: Morgan, 1959.

Cazaux, Mgr., Evêque de Luçon. "La Sainte de la Patrie, 'Les dicts de Jehanne.'" Orléans, France: Imprimerie A. PIGELET et Cie, 1945.

Colin, Paul. *La croûte: souvenirs*. Paris: La table ronde, 1957.

Cormier, Manon. *Une Bordelaise martyre de la Résistance: Manon Cormier*. Bordeaux: Imprimerie J. Pechade, 1945.

Cowburn, Benjamin. *No Cloak, No Dagger*. Barnsley, UK: Frontline Books, 2009.

de Beauvoir, Simone. *The Second Sex*. New York: Vintage Books, 1989.

de Gaulle, Charles. *Appels et Discours, 1940-1944*. Publisher and date unavailable. BNF id#: 16-LB58-206(E).

de Gaulle, Charles. *Discours et messages: pendant la guerre, juin 1940-janvier 1946*. Paris: Plon, 1970.

de Gaulle, Charles. *The Speeches of General de Gaulle*. London: Oxford University Press, 1942.

de Gaulle, Charles. *War Memoirs. Unity, 1942-1944*. Translated by Richard Howard. London: Weidenfeld & Nicolson, 1959.

Delbo, Charlotte. *Auschwitz and After*. New Haven, CT: Yale University Press, 1995.

Dior, Christian. *Christian Dior and I*. New York: Dutton, 1957.

Dior, Christian. *Talking about Fashion*. New York: Putnam, 1954.

Ferniot, Jean. *Je recommencerais bien*. Paris: Éditions Grasset, 1991.

Garby-Czerniawski, Roman. *The Big Network*. London: G. Ronald, 1961.

Giroud, Françoise. *I Give You My Word*. London: Weidenfeld & Nicolson, 1975.

Giroud, Françoise. *Portraits sans retouches, 1945-1955*. Paris: Gallimard, 2001. (3rd ed.)

Guéhenno, Jean. *Diary of the Dark Years, 1940-1944: Collaboration Resistance, and Daily Life in Occupied Paris*. Translated by David A. Bell. New York: Oxford University Press, 2014.

Hany-Lefèbvre, Noémi. *Six mois à Fresnes*. Paris: Ernest Flammarion, 1946.

Hoisne, Sabine. *Chambre 535, ou mes cinq prisons pendant l'Occupation*. Limoges and Paris: Société des Journaux et Publications du Centre, 1945.

Langellier, Alice. "V5." *The French Review* 19, no. 5 (1946): 323.

Le Breton, Auguste. *Les pégriots*. Paris: R. Laffont, 1973.

Mandelstamm, Valentin. *V5*. New York: Brentano's, 1945.

Maurel, Micheline. *An Ordinary Camp*. Translated by Margaret S. Summers. New York: Simon and Schuster, 1958.

Mornand, Germaine. *La vie et la mort de Daisy Georges-Martin, Martyre de la Résistance*. Éditions Spes: Paris, 1946.

Reboux, Paul. *Sens interdits. Sodome. Gomorrhe*. Éditions Raoul Solar, 1951.

Rey, Robert. "Vingt ans de Paris," *Exposition Paul Colin*, 1949.

Richet, Charles, Olivier Richet, and Jacqueline Richet. *Trois Bagnes*. Paris: J. Ferenczi & Fils, 1945.

Rosane. *Terre de cendres : Ravensbrück et Belsen, 1943-1945*. Paris: Les Œuvres françaises, 1946.

Rousseau, Jean-Jacques. *Émile, ou de l'éducation*. Paris: Folio Essais, 1995.

Saint-Clair, Simone. *Ravensbrück, l'Enfer des femmes*. Éditions Jules Tallandier: Paris, 1945.

Salonne, Marie-Paule. *Fends la Bise! Scènes du maquis Breton*. Éditions Bloud & Gay, 1945.

Saurel, Louis. *Les femmes héroïques de la Résistance: Berthie ALBRECHT, Danielle CASANOVA*. Part of Fernand Nathan's edited collection, "Collection Révélations: Petite encyclopédie de la Résistance." Paris, 18, rue Monsièur-le-Prince: Fernand Nathan, 1945.

Séailles, C. *Simone et ses compagnons*. Paris: Éditions de Minuit, 1947.

Soltikow, Michael Alexander. *The Cat: A True Story of Espionage*. London: Macgibbon & Kee, 1957.

Terrenoire, Elisabeth. *Combattantes sans uniforme*. Bloud & Gay, 1946.

Téry, Simone. *Du soleil plein le coeur, la merveilleuse histoire de Danielle Casanova*. Paris: Les Éditeurs Français Réunis, 1949.

Thomas, Édith. *Jeanne d'Arc*. Paris: Éditions hier et aujourd'hui, 1947.

Thomas, Édith, J. Lecompte-Boinet, général de Larminat, René Char, and Vercors. *Berthie Albrecht, Pierre Arrighi, général Brosset, D. Corticchiato, Jean Prevost: Cinq parmi d'autres*. Paris: Les Éditions de Minuit, 1947.

Tillion, Germaine. *Ravensbrück: An Eyewitness Account of a Women's Concentration Camp*. New York: Doubleday, 1975.

Vercors. *Souffrances de mon pays*. Paris: Éditions Émile-Paul Frères, 1945.

Wilborts, Suzanne. *Pour la France: Angers, La Santé, Fresnes, Ravensbrück, Mauthausen*. Paris: C. Lavauzelle, 1946.

Young, George Gordon. *The Cat with Two Faces*. New York: Coward-McCann, 1957.

Secondary sources

Abelson, Elaine S. *When Ladies Go A-Thieving: Middle-Class Shoplifters in the Victorian Department Store*. New York: Oxford University Press, 1989.

Adler, K. H. *Jews and Gender in Liberation France*. Cambridge, UK: Cambridge University Press, 2003.

Agulhon, Maurice. "De Gaulle et l'histoire de France." *Vingtième siècle* 53, no. 1 (1997): 3–12.

Agulhon, Maurice. *Les métamorphoses de Marianne: l'imagerie et la symbolique républicaines de 1914 à nos jours*. Paris: Flammarion, 2001.

Arnold, Rebecca. *Fashion, Desire and Anxiety: Image and Morality in the 20th Century*. New Brunswick, NJ: Rutgers University Press, 2001.

Aron, Robert. *De Gaulle Triumphant: The Liberation of France August 1944-May 1945*. Translated by Humphrey Hare. London: Putnam & Co., Ltd, 1964.

Aron, Robert. *France Reborn: The History of Liberation*. New York: Charles Scribner, 1964.

Arzaroli, Christine. *Le maquillage clair-obscur: une anthropologie du maquillage contemporain*. Paris: L'Harmattan, 1996.

Auslander, Leora. *Taste and Power: Furnishing Modern France*. Berkeley, CA: The University of California Press, 1996.

Auvray, Emmanuel. " Violette Morris (1893-1944): de l'héroïsme guerrier et sportif à la collaboration." In *Le sport et la guerre, XIXe et XXe siècles*, edited by Luc Robène. Rennes: Presses universitaires de Rennes, 2012.

Bard, Christine. *Les femmes dans la société française au 20ᵉ siècle*. Paris: Colin, 2001.

Bard, Christine. "Les Femmes travesties, un mauvais genre, Le 'DB58' aux Archives de la Préfecture de la Police." *Clio* 10, (1999) : 155–68.

Bard, Christine. *Les filles de Marianne: histoire des féminismes, 1914-1940*. Paris: Fayard, 1995.

Bard, Christine. *Une histoire politique du pantalon*. Paris: Éditions du Seuil, 2010.

Barnard, Malcolm. *Fashion as Communication*. New York: Routledge, 1996.

Barthel, Diane. *Putting on Appearances: Gender and Advertising*. Philadelphia: Temple University Press, 1988.

Barthes, Roland. *Mythologies*. London: Paladin, 1973.

Bartky, Sandra. "Foucault, Femininity, and the Modernization of Patriarchal Power." In *The Politics of Women's Bodies: Sexuality, Appearance, and Behavior*, edited by Rose Weitz, 25–45. New York: Oxford University Press, 2003.

Beevor, Antony and Artemis Cooper. *Paris after the Liberation, 1945-1949*. New York: Doubleday, 1994.

Bernard, Jean-Pierre Arthur. *Le Goût de Paris*, vol. 2, *L'Espace*. Paris: Mercure de France, 2004.

Bertherat, Marie, et al. *100 Ans de Mode*. Paris: Éditions Atlas, 1996.

Blaza, Franz G. "Detective/Mystery/Spy Fiction." In *Handbook of French Popular Culture*, edited by Pierre L. Horn, 39–58. New York: Greenwood Press, 1991.

Bonnet, Marie-Joseph. *Tortionnaires, truands, et collabos*. Rennes: Éditions Ouest-France, 2013.

Bonvoisin, Samra-Martine and Michèle Maignien. *La presse féminine*. Paris: Presses universitaires de France, 1986.

Bouglé-Moalic, Anne-Sarah. *Le vote des Françaises. Cent ans de débats, 1848-1944*. Rennes: Presses universitaires de Rennes, 2012.

Bourdieu, Pierre. *The Field of Cultural Production: Essays on Art and Literature*. New York: Columbia University Press, 1993.

Bouvard, Marguerite Guzman. *Revolutionizing Motherhood: The Mothers of the Plaza de Mayo*. Lanham, MD: SR Books, 2002.

Brossat, Alain. *Les tondues: un carnaval moche*. Levallois-Perret: Editions Manya, 1992.

Burch, Noël and Geneviève Sellier. *The Battle of the Sexes in French Cinema, 1930-1956*. Durham, NC: Duke University Press, 2014.

Campbell, Beth M. "High Fashion and the Reconstruction of postwar France, 1945-1960," PhD diss., Rutgers University, New Brunswick, NJ.

Cancian, Francesca M. and Steven L. Gordon. "Changing Emotion Norms in Marriage: Love and Anger in U.S. Women's Magazines since 1900." *Gender and Society* 2, no. 3 (1988): 308–42.

Capdevila, Luc. "L'identité masculine et les fatigues de la guerre (1914-1945)." *Vingtième Siècle* 3, no. 75 (2002): 97–108.

Capdevila, Luc. "The Quest for Masculinity in a Defeated France, 1940-1945." *Contemporary European History* 10, no. 3 (2001): 423–45.

Carpenter, Laura M. "From Girls into Women: Scripts for Sexuality and Romance in *Seventeen* Magazine, 1974-1994." *Journal of Sex Research* 35, no. 2 (1998): 158–68.

Cawthorne, Nigel. *The New Look: The Dior Revolution*. London: Reed International Books Limited, 1996.

Chaperon, Sylvie, "'Feminism is Dead. Long live feminism!' The Women's Movement in France at the Liberation, 1944-1946." In *When the War Was Over: Women, War and Peace in Europe, 1940-1956*, edited by Claire Duchen and Irene Bandhauer-Schöffmann, 146–60. London: Leicester University Press, 2000.

Chaperon, Sylvie. *Les années Beauvoir: 1945-1970*. Paris: Fayard, 2000.

Charles-Roux, Edmonde, ed. *Le Théâtre de la Mode*. Paris: Éditions du May, 1990.

Cheney, Liana De Girolami. "The Cult of Saint Agatha." *Women's Art Journal* 17, no. 1 (1996): 3–9.

Childers, Kristin Stromberg. *Fathers, Families, and the State in France, 1914-1945*. Ithaca, NY: Cornell University Press, 2003.

Cohen, Deborah. *Household Gods: the British and Their Possessions*. New Haven, CT: Yale University Press, 2006.

Cole, Joshua. *The Power of Large Numbers: Population, Politics, and Gender in Nineteenth-Century France*. Ithaca, NY and London: Cornell University Press, 2000.

Collins, Marcus. *Modern love: Personal Relationships in Twentieth-Century Britain*. Newark, DE: University of Delaware Press, 2006.

Coontz, Stephanie. *Marriage, a History*. New York: Viking, 2005.

Copley, A. R. H. *Sexual Moralities in France, 1780-1980: New Ideas on the Family, Divorce, and Homosexuality: an Essay on Moral Change*. London and New York: Routledge, 1989.

Coward, David. *A History of French Literature*. Oxford: Blackwell, 2002.

D'Amico, F. "The Women of Abu Ghraib." In *"One of the Guys": Women as Aggressors and Torturers*, edited by Tara McKelvey, 45–50. Emeryville. CA: Avalon Publishing, 2007.

Davis, Belinda J. *Home Fires Burning: Food, Politics, and Everyday Life in World War I Berlin*. Chapel Hill, NC: University of North Carolina Press, 2000.

Dean, Carolyn J. *The Fragility of Empathy after the Holocaust*. Ithaca, NY: Cornell University Press, 2004.

Dean, Carolyn J. *The Frail Social Body*. Berkeley, CA: University of California Press, 2000.

Dean, Carolyn J. "Intellectual History and the Prominence of 'Things that Matter.'" *Rethinking History* 8, no. 4 (2004): 537–47.

Dean, Carolyn J. "Review: *The Empire of Fashion.*" *AHR* 101, no. 2 (1996): 476–77.

Decaumont, Françoise. "La Préparation des ordonnances à Alger: Le Vote des femmes." In *Le Rétablissement de la légalité républicaine* (1944), edited by Fondation Charles de Gaulle, 101–18. Paris: Éditions Complexe, 1996.

de Grazia, Victoria. *Irresistible Empire: America's Advance through Twentieth-Century Europe.* Cambridge, MA: Belknap Press, 2005.

de Marly, Diana. *Christian Dior.* New York: Holmes & Meier, 1990.

Denoyelle, Bruno, "Canard Déchaîné et Poules Enchaînées: les premiers actes civiques des femmes au regard de la caricature satirique (1944-1946)." *Clio* 1 (1995): 272–8.

de Pietri, Stephen and Melissa Leventon. *New Look to Now: French Haute Couture, 1947-1987.* New York: Rizzoli International Publications, Inc., 1989.

de Réthy, Esmerelda and Jean-Louis Perreau. *Christian Dior: The Early Years, 1947-1957.* New York: Vendome Press, 2001.

Diamond, Hanna. "'Libération! Quelle Libération?' L'expérience des femmes toulousiennes." *Clio* 1 (1995) : 89–109.

Diamond, Hanna. *Women and the Second World War in France: Choices and Constraints.* London and New York: Longman, 1999.

Doron, Daniella. *Jewish Youth and Identity in Postwar France.* Bloomington, IN: Indiana University Press, 2015.

Dowd, James J. and Nicole R. Pallotta. "The End of Romance: The Demystification of Love in the Postmodern Age." *Sociological Perspectives* 3, no. 4 (2000): 549–80.

Duchen, Claire. *Women's Rights and Women's Lives in France, 1944-1968.* London and New York: Routledge, 1994.

Eck, Hélène, "Les Françaises sous Vichy." In *Histoire des femmes en Occident. Tome 5: Le XXe siècle*, edited by Françoise Thébaud, 185–212. Paris: Plon, 1992.

Eck, Hélène and Claire Blandin, eds. *'La vie des femmes': La presse feminine aux XIXe et XXe siècles.* Paris: Éditions Panthéon-Assas, 2010.

Farmer, Sarah. *Martyred Village: Commemorating the 1944 Massacre at Oradour-sur-Glane.* Berkeley, CA: University of California Press, 1999.

Farmer, Sarah. "Postwar Justice in France: Bordeaux, 1953." In *The Politics of Retribution in Europe: World War II and Its Aftermath*, edited by István Deák, Jan T. Gross, and Tony Judt, 194–211. Princeton, NJ: Princeton University Press, 2000.

Fayolle, Sophie, "Réagir aux premiers votes des femmes. Le cas du Parti communiste français." *Cahiers d'histoire. Revue d'histoire critique* 94–95 (2005): 223–39.

Ferguson, Marjorie. *Forever Feminine: Women's Magazines and the Cult of Femininity.* Ashgate: London, 1983.

Ferguson, Priscilla Parkhurst. *Accounting for Taste: The Triumph of French Cuisine.* Chicago: University of Chicago Press, 2004.

Firth, Raymond. *Symbols Public and Private.* Ithaca, NY: Cornell University Press, 1973.

Fishman, Sarah. *We Will Wait: Wives of French Prisoners of War, 1940-1945.* New Haven, CT: Yale University Press, 1991.

Foucault, Michel. *Discipline and Punish: the Birth of the Prison.* New York: Pantheon Books, 1977.

Gardey, Delphine. *Le Linge du Palais-Bourbon.* Lormont, France: Le Bord de l'eau, 2015.

Gates, Jr., Henry Louis and Karen C. C. Dalton. *Josephine Baker and La Revue Nègre: Paul Colin's Lithographs of Le Tumulte Noir in Paris, 1927.* New York: Harry N. Abrams, 1997.

Gentry, Caron E. and Laura Sjoberg. *Beyond Mothers, Monsters, Whores: Thinking about Women's Violence in Global Politics.* London: Zed Books, 2015.

Ghéraiche, William. "Les femmes politiques de 1944 à 1947: quelle liberation?." *Clio* 1 (1995): 1–12.

Gildea, Robert. *France since 1945.* New York and Oxford: Oxford University Press, 2002.

Gildea, Robert. *Marianne in Chains: Daily Life in the Heart of France during the German Occupation.* New York: Picador/Metropolitan Books, 2004.

Gildea, Robert. *The Past in French History.* New Haven, CT: Yale University Press, 1994.

Givhan, Robin. *The Battle of Versailles.* New York: Flatiron Books, 2015.

Gledhill, Christine and Gillian Swanson, eds. *Nationalising Femininity: Culture, Sexuality and British Cinema in the Second World War.* New York: St. Martin's Press, 1996.

Grayzel, Susan R. *Women's Identities at War: Gender, Motherhood, and Politics in Britain and France during the First World War.* Chapel Hill, NC: University of North Carolina Press, 1999.

Gorrarra, Claire. *The Roman Noir in Post-war French Culture: Dark Fictions.* New York and Oxford: Oxford University Press, 2003.

Grout, Holly. *The Force of Beauty: Transforming French Ideas of Femininity in the Third Republic.* Baton Rouge, LA: LSU Press, 2015.

Grumbach, Didier. *History of International Fashion.* Northampton, MA: Interlink, 2014.

Gubar, Susan. "This is My Rifle, This Is My Gun': World War II and the Blitz on Women." In *Behind the Lines: Gender and the Two World Wars*, edited by Margaret Higonnet et al., 227–59. New Haven, CT: Yale University Press, 1987.

Gury, Christian. *L'honneur ratatiné d'une athlete lesbienne en 1930.* Paris: Éditions Kimé, 1999.

Harris, Ruth. "The 'Child of the Barbarian': Rape, Race and Nationalism in France during the First World War." *Past and Present* 1, no. 141 (1993): 170–206.

Harsin, Jill. *Policing Prostitution in Nineteenth-Century Paris.* Princeton, NJ: Princeton University Press, 1985.

Hazareesingh, Sudhir. *In the Shadow of the General: Modern France and the Myth of de Gaulle.* New York: Oxford University Press, 2012.

Helm, Sarah. *Ravensbrück.* New York: Doubleday, 2014.

Herscher, Ermine. *Qualité de vie: objets des valeurs quotidiennes.* Paris: Editions Du May, 1991.

Hill, Daniel Delis. *As Seen in Vogue: A Century of American Fashion in Advertising.* Lubbock, TX: Texas Tech University Press, 2015.

Hoveyda, Fereydoun. *Histoire du roman policier.* Paris: Les Editions du Pavillon, 1965.

Hufton, Olwen H. *Women and the Limits of Citizenship in the French Revolution.* Toronto: The University of Toronto Press, 1992.

Hunt, Lynn. *The Family Romance of the French Revolution.* Berkeley: University of California Press, 1992.

Hunt, Lynn. *Inventing Human Rights: A History.* New York: WW Norton & Company, 2007.

Hunt, Lynn. *The Invention of Pornography: Obscenity and the Origins of Modernity, 1500-1800.* New York: Zone Books, 1996.

Hunt, Lynn. "The Many Bodies of Marie Antoinette: Political Pornography and the Problem of the Feminine in the French Revolution." In *Eroticism and the Body Politic*, edited by Lynn Hunt, 108–30. Baltimore: Johns Hopkins University Press, 1991.

Hunt, Lynn. *Politics, Culture and Class in the French Revolution.* Berkeley and Los Angeles: University of California Press, 1984.

Jackson, Julian. *Living in Arcadia: Homosexuality, Politics, and Morality in France from the Liberation to AIDS.* Chicago: University of Chicago Press, 2009.

Jackson, Julian. *The Popular Front in France: Defending Democracy, 1934-1938.* Cambridge, UK: Cambridge University Press, 1988.

Jackson, Julian. "Sex, Politics and Morality in France, 1954-1982." *History Workshop Journal* 61, no. 1 (2006): 77–102.

Jennings, Eric, "'Reinventing Jeanne': The Iconology of Joan of Arc in Vichy Schoolbooks, 1940-44." *Journal of Contemporary History* 29, no. 4 (1994): 711–34.

Jenson, Jane, "The Liberation and New Rights for French Women." In *Behind the Lines: Gender and the Two World Wars*, edited by Margaret Higonnet et al., 272–84. New Haven, CT: Yale University Press, 1987.

Judt, Tony. *Postwar: A History of Europe since 1945.* New York: Penguin, 2005.

Kaufmann, Dorothy. "The Story of Two Women: Dominique Aury and Edith Thomas." *Signs* 23, no. 4 (1998): 883–905.

Kedward, H. R. and Nancy Wood, eds. *The Liberation of France: Image and Event.* Oxford and Washington, DC: Berg, 1995.

Keenan, Brigid. *Dior in Vogue.* New York: Harmony Books, 1981.

Kelly, Michael, "The Reconstruction of Masculinity at the Liberation." In *The Liberation of France*, edited by H. R. Kedward and Nancy Wood, 117–28. Oxford and Washington, DC: Berg, 1995.

Kerber, Linda K. *No Constitutional Right to be Ladies: Women and the Obligations of Citizenship.* New York: Hill and Wang, 1998.

Kirsch, Jonathan. *The Short, Strange Life of Herschel Grynszpan: A Boy Avenger, A Nazi Diplomat, and a Murder in Paris.* New York: WW Norton, 2013.

Koreman, Megan. *The Expectation of Justice: France, 1944-1946.* Durham, NC: Duke University Press, 1999.

Kuisel, Richard. *Seducing the French: The Dilemma of Americanization*. Berkeley, CA: University of California Press, 1993.

LaCapra, Dominick. "History, Language, and Reading: Waiting for Crillon." *AHR* 100, no. 3 (1995): 799–828.

Landes, Joan. *Women and the Public Sphere in the Age of the French Revolution*. Ithaca, NY: Cornell University Press, 1988.

Lang, Kurt and Gladys Engel Lang. "The Power of Fashion." In *The Fashion Reader*, edited by Linda Welters and Abby Lillethun, 83–6. Oxford: Berg, 2011.

Langhamer, Claire. "Adultery in Post-war England." *History Workshop Journal* no. 62 (Autumn 2006): 86–115.

Laszlo, Pierre and Roxanne Lapidus. "Nothing Added, Nothing Subtracted." *SubStance* #105, 33, no. 3 (2004): 108–25.

Latimer, Tirza True. *Women Together/Women Apart: Portraits of Lesbian Paris*. New Brunswick, NJ: Rutgers University Press, 2005.

Le Moigne, Frédéric. "1944-1951: Les deux corps de Notre Dame de Paris." *Vingtième Siècle* #78 (avril-juin 2003): 75–88.

Lipovetsky, Gilles. *The Empire of Fashion: Dressing Modern Democracy*. Princeton, NJ: Princeton University Press, 1994.

Lloyd, Christopher. *Collaboration and Resistance in Occupied France: Representing Treason and Sacrifice*. New York: Palgrave Macmillan, 2003.

Lloyd, Christopher. "In the Service of the Enemy: The Traitor in French Occupation Narratives." *French Cultural Studies* 22, no. 3 (2011): 239–49.

Lottman, Herbert R. *The Purge*. New York: Morrow, 1986.

Lystra, Karen. *Searching the Heart: Women, Men, and Romantic Love in Nineteenth-Century America*. New York: Oxford University Press, 1989.

Mansker, Andrea. *Sex, Honor and Citizenship in Early Third Republic France*. New York: Palgrave MacMillan, 2011.

Marilley, Suzanne M. *Woman Suffrage and the Origins of Liberal Feminism in the United States*. Cambridge, MA: Harvard University Press, 1997.

Maza, Sarah. *Private Lives and Public Affairs: The Causes Célèbres of Prerevolutionary France*. Berkeley: University of California Press, 1993.

May, Elaine Tyler. *Homeward Bound: American Families in the Cold War Era*. New York: Basic Books, 1988.

McKelvey, Tara. *One of the Guys: Women as Aggressors and Torturers*. Emeryville, CA: Seal Press, 2007.

Meltzer, Françoise. *For Fear of the Fire: Joan of Arc and the Limits of Subjectivity*. Chicago: The University of Chicago Press, 2001.

Michallat, Wendy. "Droit au but: Violette Morris and Women's Football in 'les années folles'." *French Studies Bulletin* 26, no. 97 (2005): 13–17.

Miller, Laurent. *La presse écrite en France au XXe siècle*. Paris: Librairie Générale Française, 2005.

Mosse, George. *Nationalism and Sexuality*. New York: H. Fertig, 1985.

Muel-Dreyfus, Francine. *Vichy and the Eternal Feminine: A Contribution to a Political Sociology of Gender*. Durham, NC: Duke University Press, 2001.

Muncy, Robyn. *Creating a Female Dominion in American Reform, 1890-1935*. New York: Oxford University Press, 1991.

Neveu, Eric. "Trente ans de litterature d'espionnage en France (1950-1980)." *Vingtième siècle* 10, no. 1 (1986): 51–65.

Newman, Louise. *White Women's Rights: The Racial Origins of Feminism in the United States*. New York: Oxford University Press, 1999.

Nye, Robert A. *Masculinity and Male Codes of Honor in Modern France*. Berkeley: University of California Press, 1998.

Nye, Robert A. "Michel Foucault's Sexuality and the History of Homosexuality in France." In *Homosexuality in Modern France*, edited by Jeffrey Merrick and Bryant T. Ragan, Jr., 225–41. New York: Oxford University Press, 1996.

Offen, Karen. "Women, Citizenship and Suffrage with a French Twist." In *Suffrage and Beyond: International Feminist Perspectives*, edited by Caroline Daley and Melanie Nolan, 151–70. Auckland, NZ: Auckland University Press, 1994.

Okawa, Tamiko. "Licensing Practices at the Maison Dior." In *Producing Fashion: Commerce, Culture, and Consumers*, edited by Regina Lee Blaszczyk, 82–107. Philadelphia: University of Pennsylvania Press, 2008.

Olmstead, Kathryn S. "Blond Queens, Red Spiders, and Neurotic Old Maids: Gender and Espionage in the Early Cold War." *Intelligence and National Security* 19, no. 1 (2004): 78–94.

Palmer, Alexandra. *Dior: A New Look, A New Enterprise (1947-1957)*. London: V&A Publishing, 2009.

Parkins, Ilya. *Poiret, Dior and Schiaparelli: Fashion, Femininity and Modernity*. London: Berg, 2012.

Partington, Angela. "Popular Fashion and Working-Class Affluence." In *Chic Thrills: A Fashion Reader*, edited by Juliet Ash and Elizabeth Wilson, 145–61. Berkeley, CA: The University of California Press, 1993.

Pateman, Carole. "Equality, Difference, Subordination: the Politics of Motherhood and Women's Citizenship." In *Beyond Equality and Difference: Citizenship, Feminist Politics, Female Subjectivity*, edited by Gisela Bock and Susan James, 17–31. New York and London: Routledge, 1992.

Paxton, Robert O. *Vichy France: Old Guard and New Order, 1940-1944*. New York: Alfred A. Knopf, 1972.

Pedley, Alan. *As Mighty as the Sword: A Study of the Writings of Charles de Gaulle*. Exeter: Elm, 1996.

Peiss, Kathy. *Hope in a Jar: the Making of America's Beauty Culture*. New York: Henry Holt & Co., 1998.

Périer, Anne-Marie and Jean-Dominique Bauby. *Les Années* Elle, *1945-2000*. Levallois-Perret: Filipacchi, 1999.

Perrault, Gilles and Pierre Azéma. *Paris under the Occupation*. New York: Vendome Press, 1989.

Peterson, Anna L. *Martyrdom and the Politics of Religion: Progressive Catholicism in El Salvador's Civil War*. Albany, NY: State University of New York Press, 1997.

Pollard, Miranda. *Reign of Virtue: Mobilizing Gender in Vichy France*. Chicago: The University of Chicago Press, 1998.

Pringle, Colombe. *Telles qu'Elle*. Paris: Bernard Grasset, 1995.

Proctor, Tammy M. *Female Intelligence: Women and Espionage in the First World War*. New York: New York University Press, 2003.

Pulju, Rebecca. "Consumers for the Nation: Women, Politics, and Consumer Organization in France, 1944-1965." *Journal of Women's History* 18, no. 3 (2006): 68–90.

Pulju, Rebecca. *Women and Mass Consumer Society in Postwar France*. New York: Cambridge University Press, 2011.

Rabinowitz, Lauren. *For the Love of Pleasure: Women, Movies, and Culture in Turn-of-the-Century Chicago*. New Brunswick, NJ: Rutgers University Press, 1998.

Ramsay, Raylene L. *French Women in Politics: Writing Power*. New York: Berghahn Books, 2003.

Rappaport, Erika Diane. *Shopping for Pleasure: Women in the Making of London's West End*. Princeton, NJ: Princeton University Press, 2000.

Rauch, André. "La virginité de sainte Odile et la liberté de Marianne." In *La République en représentations: autour de l'œuvre de Maurice Agulhon*, edited by Maurice Agulhon, Annette Becker, and Évelyne Cohen, 265–78. Paris: Publications de la Sorbonne, 2006.

Read, Geoff. *The Republic of Men: Gender and the Political Parties in Interwar France*. Baton Rouge, LA: LSU Press, 2014.

Reineke, Sandra. *Beauvoir and Her Sisters: The Politics of Women's Bodies in France*. Urbana: University of Illinois Press, 2011.

Rendall, Jane. *Origins of Modern Feminism: Women in Britain, France, and the United States, 1780-1860*. Chicago: Lyceum Books, 1990.

Rennert, Jack. *100 Posters of Paul Colin*. New York: Images Graphiques, 1977.

Reynolds, Helen. *The 40s and 50s: Utility to New Look*. Milwaukee, WI: Gareth Steven Publishing, 2000.

Rigby, Brian and Nicholas Hewitt. "Introduction." In *France and the Mass Media*, edited by Brian Rigby and Nicholas Hewitt, 1–4. London: MacMillan, 1991.

Riot-Sarcey, Michèle. *Histoire du féminisme*. Paris: Éditions la Découverte, 2002.

Rioux, Jean-Pierre. *Au bonheur la France: des Impressionistes à de Gaulle, comment nous avons su être heureux*. Paris: Perrin, 2004.

Rioux, Jean-Pierre. *The Fourth Republic, 1944-1958*. Cambridge and New York: Cambridge University Press, 1987.

Roberts, Mary Louise. *Civilization without Sexes: Reconstructing Gender in Postwar France, 1917-1927*. Chicago: The University of Chicago Press, 1994.

Roberts, Mary Louise. "Making the Modern Girl French." In *The Modern Girl around the World*, edited by Alys Eve Weinbaum et al., 77–95. Durham, NC: Duke University Press, 2008.

Rosbottom, Ronald C. *When Paris Went Dark: The City of Light under German Occupation, 1940-1944*. New York: Little, Brown, and Company, 2014.

Ross, Kristin. *Fast Cars, Clean Bodies: Decolonization and the Reordering of French Culture*. Cambridge, MA: The MIT Press, 1996.

Rossiter, Margaret L. *Women in the Resistance*. New York: Praeger, 1986.

Rouquet, François, Danièle Voldman, Fabrice Virgili, and Luc Capdevila. *Hommes et femmes dans la France en guerre (1914-1945)*. Paris: Payot, 2003.

Rousso, Henry. *Le Syndrome de Vichy*. Éditions du Seuil, octobre 1987 et mai 1990.

Rousso, Henry *The Vichy Syndrome: History and Memory in France since 1944*. Cambridge, MA: Harvard University Press, 1991.

Rousso, Henry and Eric Conan. *Vichy: An Ever-Present Past*. Hanover, NH: University Press of New England, 1998.

Ruffin, Raymond. *Violette Morris: l'hyène de la Gestap*. Paris: Cherche-Midi, 2004.

Scanlon, Jennifer. *Inarticulate Longings: The Ladies' Home Journal, Gender, and the Promises of Consumer Culture*. New York: Routledge, 1995.

Schirmer, Jennifer. "The Seeking of Truth and the Gendering of Consciousness: The Comadres of El Salvador and the Conavigua Widows of Guatemala." In *Viva: Women and Popular Protest in Latin America*, edited by Sarah A. Radcliffe and Sallie Westwood, 30–64. London: Routledge, 1993.

Schwartz, Paula. "*Partisanes* and Gender Politics in Vichy France." *French Historical Studies* 16, no. 1 (1989): 126–51.

Scott, Joan Wallach. "Fantasy Echo: History and the Construction of Identity." *Critical Inquiry* 27, no. 2 (2001): 284–304.

Scott, Joan Wallach. *Gender and the Politics of History*. New York: Columbia University Press, 1999.

Scott, Joan Wallach. *Only Paradoxes to Offer: French Feminists and the Rights of Man*. Cambridge, MA: Harvard University Press, 1996.

Scott, Joan Wallach. *Parité! Sexual Equality and the Crisis of French Universalism*. Chicago: The University of Chicago Press, 2005.

Scott, Joan Wallach. "Rewriting History." In *Behind the Lines: Gender and the Two World Wars*, edited by Margaret Higonnet et al., 19–30. New Haven, CT: Yale University Press, 1987.

Scott, Joan Wallach. *The Politics of the Veil*. Princeton, NJ: Princeton University Press, 2007.

Seidman, Steven. *Romantic Longings: Love in America, 1830-1980*. New York: Routledge, 1991.

Seymour, Miranda. *Bugatti Queen: In Search of a French Racing Legend*. New York: Random House, 2004.

Sigel, Lisa Z. "Filth in the Wrong People's Hands: Postcards and the Expansion of Pornography in Britain and the Atlantic World, 1880-1914." *Journal of Social History* 33, no. 4 (2000): 858–85.

Sigel, Lisa Z. *Governing Pleasures: Pornography and Social Change in England, 1815-1914*. New Brunswick, NJ: Rutgers University Press, 2002.

Smith, Bonnie G. *Changing Lives: Women in European History since 1700*. Lexington, MA: DC Heath & Co, 1989.

Smith, Paul. *Feminism and the Third Republic: Women's Political and Civil Rights in France, 1918-1945*. Oxford: Oxford University Press, 1995.

Soley-Beltran, Patrìcia. "Modelling Femininity." *European Journal of Women's Studies* 11, no. 3 (2004): 309–26.

Stearns, Peter N. and Mark Knapp, "Men and Romantic Love: Pinpointing a Twentieth-Century Change." *Journal of Social History* 26, no. 4 (1993): 769–95.

Steele, Valerie. *Paris Fashion*. 2nd edn. Oxford: Berg, 1998.

Sullerot, Evelyne. *La presse féminine*. Paris: Armand Colin, 1963.

Surkis, Judith. *Sexing the Citizen: Morality and Masculinity in France, 1870-1920*. Ithaca, NY: Cornell University Press, 2006.

Tiersten, Lisa. *Marianne in the Market: Envisioning Consumer Society in fin-de-siècle France*. Berkeley: University of California Press, 2001.

Vasey, Ruth. *The World According to Hollywood, 1918-1939*. Madison, WI: University of Wisconsin Press, 1997.

Veillon, Dominique. *Fashion under the Occupation*. New York: Berg, 2002.

Vienne, Véronique, "The Woman Who Was *ELLE*: Hélène Gordon-Lazareff." In *The Education of An Art Director*, edited by Steven Heller and Véronique Vienne, 189–94. New York: Allworth Press, 2006.

Vinen, Richard. *A History in Fragments: Europe in the Twentieth Century*. Cambridge, MA: Da Capo Press, 2001.

Virgili, Fabrice. *Shorn Women: Gender and Punishment in Liberation France*. Oxford and New York: Berg, 2002.

Virgili, Fabrice. "Les tondues à la Libération: le corps des femmes, enjeu d'une réappropriation." *Clio* 1, no. 1 (1995): 1–12.

Wallach, Janet. *Chanel: Her Style and Her Life*. New York: Doubleday, 1998.

Walkowitz, Judith R. *City of Dreadful Delight: Narratives of Sexual Danger in Late-Victorian London*. Chicago: The University of Chicago Press, 1992.

Walkowitz, Judith R. *Prostitution and Victorian Society: Women, Class, and the State*. Cambridge, UK and New York: Cambridge University Press, 1980.

Warner, Marina. *Joan of Arc: The Image of Female Heroism*. New York: Alfred A. Knopf, 1981.

Warner, Marina. *Monuments and Maidens: The Allegory of the Female Form*. New York: Atheneum, 1985.

Weber, Eugen. *The Hollow Years: France in the 1930s*. New York: Norton, 1994.

Weill, Alain and Jack Rennert. *Paul Colin, Affichiste*. Paris: Éditions Denoël, 1989.

Weiner, Susan. "Two Modernities: From 'Elle' to 'Mademoiselle'. Women's Magazines in Postwar France." *Contemporary European History* 8, no. 3 (1999): 395–409.

Weitz, Margaret Collins. "Art in the Service of Propaganda: the Poster War in World War II." *Religion and the Arts* 4, no. 1 (2000): 43–75.

Weitz, Margaret Collins. *Sisters in the Resistance: How Women Fought to Free France, 1940-1945*. New York: John Wiley & Sons, Inc., 1995.

Wheelwright, Julie. *The Fatal Lover: Mata Hari and the Myth of Women in Espionage*. London: Collins & Brown, 1992.

Wieviorka, Olivier. *The French Resistance*. Cambridge, MA: Harvard University Press, 2016.

Woloch, Nancy. *Women and the American Experience*. Boston: McGraw-Hill, 2006.

Zdatny, Steven. *Fashion, Work, and Politics in Modern France*. Palgrave McMillan: New York, 2006.

Index

9 781350 105553